W9-BTE-604

Counseling
and
Psychotherapy

Science and Behavior Books brings to those interested in the behavioral sciences important and timely books produced economically in durable vinyl covers. We solicit opinions and ideas from our readers.

This is an Original Edition
in vinyl covers

Counseling and Psychotherapy

CLASSICS

on Theories

and Issues

Edited by

Ben N. Ard, Jr.

Professor of Counseling
San Francisco State College

SCIENCE AND BEHAVIOR BOOKS, INC.
577 College Avenue, Palo Alto, California 94306

BF 637. C6 A68

Copyright © 1966 by Science and Behavior Books,
Inc. Printed in the United States of America.
All rights reserved. This book, or parts thereof,
may not be reproduced in any form without
permission of the publisher.

Library of Congress Catalog Card 66-23291

*"A clash of doctrines is not a disaster—it is
an opportunity."*

—*A. N. Whitehead*

INTRODUCTION

Many practitioners in the field of counseling and psychotherapy operate from within the framework of one theoretical outlook, frequently because, during their training, they studied under a teacher who espoused one theory as the only way to view problems and issues. This book is offered as an aid both to students in training and to practitioners already in the field in the hope that it will provide a broader background by considering a variety of theories and several different positions on some significant issues, as expressed first-hand by the authors of the ideas themselves.[1]

Before getting into a discussion of the role of theory in this field, perhaps a few general remarks on counseling and psychotherapy are not out of order. A fine-line distinction between counseling and psychotherapy is admittedly difficult if not impossible to draw. Consequently many of the papers in this book will deal with psychotherapy while others are concerned with counseling. It is hoped that this usage will not confuse or bother the reader unnecessarily.

The papers selected for this book deal basically with any psychological technique used in the treatment of what might be roughly termed the normal range of problems faced by children, adolescents, and adults. This excludes from consideration most of the psychiatric therapies intended for psychotics, the therapies involving drugs or other medical treatment, shock treatments, conditioning treatments, and the so-called "behavior" therapies, as well as the Freudian and neo-Freudian theories (which have been presented elsewhere in abundance). Most of the aforementioned approaches require a medical degree and other specialized training (e.g., at a psychoanalytic training institute). The theories in this book deal with verbal interaction between client and counselor or psychotherapist and do not, therefore, require the medical

---

[1]These papers have been reprinted exactly, without further editing, except for Chapter IV which was abridged with the author's permission. However, italics which were not essential for meaning and emphasis have been eliminated in the interest of readability.

training presupposed in the above theories. Therefore the theories and issues discussed here should be of interest to practitioners who function as counselors, psychologists, social workers, and other members of the helping professions.

A professional counselor or psychotherapist needs to know not only what to do in various situations with a wide variety of clients but also why. The <u>what</u> may be considered to be the <u>techniques</u> of counseling and psychotherapy. But these techniques depend, or at least should depend, upon prior conceptions of <u>why</u> a given technique is called for in a particular situation. Thus techniques, ideally, depend upon prior <u>theories</u>.

The growth of science depends, at least in an important part, upon tracing the consequences of false hypotheses. Similarly, growth in enlightenment can result from the drawing and elaboration of the consequences of any theory—provided that a proper climate of opinion encourages the development of theory, and provided that its espousal remains in the universe of discourse and debate. This book is intended to make a contribution to the field by aiding just such discourse and debate.

In common usage "theory" is usually contrasted with "practice." However, as Norman R. Campbell (1953, p. 289), in a discussion of the structure of theories, has pointed out,

> The desire of many half-educated persons to rely on "practical conclusions" rather than on the reasoning of the "theorist" is founded merely on ignorance and on an inability to differentiate between the kinds of thought likely to lead to truth and those which may be associated with error.

Nevertheless, as Campbell (1953, p. 289) has also noted,

> The views of "practical men" are usually derived from assumptions and arguments no less complex than those on which theory is based; they are more and not less liable to error because they are less openly expressed. The idea that there are no propositions "true in theory but false in practice" has its foundation only in the incompetence of the uninitiated to understand theory, and in their habit of applying propositions to circumstances entirely foreign to the theory. To those who have not the power to think, theory will always be dangerous.

Some people are critical of theorizing because they say theories cannot be proven true, or at least not completely so. Following this line of reasoning, these people are loath to "waste time" with theories. But, as Campbell (1953, p. 300) has pointed out,

> Theories are often accepted and valued greatly, by part of the scientific world at least, even if it is known that they are not quite true and are not strictly equivalent to any experimental laws, simply because the ideas which they bring to mind are intrinsically valuable.

The reader is urged to keep this thought in mind as he considers the various theories in this book.

Finally, in this consideration of some of the antitheoretical views in the field, Ford and Urban (1963, pp. 24-25) have noted that

> Some theorists, such as phenomenologists, are concerned about imposing an inappropriate conceptual scheme on an individual's behavior. This is a legitimate concern, but the solution is not the alternative of simply adopting the individual's own conceptual scheme which may be loaded with many inadequacies, as in disordered individuals, although some extremists in the phenomenological movement propose its adoption.

Too often some practitioners operate in the field simply on the basis of what "feels" to them at the moment like the proper thing to do. Some authorities have even urged this attitude be adopted toward counseling and psychotherapy in general. Hopefully, a thoughtful consideration of a variety of theoretical approaches may provide a more justifiable basis for practice.

There are too many practitioners, also, who do what they do in counseling and psychotherapy merely because (by chance factors usually) that is what they were taught to do in their professional training. That is, practitioners in their training have too often been taught only one theoretical approach. After they enter the field, they work in only one fashion—that of their major professor. Rather than creating such a specific image so early in training, it would seem wiser to clarify more fully the range of possibilities. Thus we must attempt to build into training programs the many possible theories and procedures within that range of possibilities.

This book is intended to provide just such a broad introduction to a variety of theoretical approaches to counseling and psychotherapy. It is intended to provide another approach—what might be called a multi-track approach rather than a single-track approach.

Some authorities in the field have recommended that the student in training adopt a particular theoretical position without reservation—that he become a "true believer." It has even been suggested that the student be enthusiastically imbued with the theory before he commences to examine it critically. However, not everyone would agree with this blind acceptance of one theory to the exclusion of all other possibilities. Carl Rogers (1959, p. 191) has commented in this regard, ". . . I am distressed at the manner in which small caliber minds immediately accept a theory—almost any theory—as a dogma of truth."

The present book takes an entirely different approach. The assumption here is that it is better for the student to become aware of the variety of different theories available in the field. It is hoped that the student will read each of the theories critically and not merely absorb one theory, revel in it, and identify with it as practically a religious badge of honor.

This book of theories and issues, then, presents the student or the practitioner in the field with a variety of points of view or frames of reference. They are purposefully chosen as provocative, opposing, controversial points of view. Most of these papers have appeared previously in professional journals or in books presenting one point of view. In order to make it more feasible for the student or practitioner to consider these contrasting views, they have been grouped in such a fashion as to bring their opposing positions into sharp contrast.

The reader is urged to consider each theory in relation to each of the others, to contrast them, to weigh them critically and thoughtfully, and not to agree with any author unless he feels he is forced to by the weight of the author's evidence and arguments.

San Francisco, 1966   Ben N. Ard, Jr.

REFERENCES

Campbell, Norman R. The structure of theories. In Feigl and
    Brodbeck (Eds.) Readings in the philosophy of science. New
    York: Appleton-Century-Crofts, 1953. Pp. 288-308.

Ford, Donald H. and Urban, Hugh B. Systems of psychotherapy: a comparative study. New York: Wiley, 1963.

Rogers, Carl R. A theory of therapy, personality, and interpersonal relationships, as developed in the client-centered framework. In Sigmund Koch (Ed.), Psychology: a study of a science. Vol. 3. New York: McGraw-Hill, 1959.

Whitehead, A. N. Science and the modern world. New York: Macmillan, 1925.

CONTRIBUTORS

BEN N. ARD, JR., Ph. D., Professor of Counseling, San Francisco State College, San Francisco, California.

NATHANIEL BRANDEN, M. A., Director, Nathaniel Branden Institute, Inc., New York City.

ROBERT L. BROWNING, Ph. D., Associate Professor of Christian Education, Ohio Methodist Theological School, Delaware, Ohio.

ROBERT CALLIS, Ph. D., Dean, Extra-divisional Administration, University of Missouri, Columbia, Missouri.

ALBERT ELLIS, Ph. D., Executive Director, Institute for Rational Living, Inc., New York City.

WILLIAM GLASSER, M. D., Consulting Psychiatrist, Ventura School for Girls, Camarillo, California.

ABRAHAM H. MASLOW, Ph. D., Professor of Psychology, Brandeis University, Waltham, Massachusetts.

O. HOBART MOWRER, Ph. D., Research Professor, University of Illinois, Urbana, Illinois.

HERMAN J. PETERS, Ph. D., Associate Professor of Education, Ohio State University, Columbus, Ohio.

CARL R. ROGERS, Ph. D., Resident Fellow, Western Behavioral Sciences Institute, La Jolla, California.

JOSEPH SAMLER, Ph. D., Chairman, Vocational Rehabilitation Board, Veterans Administration, Washington, D. C.

FREDERICK C. THORNE, M. D., Ph. D., Editor, Journal of Clinical Psychology, Brandon, Vermont.

LEONA E. TYLER, Ph. D., Dean, Graduate School, University of Oregon, Eugene, Oregon.

E. G. WILLIAMSON, Ph. D., Dean of Students, University of Minnesota, Minneapolis, Minnesota.

C. GILBERT WRENN, Ph. D., Professor of Educational Psychology, Arizona State University, Tempe, Arizona.

CONTENTS

GENERAL INTRODUCTORY PAPERS

COUNSELING AND PSYCHOTHERAPY THEORIES

SPECIFIC ISSUES IN COUNSELING AND PSYCHOTHERAPY

APPENDIXES

INDEXES

General Introductory Papers

I

TOWARD AN INTEGRATED THEORY OF COUNSELING

Robert Callis

First, let me apologize for being so presumptuous as to choose to talk about an integrated theory of counseling. I feel very inadequate to the task. However, I have chosen this topic more because of its need to be considered than because of what I will be able to do with it. There is entirely too much talk abroad in the land of counseling of the "either-or" and "what school do you belong to?" variety. Such talk is unhealthy for the profession in that it substitutes belief and convictions for creative thought and research. We need to organize our knowledge (theories and facts) in such a manner that the result is a consistent and unified guide to counseling thought, research and practice. We need a theory that is useful in our day by day practice; one that is not just a rag-bag collection of unrelated constructs, but a unified theory with high internal consistency. This paper is an attempt to take a step in that direction.

Before we get into the age-old hassle of theory vs. practice, let me commit myself at least to the notion that the most practical thing I know of is a good theory. The definition of a theory is an organized set of ideas which will explain a maximum amount of the phenomena with which we are concerned. The test of a theory is—will it work? A good theory will work more often and in a greater variety of situations than a poor theory. Actually, there is no dichotomy between theory and practice. If a theory is adequate it is practical.

This paper is organized around three questions: (a) What energizes behavior? What causes the human organism to move, to act, to respond, to behave? (b) How does the human organism de-

Reprinted by permission of the author and the Journal of *College Student Personnel,* 1960, 1:2-9.

velop a behavior repertoire? When is one's behavior repertoire adequate or inadequate? What is the nature of the inadequacies? (c) How can the several kinds of inadequacies in behavior repertoire be corrected? Which counseling method is most effective in correcting which inadequacy in behavior repertoire?

WHAT ENERGIZES BEHAVIOR?

Perhaps first we should state what appears to be a basic law of behavior: The primary goal of an organism is to behave in such a fashion that he is able to extract from his environment the satisfaction of his needs not only at the moment but in a sustained manner in the future. Most behavioral scientists agree that the stuff that energizes behavior is the need of the organism. Thus, if we are to understand behavior, we must understand the needs that the organism is trying to satisfy. So that we won't get bogged down by terminology, let us assume that needs and drives have to energize behavior.

Various authors have developed lists of needs. Maslow (1954) has ordered these needs into a hierarchy according to their power or priority relative to each other. This order is typical but individual variation from it can be observed. The following list is a modification of Maslow's list. It contains seven needs: two biological and five psycho-social. These are presented in order of their power or priority with the most powerful one first.

1. Self-preservation. This drive to survive physically has been rather well established in all forms of life. Immediately, we can think of instances in which some other need supercedes this supposedly most basic and powerful one. Suicide, for example, violates this basic drive. It seems to me that in the human organism we must introduce an additional construct here in order to understand self-preservation. Biologists describe self-preservation as a drive for physical survival. However, as we grow and develop, we develop a psychological self as well as a physical self. Somehow these two selves get intertwined. If we consider this drive for self-preservation to encompass both the physical and the psychological self, we can leave it stand as the highest priority and most powerful drive. Take, for example, the soldier who throws himself on a live grenade to protect his buddies from certain death; knowing full well that in doing so he will be killed. Some need more powerful than that to survive physically has motivated him. We can explain this act of heroism by invoking the notion of preservation of the psychological self and

postulating that the soldier was acting in accordance with a concept of himself as a good soldier, one loyal to his buddies and one willing to risk his life to protect his buddies.

2. <u>Reproduction of the species.</u> This is the second most powerful drive which biologists have identified. It also seems to be biologically inherited. The absence or malfunction of either the drive to physical survival or the drive to reproduce the species will cause that particular genetic strain to die out. We are here today only because our ancestors possessed these two drives in sufficient quantity. The genetic argument is perhaps the most powerful argument for these two biological drives being considered first in priority in relation to all the other drives. This puts preservation of the psychological self in second place. Dead heroes do not reproduce themselves.

3. <u>Security</u>. Security is a widely used term and perhaps loosely so at times. Security here has to do with a feeling of confidence within the individual that he will be able to satisfy his needs now and continuously in the future. When this security need is not satisfied, the person is fearful and apprehensive that he will not be able to interact with his environment in such a way that his needs will be satisfied. The magnitude of this fear may reach catastrophic proportions producing extreme anxiety and panic.

4. <u>Respect for self.</u> Each person needs to feel that he is worthy of dignity and respect. This is an attitude toward self; an approval of oneself. It is not necessarily associated with social or economic status. It is a need of everyone regardless of his status in life.

5. <u>Acceptance by others</u>. This includes heterosexual love, family and other close friendships, and general gregariousness. In adolescence acceptance by peers is highlighted.

6. <u>Self expression and accomplishment.</u> We have a need to use our abilities in manners suggested by our interests to create or accomplish something. Ability in itself has drive properties. This expression may take occupational forms or it may take recreational and hobby forms. Ability here is not restricted to intellectual ability.

7. <u>Esthetic experiences.</u> The need for esthetic experience accounts for the existence of art, music, drama, etc.

Maslow's hierarchy principle states that in general until the most basic need has been satisfied in our perception or expectation, but not necessarily in reality, we cannot attend to the higher order but less powerful needs. The implications for the counselor are two-fold: (1) at what need level is the client functioning or having difficulty functioning? and (2) at what level is the counselor functioning and is the counselor able to distinguish between his own need level and that of his client? When the counselor understands at what need level the client is having difficulty, he is able to see more clearly the goal of counseling and is able to choose an appropriate counseling method for this instance.

Once we have satisfied our more basic needs, we are then able to "upshift" and attend to higher order needs. When the satisfaction of these lower order needs is threatened, we "downshift" to attend to them.

If we can accept the notion that needs motivate our behavior, we are ready to consider the behavior repertoire that we have at our command which we can use to interact with our environment for the purpose of satisfying our needs.

HOW DOES ONE DEVELOP HIS BEHAVIOR REPERTOIRE?

Needs provide the motivating force which energizes behavior and sets the goal to be attained as well. But what sort of behavior does one employ in attempting to satisfy his needs? What patterns of behavior response does he have at his command; i.e., what repertoire of behavior responses does he have abailable for use? How does he choose a single course of action from among the several that may be in his repertoire? What happens if the choice is wrong? What happens if the behavior repertoire cupboard is bare? Where does counseling fit into such a scheme? These are a few of the questions which must be answered. Pepinsky and Pepinsky (1954) have dealt with several of these questions at length. You will see that my treatment of the questions has been influenced by the Pepinskys'.

We can define behavior repertoire as the total of all behavior response that the individual is capable of making. We start with our inherited capacities and through maturation and experience build a behavior repertoire. Our behavior repertoire changes or is subject to change with each new experience. Thus, experience becomes the first level in a schematic diagram (Figure 1) which we can construct to represent behavior repertoire.

For our purposes here, the unit of experience can be conceived of as being of any size. Experience is an objective occurrence external to the "psyche."

The second element is perception. Perception is the individual's interpretation of the experience or that which is interiorized by the individual.

The third element is <u>generalization.</u> We seem to have a natural tendency to group perceptions which appear to us to be of a similar kind and draw one rule or generalization from the whole class of events. We use this generalization to guide our behavior at any time in the future when we encounter an event perceived to be the same class of events as those about which the generalization was drawn. For example, if we go into a strange room which is dark and wish to turn on the light, where would we look for the light switch? Most of us have had experiences with light switches and from these experiences and our perceptions of them, we have concluded or generalized that usually the light switch is located on the wall adjacent to the door frame a little above waist high. We have also learned, that is, concluded or generalized that light switches are not to be found on the ceiling or in the floor. Consequently, we look for the light switch near the door and not on the floor or ceiling. Thus, the generalization based on past experience guides our behavior in this present situation.

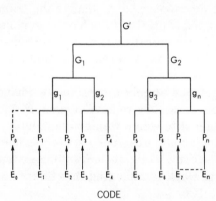

CODE
E-EXPERIENCE; P-PERCEPTION; g-FIRST
ORDER GENERALIZATION; G-SECOND ORDER
GENERALIZATION; G'-THIRD ORDER GENERAL-
IZATION

Before we apply a generalization to a new situation we must determine that the new situation is identical for our purpose to the class of situations from which our generalization came. Thus, if the dark room mentioned above were in a rustic log cabin in an isolated wooded area we should suspect that there would be neither lights nor light switches in the room. The ability to differentiate between apparently identical situations and actually identical situations must be admitted into the scheme of thinking which we are developing here. Dollard, Auld and White (1953) have indicated that improvement in accuracy of differentiation and discrimination is a major goal in psychotherapy. They describe instances in which psychiatric patients try to apply generalizations developed out of childhood experiences to situations which they encounter as adults. Although the generalizations were valid for the childhood situations, the apparently identical adult situations were in reality not identical, and, consequently, the behavior repertoire employed was ineffective in satisfying the patient's needs.

The constellation of all generalizations developed out of past experience gives direction and selectivity to our behavior tendencies in our attempts to interact with present environment to satisfy present needs. If this constellation of generalization which we have labelled behavior repertoire directs our behavior in such a way that our needs are satisfied we can consider it adequate.

When a client comes to a counselor saying, "I have a problem. I would like for you to help me with it," he is, in effect, saying, "My behavior repertoire is inadequate. Will you help me correct the inadequacies?" No matter what language he uses, in the model we are developing here, that is the translation.

What kinds of inadequacies in behavior repertoire can there be? There are three general classes of inadequacies: (1) lack of experience, (2) distortions in perception, and (3) errors in generalization.

Lack of experience simply means that we have not had the kind of experience necessary to develop generalizations appropriate for the situation with which we are confronted. This includes lack of information about ourselves as well as our environment. Most counseling effort devoted to increasing understanding of self and of the world of work is attacking this first kind of inadequacy. (See Eo in Figure 1.)

Distortion in perception can occur even though our experience or exposure is adequate. For example, our need to regard ourselves highly may be so pressing that we distort or deny all evidence or experience which suggests that we may not be as intelligent or popular as our current self-concept suggests. Generalizations based on distorted perceptions are apt to be invalid and will direct us into behavior which will not satisfy our needs.

Errors in generalization are more difficult to describe in concrete terms. We could say that they are faulty logic but this is not very helpful. Errors in grouping perceptions from which we draw a generalization would produce a faulty generalization, but, also, there can be errors in actual generalization itself. The process of creating an idea resists definition and description. We can test the validity of an idea, hypothesis or generalization once it has been invented, but we know very little about how these inventions were produced. In our model, we must include errors in generalization even if we cannot describe exactly how they occur.

In addition to the three types of inadequacies, there is a fourth notion that needs mentioning. That is the spread of effect of errors. Lack of experience or distortion in perception does not stop there. They cause, in turn, erroneous generalization based this time on the original error. One is reminded here of the children's ditty: "For the lack of a nail, the shoe was lost. For the lack of a shoe, the horse was lost. For the lack of a horse, the rider was lost. For the lack of the rider, the battle was lost."

Let us return to our client who has said to us (translated), "My behavior repertoire is inadequate. Will you help me correct the inadequacies?" It seems to me that the problem calls for two discoveries: (1) discovery of the error, and (2) discovery of a way to correct the error. Who is to make the discoveries? We have two choices—the counselor or the client. Or, to say it another way, there are two general methods of counseling—(1) client self-discovery and (2) counselor discovery followed by interpretation.

WHICH COUNSELING METHOD IS MOST EFFECTIVE IN CORRECTING WHICH INADEQUACY IN BEHAVIOR REPERTOIRE?

This question suggests that the counselor's behavior repertoire should include more than one counseling method. Is there any justification for a counselor being competent in and using more than one counseling method? Or, is some one counseling method sufficient to solve all client problems as many counselors contend? Reasoning by analogy does not always lead to valid conclusions but let's take that risk for a moment.

Suppose that you move to a new town and shortly thereafter you develop a severe head cold. You consult a physician and he gives you a shot of penicillin. You get well. You conclude that he is a good physician. Later on you break your arm. You go back to your physician. He gives you a shot of penicillin and starts to dismiss you. You say, "But Doc, how about this broken bone? Aren't you going to set it?" He replies, "I don't believe in bone setting. I'm a penicillin man." Do you still consider him a good physician? If not, why not? Because he is a one-tool physician. He refuses to vary his treatment according to the problem. Should we not also condemn counselors for this "one-tool" attitude?

Suppose your car has blown a head gasket. You take it to a garage for repair. The mechanic starts banging on the head bolts

with a screwdriver. You say, "Why don't you use a wrench on
these head bolts?" and he replies, "Oh, I couldn't do that, you
see, I'm a screwdriver man." Would you judge him to be a competent mechanic? If not, why not? Would you really condemn
him for being a one-tool mechanic? He has such strong faith in
his screwdriver and such strong conviction that it is proper to
limit himself to only one tool. Isn't faith and conviction a sufficient basis for determining one's professional behavior? Since it
seems to be a sufficient basis for many counselors, it would seem
only fair that we also permit physicians and mechanics the privilege of restricting their tools on the basis of faith and conviction.

Many counselors restrict themselves to the client self-discovery method solely. Since all of us must agree that counseling
is a learning process, at least in some broad sense of the word,
let's try another reduction to absurdity. Suppose we instruct
every third grade teacher that he is to employ the self-discovery
method solely, and, in addition, we set the standard that every
third grader must know the multiplication tables before he can go
on to the fourth grade. How many grey-bearded third graders
would we have hobbling around in our schools because they hadn't
yet discovered the multiplication tables? Of course, someone did
discover the multiplication tables years ago, but, it was not a
third grader. However, millions of third graders have learned
the multiplication tables by having them interpreted to them. Many
a client has learned what occupational groups his interests are
similar to through interpretation within a few hours time. Most
of these would expend hundreds of hours to acquire the same understanding of themselves by self-discovery method.

I have tried to show that a single counseling method cannot
solve all types of problems, and that client self-discovery method
of counseling cannot solve certain client problems and will be
grossly inefficient with others. But, how about the converse?
Can counselor discovery and interpretation be effective in all instances? Let's return to our discussion of distortion in perception. It was shown that distortion in perception can occur even
though the client has had adequate and appropriate experience or
exposure. Certainly, interpretation by the counselor is an experience or exposure for the client. Therefore, it is quite possible
and conceivable that the client may distort or reject a counselor's
interpretation which would in turn produce an erroneous generalization. An erroneous generalization is an inadequacy in behavior
repertoire so the client is still unable to satisfy his needs. Counseling has failed.

We now come to the major point in this paper. Clients consult counselors because they have found that their behavior repertoire is inadequate. Inadequacies in behavior repertoire can be of three different kinds and counseling methods are basically of two kinds, neither of which can be effective with all kinds of inadequacies. Therefore, it is absolutely necessary that counseling include differential diagnosis which will form the basis for differential choice of treatment, i.e., counseling method. The one-tool counselor must go. He is just as unscientific, unprofessional, unethical and immoral as the penicillin physician or the screwdriver mechanic. The only instance in which a counselor would be justified in restricting himself to one method, would be for him to limit his practice to one type of inadequacy. Even then, he would have to engage in diagnosis to determine if this particular client is the type of case he would accept. Diagnosis in counseling is not a new topic, nor is it a completely forgotten one. (See Apostal and Miller, 1959; Berezin, 1957; Bordin, 1946; Pepinsky, 1948; Weiner, 1959; Williamson and Darley, 1937.)

In spite of all of the important contributions Rogers (1931, 1939, 1942, 1951) has made, he has damaged the field quite significantly by making most of us feel guilty about diagnosis, and yet if you read his works carefully this should not have happened. Rogers limits his method to certain kinds of cases and makes the determination (diagnosis) at the outset that the case is appropriate to his method (client self-discovery) before accepting the case. I have a bone to pick with the pseudo-Rogerians, not Rogers himself.

If the word diagnosis makes you feel squeamish, if it rankles you, I believe we can avoid that very nicely by substituting "working hypothesis" for "diagnosis." Of course, we are still talking about the same thing, but "working hypothesis" may be more palatable to many counselors. Each counselor, whether he admits it or not, draws generalizations (working hypotheses) about his client on a moment-to-monent basis throughout the entire counseling process. On the basis of these hypotheses the counselor determines what his behavior will be, what method he will employ at the next moment. In reality, every counselor employs differential diagnosis and differentially chooses his treatment method accordingly. My plea, simply, is to make these operations explicit so that we can begin to think about and conduct some research on the effectiveness of various counseling methods in correcting the several kinds of inadequacies in behavior repertoire.

As a starting point for this line of investigation, let me pro-

pose two hypotheses. Earlier three kinds of inadequacies in behavior repertoire were described: (1) lack of experience, (2) distortion in perception and (3) erroneous generalization. I will deal
here with the first two only. Also, I will not attempt to distinguish
between the two kinds of discoveries to be made. However, I suspect that the following hypotheses are more appropriate to discovery of a way to correct an inadequacy than to discovering the inadequacy in the first place.

Hypothesis A. Lack of experience is most effectively dealt
with by the method of counselor discovery and interpretation.

Hypothesis B. Distortion in perception is most effectively
dealt with by the method of client self-discovery.

There are several arguments to support these two hypotheses
as a starting point. Lack of experience includes lack of information about self and the environment. Experience can be direct or
vicarious. The client is motivated by his needs to obtain the result of the experience which he is lacking. Typically the counselor
is able to obtain the necessary information, understandings and insights by virtue of his superior knowledge of human behavior, his
superior knowledge of environment, and his superior methods of
assessing psychological characteristics. The counselor can supply the client with the proper information (experiences) and the
client can correct his inadequacies in a straightforward learning
situation. However, if the client is unable to utilize these counselor discoveries, the problem is not one of lack of experience
but one of distorted perceptions. The client does not need more
information or experience to distort. He needs to correct his distortions. Since his distortions are in part a defense against en-
croachment from the outside, he cannot accurately utilize information from the counselor. Therefore, he must discover for himself.
The counselor can aid by creating a situation in which the client
need not spend all of his attention and energy defending himself
against his environment but can attend to the things in this own
make-up which are causing him trouble. The counselor can provide a safe situation in which the client can work on material he
already has on hand.

To summarize very briefly, I have suggested a theoretical
model for counseling which includes the following points:

1. Biological and psycho-social needs are the energizers of
   behavior.
2. Behavior repertoire is made up of three elements—experience,
   perceptions and generalizations.

3. Behavior repertoire may be inadequate for any of three reasons—lack of experience, distortion in perception or erroneous generalizations.
4. The goal of counseling is to discover and correct inadequacies in behavior repertoire.
5. These discoveries can be made by either client or counselor. Therefore, counseling methods can be grouped under general methods; client self-discovery, and counselor discovery accompanied by interpretation.
6. Any one counseling method will not be equally effective in discovering and correcting all types of inadequacies in behavior repertoire.
7. There is an urgent need for attention to the problem of differential diagnosis leading to differential choice of treatment. Two attractive research hypotheses as a start on the problem are: (a) Lack of experience can be most effectively dealt with by counselor discovery and interpretation. (b) Distortions in perceptions can be most effectively dealt with by client self-discovery.

REFERENCES

Apostal, R.A., & Miller, J.G. A manual for the use of a set of diagnostic categories. Columbia: University of Missouri Testing and Counseling Service Report No. 21, 1959.

Berdie, R. F. Counseling principles and presumptions. J. counsel. Psychol., 1959, 6: 175-182.

Berezin, Annabel G. The development and use of a system of diagnostic categories in counseling. Unpublished doctoral dissertation, Univer. of Missouri, 1957.

Bordin, E. S. Diagnosis in counseling and psychotherapy. Educ. Psychol. Measmt., 1946, 6: 169-184.

Dollard, J., Auld, F. W., & White, Alice M. Steps in psychotherapy. New York: Macmillan, 1953.

Maslow, A. H. Motivation and personality. New York: Harper, 1954.

Pepinsky, H. B. The selection and use of diagnostic categories in clinical counseling. Psychol. Monogr., 1948, No. 15.

Pepinsky, H. B. and Pepinsky, Pauline N. Counseling: Theory and practice. New York: Ronald, 1954.

Rogers, C. R. Test of personality adjustment. New York: Association Press, 1931.

Rogers, C. R. The clinical treatment of the problem child. Boston: Houghton Mifflin, 1939. .

Rogers, C. R. Counseling and psychotherapy. Boston: Houghton Mifflin, 1942.

Rogers, C. R. Client-centered therapy. Boston: Houghton Mifflin, 1951.

Weiner, I. B. The role of diagnosis in a university counseling center. J. counsel. Psychol., 1959, 6: 110-115.

Williamson, E. G., & Darley, J. G. Student personnel work. New York: McGraw-Hill, 1937.

II

CRITIQUE OF RECENT DEVELOPMENTS IN PERSONALITY COUNSELING THEORY

Frederick C. Thorne

The progress of science would be expedited greatly if the originators of significant contributions would make periodic progress reports concerning their latest thinking about recent developments related to theoretical systems. Much speculative controversy could have been avoided if Freud, Adler, John B. Watson and other theorizers had issued periodic statements bringing their latest viewpoints up-to-date publicly, and particularly where important revisions of earlier viewpoints had occurred. These comments are particularly true of the field of psychotherapy where there is great need for systematically relating and validating a large number of theoretical contributions which too often have not been assimilated into the body of scientifically established facts but have become the foundations of isolated schools or systems. The purpose of this article is to present a critique of personality counseling theory bringing up-to-date our most recent thinking on the subject.

GENERAL REMARKS CONCERNING THEORIZING AND SYSTEM-BUILDING

No one would voluntarily restrict creative theorizing which may supply hypothetical models for lucrative research design. There are definite dangers, however, in applied fields such as

Reprinted by permission of the author and the *Journal of Clinical Psychology,* 1957, 13:234–244.

psychotherapy when theorizing and system-building far outstrip anything which has been established scientifically so that unvalidated theories are given large scale clinical application. It must be emphasized that in psychodiagnosis and psychotherapy, unproven theories and unvalidated practices are in current use far more widely than in any other clinical field. Unlike modern medicine in which schools and cults are practically extinct and where the subject matters consist largely of what has been established scientifically, in the field of psychotherapy we find a large number of competing theoretical systems and schools all being widely applied in the almost complete absence of validation and standardization.

Theory-centeredness may lead to metaphysical and dialetic confusion which actually impedes the forward progress of science. One example of such tendencies exists in the current contents of many psychoanalytic and psychiatric journals of which a formal analysis of topics and methods reveals that 80-90% of the articles are purely speculative or anecdotal in contrast with a content of about 80 or 90% of experimental-statistical studies in basic-science oriented psychological journals. Unending speculative controversy goes on concerning the theoretical implications of even chance remarks made by Freud and other "authorities." The situation is comparable to the centuries-long speculations of the greatest minds of ancient times concerning the nature of the human circulatory system which was settled forever by Harvey's simple emperic observation of the direction of blood flow in the veins by compressing and then releasing pressure on a vein on the back of the hand. The attempt to validate theories logically by constructing supposedly comprehensive and consistent systems is obsolete in an era when experimental-statistical validation is possible. It is regrettable that so much time is being currently spent in the attempt to secure respectibility [sic] for unvalidated clinical methods by relating them to theories which have some systematic prestige.

PSYCHOANALYTICALLY ORIENTED PSYCHOTHERAPIES

Psychoanalytically-oriented practices probably have the largest current following and prestige in the fields of counseling and psychotherapy, particularly in educational institutions and clinics which are administered by psychoanalysts. Since 1945, the psychiatry departments of several major universities have been taken over by psychoanalysts and we have reports from such installations or cities that personnel without psychoanalytic training find it difficult to obtain or retain appointments.

There is little evidence that basic science psychology is either well understood or utilized in many psychoanalytic centers. Indeed, a large portion of the time of many analysts is devoted to the training of other analysts in the same unvalidated methods, which condition may continue to exist as long as it is necessary to obtain such qualifications to gain local professional recognition.

This phenomenon of the contemporary prestige of psychoanalysis exists in spite of the fact that today, more than 50 years after the appearance of Freud's basic theories, there is still no adequate experimental-statistical validation of the system either in whole or part. While psychoanalytic formulations may receive empiric validation in individual cases, there is little acceptable evidence that they may be universally applied to all persons at all times. Without in any way disparaging the brilliance of Freud's contributions or minimizing their importance as clarifying certain classes of behavior data, there is still room for sound skepticism concerning current practices of projecting psychoanalytic interpretations on all case materials. In personal observations of psychoanalytic approaches (as well as many others), we have frequently noted therapists displaying considerable intellectual ingenuity trying to match standard theoretical interpretations to samples of behavior data but without much apparent awareness of the evident invalidity of such practices. This constitutes an example of extreme directiveness in which the therapist projects diagnoses and interpretations uncritically whether they fit or not. Our conclusion concerning psychoanalytic approaches must be that this method is essentially intuitive, anecdotal, empiric and unvalidated in its present stage of evolution since there is a dearth of experimental-statistical data. Individual applications, no matter how brilliant and productive, are at present empiric and intuitive. A great deal of the difficulty will be obviated, undoubtedly, as the phenomena uncovered by the psychoanalytic method are integrated and interpreted in terms of basic science psychology. Expediently, however, we will all go on making psychoanalytic interpretations until some better methods become available, but dangers can be minimized if greater criticality and caution are used.

Similar comments apply to projective techniques based largely on Freudian interpretations. Many clinicians go to extremes in applying projective interpretations to all behaviors ranging from global integrations down to the most incidental mannerisms. Such methods would not be too objectionable if diagnoses were properly qualified with limiting statements indicating their hypothetical and essentially unvalidated nature, but they become grossly unscientific and bordering on charlatanism when stated with absolute positivity which rules out the consideration of other possibilities. It would be wise not to forget the lessons taught by the fate of the early methods of Freudian dream interpretation. While dreams may have symbolic significance, their latent meanings only can be understood in terms of the dynamics of the individual case to which an universal dream vocabulary or symbolism can rarely be applied. It is unwise to apply projective interpretations unless there is definite evidence that projective mechanisms indeed are operating.

CLIENT-CENTERED COUNSELING

Nondirective, client-centered methods of personality counseling have reached a stage of empiric validation where they are now widely accepted as a valuable part of our personality counseling armamentarium within the limits of their indications and contraindications. Utilized with clients who are motivated to understand and change themselves, and who have sufficient personality resources to work through to their own solutions once emotional blocks have been resolved, nondirective methods permit the client to reach his own solutions with maximum freedom. They are also valuable in many other clinical situations where acceptance, permissiveness and reflection of feelings facilitate the building of rapport, lead to more complete self-expression, and encourage the development of initiative and responsibility in solving one's own problems. When such methods are utilized within their indications and contraindications, along with such other more active methods as may be indicated, and without making excessive claims for their achievements unsupported by actual research results, there can be no quarrel with their use.

Although it is too early to make a definitive statement, evidence appears to be accumulating that use of the nondirective approach is indicated more positively with "ego-negative" persons who are dissatisfied with themselves and anxious to change, and may be contraindicated with "ego-positive" persons who are satisfied with themselves and have no insight into the fact of maladjustment or the desirability of changing. Negative self-regarding attitudes, at least when not on an obsessive or psychotic basis, tend to motivate the client to face problems and work out solutions, and a minimum of therapist activity is indicated, at least until such time as direct intervention is proven more efficient. In our experience, the nondirective approach tends to fail or reach an impasse with self-satisfied clients who either see nothing wrong or who do not want to change. This includes the large group of psychoneurotic persons whose unconscious defenses may resist even massive intervention.

Much of the dissatisfaction and published criticism of nondirectivism appear to have been stimulated more by the way in which such methods have been presented or advocated rather than with the techniques themselves. If nondirectivism had been advanced as simply a promising group of new methods to be integrated with older methods according to their indications and contraindications, it probably would have been widely accepted without controversy. However, the active promotion of the client-centered principle as the basis for a new and inclusive school of theory and practice, often advocated somewhat uncritically as a new panacea suitable for all clinical situations, and even as a philosophy for the conduct of all human affairs, has stimulated critical reactions which have sought to cut the new movement down to size and integrate its contributions into existing knowledge. The efforts of nondirectivism to erect a theoretical rationale in support of its empiric achievements often have led to the making of claims which did not seem validated by actual research findings. Finally, the tendency of some nondirectivists to refer to themselves and act as if they were the exclusive proprietors of a new school whose methods would soon make obsolete all older techniques has quite understandably stimulated criticism from those who believe that all new findings must be integrated into basic science knowledge and methods.

More than ten years ago, this writer published a critique (Thorne, 1944) of nondirective methods of counseling and psychotherapy motivated by our concern over the apparent failure of this new school to incorporate certain standard principles of objective methodology in research and clinical approaches. A restatement of our basic criticisms in 1957 would point up five major defects of research design which seriously vitiate the conclusions which can be drawn from most of the research to date.

(a) The persistent failure of nondirectivists to recognize the importance of valid diagnosis in all scientific case study, and particularly in research design, makes it impossible to evaluate clinical claims and research results.

(b) The failure to attempt to identify all pertinent variables diagnostically has made it impossible to utilize standard research designs involving use of equated samples, rigorous identification and manipulation of dependent and independent variables, and the objectification of all factors and steps known to be involved.

(c) The failure to control, or otherwise partial out, the effects of other therapeutic factors (such as suggestions, catharsis, desensitization, etc.), which are known to be operating, makes it impossible to draw any valid conclusions as to what is actually occurring in nondirective therapy.

(d) The failure to check conclusions drawn from phenomenological data obtained from the client (or inferred by the therapist) with actual objective measurements of known factors or status may result in serious misinterpretations of the realities of the therapeutic situation.

(e) Even if positive therapeutic results are demonstrable using nondirective methods, it still remains to be proven that such effects could not have been achieved just as well or even more expeditiously with other methods.

In conclusion, then, the failure to rigorously identify, diagnose and control all factors known to be operating in psychotherapy has seriously invalidated much of recent research on nondirective methods. We are not told whether the subjects are normal or abnormal, the nature and pathogenicity in terms of actual case history findings of the factors being therapized, and we are not convinced that the postulated factors actually explain the results obtained. In other words, most of the factors which we need to know about have been left undifferentiated and uncontrolled. In effect, it appears that nondirectivism postulates one standard diagnosis for all clients, namely that emotional factors blocking growth are the most important cause of all disorder, hence diagnosis is not necessary and only one standard method (nondirectivism) is indicated.

The most prominent success of client-centered methodological research has been in objectively demonstrating the actual operations which take place in this method. Nondirectivism has made a very great contribution in developing passive methods of counseling emphasizing acceptance, permissiveness, reflection and clarification of feelings, and placing the responsibility upon the client for working out his own problem solutions. Conversely, the dangers of crude directiveness, counselor-centerdness, and the invalid projection of interpretations upon the client's behavior are all better understood as a result of insistence on the client-centered principle. The issue still remains, however, concerning indications and contraindications for use of nondirective methods with different types of clients, pathological processes, degrees of pathogenicity and other factors determining outcomes.

Proponents of nondirectivism have been less successful in trying to construct a systematic theoretical rationale for their viewpoint. It appears that Rogers' earliest contributions were developed by intuitive-empiric methods, interpreted at first (Rogers, 1942) in terms of somewhat mystical concepts of self-realization and growth, and more recently developed in terms of a thoroughgoing phenomenological approach (Rogers, 1955). While such preoccupation with the self-concept and other phenomenological data as experienced by the subject himself and understood empathically by the therapist is very intriguing and commendable in itself, considerable criticsm may be directed toward the attempt to construct a complete system on such a limited approach. Even more caution should be invoked in evaluating claims by nondirectivists for unique processes and results from their methods, particularly when it is known that all therapeutic methods have their successes. Before we can ascribe much validity to claims made, for example, from changes on Q sorts given pre- and post-client-centered therapy, it will be necessary to obtain comparable Q sorts from clients treated with Coueism, Christian Science, Dianetics, psychoanalysis and many types of directive methods (all of which have very enthusiastic clients and practitioners). It may be that certain standard factors underly [sic] all these methods and that specific philosophical rationales are superfluous. Snyder recognizes this dilemma when he states that "Perhaps it doesn't make very much difference which philosophies guide a therapist's work" (Snyder, 1956). While it is interesting to attempt to trace the philosophical antecedents of recent theoretical developments as when Walker (1956) perceives Freud as the intellectual disciple of Augustine, and Rogers the intellectual descendent of Jesus, Confucius or Rousseau, there are dangers in implying that psychoanalysis or nondirectivism have some face validity from being related to such respected authorities. Similar comments apply to the currently popular practice of using laudatory or discriminatory designations to categorize accepted or rejected concepts as when Snyder (1956) categorizes neofundamentalism, scholasticism, behaviorism, psychobiology, learning theory and directive counseling as being "authoritarian", while nondirectivism is identified with "self-actualism" or "self-determinism", idealism, democratic government, humanism, progressive education, hormic psychology and phenomenology. Such a dichotomy is purely arbitrary and probably artifactual, and even worse are the self-reflexive connotations of the term "authoritarian" as interpreted against the recent associative contexts of Fascism, Communism, regimentation and exploitation as contrasted with other possible connotations involving such positive contexts as love, protection, paternalism, guidance, help and wise counseling. The use of such self-reflexive terms in purportedly scientific communications is very undesirable.

While we would defend to the end the right of Carl R. Rogers (1955) to expound his own philosophical queries and experiences in relation to problems of science and phenomenology, we must insist that the evidential value of such observations must be rigorously evaluated by scientific methods before being accepted as anything but expressions of personal opinion and faith. The quandaries of Rogers in relation to "Persons or Science" (1955) appear to be rationalizations of the deficiencies of his ideological approach. Rogers' rejection of diagnosis as a basic method of research and of clinical practice has seriously limited the scope of his whole approach, and his failure to modify his position, to publicly indicate the limitations and contraindications of nondirectivism, or to discuss their integration with older methods, may actually inhibit the acceptance of the whole movement. Snyder appears to admit this in his somewhat despairing comment of a "pox on both sides" as he concludes that "as long as Rogers cares and the Freudians care, both seem to be meeting the needs of clients" (Snyder, 1956).

Actually, the defects of the research design under which most nondirective research has been done could be avoided by the simple procedure of having some independent authority select and thoroughly study samples of cases before submitting them for nondirective treatment. This device would simultaneously objectify the nature of the case materials while at the same time free the client-centered therapist from introducing any sort of diagnostic procedure during his case handling. After the termination of therapy, the independent authority could again study the cases for the presence and nature of any changes occurring from therapy. Such results could then be compared with other samples treated by other standard methods, and the data subjected to factor analysis to discover any common factors underlying all methods.

ECLECTIC COUNSELING

The eclectic method of selecting appropriate theories and methods to fit the indications and contraindications of each individual case has long been the standard procedure in the older clinical sciences such as medicine. In personal reaction to the seeming one-sidedness of nondirective and psychoanalytic approaches, publication of a series of articles on directive therapy was begun in 1945 and later expanded into a systematic textbook (Thorne, 1950). Our adoption of the term directive was intended only to emphasize the existence of a large number of therapeutic methods (including nondirectivism) within the larger framework of all that was known about influencing personality. Our use of this term was not intended to imply any preference for any special group of methods or philosophical viewpoint, and we regret that many readers immediately projected many unintended meanings which now we do not wish to be identified with. The term eclectic would have been more accurate semantically and, by 1948, we specifically attempted to limit the term directive to the systematic attempt to use all methods of therapy eclectically based on a formal plan for the identification and modification of etiologic factors in maladjustment (Thorne, 1948). Now, we prefer to abandon all terms such as directive, nondirective, psychoanalytic, etc., as tending to create artificial continua and semantic artifacts, and instead to substitute operational descriptions and nomenclature for the dynamics of any method. The term eclectic has value only to differentiate an approach which refuses to subscribe to any one operational viewpoint or method, and becomes entirely objectionable if given self-reflexive connotations such as "authoritarian".

The eclectic approach to scientific case handling basically depends upon adequate diagnosis as the cornerstone of all case handling in order to identify etiologic causes and apply appropriate therapeutic methods according to their indications and contraindications. Currently, the most important theoretical issue in personality counseling and, indeed, all psychotherapy, is the matter of the relation of diagnosis to valid therapy. Far from attempting to establish any new school or system based on "directive" methods, our sole purpose has been to emphasize the importance of diagnosis as the cornerstone underlying the rationale for knowing the indications and contraindications of all known methods utilized without systematic bias of any kind. Frankly, we have been very much disturbed over the past few years by the discovery that many teachers and clinicians have entirely misunderstood our fundamental theoretical position which stresses a thorough-going basic-science-oriented eclecticism by erroneously identifying us with directivism as a method or end in itself. Our original selection of the term "directive psychotherapy" was intended only to emphasize that an important group of methods exists in contrast to nondirectivism, and it was not intended to identify a new school or system.

Now the need for emphasizing such a difference has long since passed, and we would prefer to use the term directive only to indicate one end of a continuum of passivity vs. activity in the therapist. In our own practice, we try to be passive or active according to the indications of the situation rather than following any ideological bias.

One of the criticisms advanced, particularly by nondirectivists, against eclecticism in its present status of development, relates to the voluminous research which has been accumulated by special schools in contrast with the meagre or nonexistent research output achieved by the exponents of eclecticism. Such criticisms have been directed against eclectic or directive counseling as where Shoben says that "Thorne is unable to escape an authoritarian tone that could not be challenged in itself if it were buttressed either by experimental evidence or convincing case material" (Shoben, 1956a, p. 43), and which comment has appeared repeatedly in many forms. Such a criticism appears to reflect a lack of understanding concerning the differing problems and responsibilities placed upon those who accept eclecticism in contrast with those who support more limited special methods. Our original aim in attempting to compile a unified systematic approach to diagnosis and therapy was to attempt to gather in one place all that was scientifically valid and fairly well accepted from all sources or schools, both clinical and experimental-statistical, eclectically. We have never made any claims for any of these methods beyond what had been advanced in the literature or appeared valid in terms of personal clinical experience. We submit that this was all that could be accomplished at time and place, and we make no special claims for any superiority of any of these methods beyond what has been empirically established. Our role was simply to attempt an integration of all that seemed to be accepted in terms of the accumulated clinical experience of our generation and without favor or prejudice for any method beyond the known indications and contraindications as currently understood. This task of attempting to integrate, in one internally-consistent presentation, the accumulated experience of clinical science is in itself so gigantic as to preclude any personal research attack upon the vast number of problems and methods, and certainly beyond our personal resources which have been invested maximally in the attempt to integrate existing research interpretively. We can only state, then, that our conclusions represent only the concentrate of human knowledge at time and place as we have interpreted it. We feel that there is a definite need not only for researchers who can provide valid data but also for global interpreters who must attempt to relate the many disparate findings which are in themselves more or less meaningless until oriented in some master frame of reference.

Any deficiencies of eclecticism or directivism simply reflect either (a) the relatively primitive state of human knowledge concerning these methods, or (b) the inadequacies of breadth of viewpoint among those who attempt an integrative interpretation. To the degree which eclecticism is able to integrate all operational methods and findings available at time and place, it appears to us that it must represent the last word concerning what we can validly understand and apply in practice. We may accept, as a basic premise, the axiom that clinical methods are simply individual applications (within the limits of validity of clinical judgment) of basic science experimental-statistical methods and data. We seek to protect the validity of our judgments and conclusions by rigorously seeking to discriminate cause-effect relationships by the most advanced diagnostic methods. We submit that this is all which can be done for time and place within any clinical orientation. Eclectic methodology is so diverse and complex that a general advance on all fronts simultaneously can come only very gradually and certainly beyond the scope of any one person or generation to advance them very markedly. In spite of this admitted deficiency based on the primitive status of existing knowledge, we can be assured of some degree of face, content, empirical and factorial validity by constantly seeking to relate our practices to the most advanced basic science thinking of time and place.

In contrast, the proponents of special methods have a particular obligation to demonstrate that new ingredients have been added over and above existing knowledge. Considering the impressive basic science advances of the last century, both by science in general and by special schools, the burden of the proof rests upon proponents of new schools to show where and how they have advanced human knowledge beyond merely introducing new terms or rehashing the known. Modern medicine for example, has reached a status of solid basic science achievement where we can expect new discoveries in special areas by experimental-statistical methods, but we do not anticipate any revolutionary philosophical advances which will change our basic methods of scientific discovery or thinking. Science supersedes schools of philosophy or metaphysics as soon as it accumulates sufficient objective knowledge in any field to provide valid bases for clinical applications. We believe that clinical psychological science has already achieved such a solid basic sci-

ence foundation of proven facts as to make obsolete the need for
metaphysical theorizing and special schools. If new advances are
made, they must be integrated into the broad foundation of scientific
knowledge rather than being offered as revolutionary panaceas to
replace all that is eclectically known.

Eclecticism in clinical practice is always held back in situations where students are trained in only one method, and are either
oblivious of other methods or insecure in their application. Until
such time as students are provided training experiences with all
known operational methods of diagnosis and therapy, it is evident
that their capacity or competence in applying all known methods
eclectically will be limited. The need to build up one's confidence
clinically be becoming a "master" in some specific school, such
as nondirectivism or psychoanalysis, disappears as personal competence with all known methods broadens and one is sustained by
the knowledge that one knows all there is to know for time and
place, i.e., broad scientific knowledge and clinical competence
reduce the need for speculative theorizing.

DISCIPLINARY COUNSELING

Williamson and Foley (1949) have presented a detailed reporting of the use of "counseling" in the disciplinary management of
student conduct problems as developed since 1941 in the office of
the dean of students at the University of Minnesota. Although the
authors evidently are aware of the classically therapeutic basic
role of personality counseling, and repeatedly emphasize the re-
habilitational and reeducative objectives of their program, it becomes immediately apparent that the term "management" would be
a much more realistic designation of their methods of case handling
than is the term "counseling". Although in defining their concept
of the role of counseling in student discipline, the authors are careful to structure their activities as not being authoritarian, regulatory or punitive, an analysis of their outline of case handling methods and the actual transcripts of individual cases indicates that
their activities are conducted within a plainly authoritarian judgmental framework which can hardly be perceived as anything else
by the students. In spite of what Williamson and Foley theorize
the situation to involve, the critical element in categorizing the
nature of the situation must be in terms of what the subjects of the
counseling perceive it to be. In discussing their procedures of
disciplinary counseling, their schematic outline (Shoben, 1956a,
p. 61), includes such steps as (a) making of charges against the

student, (b) compulsory interviewing for counseling purposes, (c) reporting and review by a disciplinary committee in a face-to-face situation with the student, and (d) disciplinary action by the committee involving the imposition of further regulatory actions upon the student. Whatever the professed intentions of the disciplinary committee, the execution of its functions in such a framework cannot avoid the connotation of a judgmental, regulatory and, perhaps, punitive orientation to case handling as the whole situation is perceived by the student from the implications of what goes on. That many students may, indeed, perceive the situation as basically judgmental and punitive is clearly evident in the case of Milton Reed (Shoben, 1956a, p. 229) where not only the accused but also two friends openly profess their fears that unreasonable judgments and/or punishments are going to be administered.

In our opinion, no method of case handling deserves to be designated as counseling unless healing is the basic and primary objective beyond which all other considerations are secondary. In order to retain its basically therapeutic functions, the counseling situation must be thoroughly safeguarded to preserve its purpose of being the one place (in addition to psychiatry) where a person may frankly discuss his problems in a completely healing atmosphere unthreatened by any question of judgment or punishment. We are in agreement with Rogers (1942) in his contention that any other structuring of the situation destroys the therapeutic context.

Implicit in the approach of Williamson and Foley is the questionable assumption that misbehavior is classifiable into voluntary and involuntary types for which discipline and therapy are the solutions respectively. While the authors recognize that immaturity and personality deviations may interact with unhealthy environmental forces to produce misconduct, the installation of such complicated judicial machinery and practices only succeeds in advancing the implication that we are really dealing with deliberate misbehavior, bordering on criminality, and which can be handled best by punitive procedures progressively applied until the miscreant sees the light and voluntarily controls himself better. We must insist that such methods of case handling are more properly designated as management and do not qualify as counseling because the basic operational framework is not primarily therapeutic but rather is regulatory and administrative. This is not to imply that counseling cannot be carried on within disciplinary or administrative auspices where the healing motive is primary and disposition is secondary. We would prefer to base all counseling on the postulate that all misbehavior reflects immaturity, personality deviation or personality reactions to situations, reflecting various degrees of lack of control, and arising etiologically in the domain of psychopathology. From such a viewpoint, all disciplinary problems should be handled within a completely therapeutic frame of reference, only being referred for regulatory action in the event of a breakdown of therapeutic progress and poor prognosis. The authorities could take notice of misconduct by anonymous comments on the situation, clearly indicating its position that such behavior must be the result of unhealthy thinking, and further indicating that gross regulatory methods would be enforced only in the event of the breakdown of rehabilitation.

There is serious question whether disciplinary counseling as practiced in the case of Janet Larson (Shoben, 1956a, p. 261) may be actually untherapeutic and dangerous to the health of the subjects concerned. We can think of few situations more traumatic and guilt-productive than for students to be detected in the act of sex intercourse in the bushes by the university watchman and such detection is usually punishment enough. Pschiatrically, there is great danger of the girl (at least) developing incapacitating mortification and guilt reactions which may lead to life-long neuroticism and frigidity. When this student was interrogated by F. L. Crane in the presence of John D. Foley on July 22, 1945 in great detail concerning what took place, the circumstances of the interview indicate that it was conducted somewhat like a third degree solely for the purpose of securing a signed confession and with nothing therapeutic taking place. Further, on July 23, the accused Janet Larson and William Burton were called before the faculty disciplinary committee and interrogated together about their marriage intentions, guilt reactions and penitent attitudes. The trend of the questioning seemed to hint that the university would be satisfied if the couple married (shotgun influence?) but it actually did not accomplish this purpose, perhaps because Burton was led to admit previous intercourse before Miss Larson and also did not seem completely enthusiastic about marriage. The most therapeutic action taken was the decision of the disciplinary committee to put the students on probation while continuing at the university. It is interesting to note that on May 11, 1946, counselor G. E. K. spontaneously notes that Miss Larson no longer has "a vivacious, energetic enthusiasm" in her manner but has changed to "quiet winsomeness", which might be interpreted as reflecting deep anxiety or guilt. In any case, a perusal of the case record reveals no evidence of therapeutic counseling but only the administrative details of handling student misbehavior.

An analysis of the entire 15 cases cited as examples of disciplinary counseling reveals that the counselor activity seems to consist in acting as the representative of university authority in identifying alleged misbehavior, identifying the students involved, obtaining signed confessions before witnesses, conducting judicial hearings, and later advising the student how to behave in order to stay out of trouble again. While some secondary therapeutic results may be achieved where leniency, tolerance, and patience may operate to keep the student in the university until he can learn to handle objective behaviors more adaptively, there is little evidence either that the primary emphasis is therapeutic or that modern counseling methods have been used under maximally effective conditions to secure deep personality changes.

DIFFERENT OPERATIONAL APPROACHES

Order may be brought into the current confusion of competing psychotherapies by reducing or translating each approach to its lowest operational common denominator. As pointed out elsewhere (Thorne, 1953a, p. 138), behavior analysis may be attempted from the operational viewpoints of instinct theory, perceptual field theory, learning theory, motivation theory or the psychology of the emotions. Each diverse approach utilizes its own operational levels of personality study and achieves its own distinctive results which may reflect determination by general, group or specific factors. Clinicians trained primarily in one operational approach tend to have trouble comprehending the methods and results from other operational approaches. The advantage of a thoroughgoing operational approach is that it permits the study of raw behavior data directly and with the formulation of diagnostic impressions induc-tively to fit the individual case with the progressive interpretation of data. The problem is to construct a theory to fit the case inductively rather than trying to apply theories deductively. Operationism renders unnecessary undue speculation and theorizing if carried out in sufficient detail to uncover the major etiologic factors in each case.

The fact that many methods appear to produce results can only have two possible explanations. Either similar dynamic factors are operating in diverse methods, or there is more than one method for achieving the same specific goals. For example, as pointed out by Snyder (1956, p. 92), perhaps a theory of psychotherapy does little more than to inspire the therapist with confidence which is transmitted to the client and becomes the basis of a relationship

which shows the client that "somebody" cares. Or perhaps suggestion effects and emotional release are enough to help most clients.
Or perhaps merely doing something until time and nature heal is
enough. Such important questions can only be solved with a research design complex enough to identify and control all relevant
variables. In the meantime, symposia on perceptual field theory
or learning theory in relation to psychotherapy may be very valuable in casting light on what these various operational approaches
may contribute but it should not be expected that any one operational
approach can provide the complete answer. Combs (1954) may be
correct in concluding that traditional learning theories offer little
towards the improvement of counseling (that is, beyond the general
recognition that all therapy involves learning according to well-
known psychological laws), but we feel that he is overoptimistic in
assuming that all behavior is a function of the field of perception at
the moment of behaving so that the process of counseling becomes
one of altering perceptions in desired directions. Shaw (6) apparently takes a much more valid position (in agreement with our
eclectic viewpoint) that varied conditions of learning in persons
may produce a variety of etiologic factors operating on many levels
of personality integration. We agree with Shoben (7) that contemporary learning theories are most interested in principles of learning while the clinician must attempt, as we have also previously
pointed out, to (a) establish suitable conditions so that learning can
take place, and then (b) to actually introduce new conditionings in
more healthy directions (Thorne, 1953b, p. 278). Our own detailed
viewpoint is that personality integration may be organized by many
levels of factors, which may be perceptual, learned, motivational,
affective or instinctive, operating at various levels of generality or
specificity, and each requiring their own particular operational
methods for diagnosis or treatment (Thorne, 1955, pp. 14-15). It
will probably require complex experiments of factor analytic design
to differentiate prototypical patterns of syndrome organization.

SEMANTIC PROBLEMS

A most urgent problem in the whole field of diagnosis and
therapy concerns the early adoption of a uniform and universal system of nomenclature so that the coordinates and boundaries of psychological space may become standardized. Every few months
some authority launches a new theory replete with its own distinctive terminology which usually is not related to the coordinates of
accepted knowledge. Two recent examples of such system-building

with difficult new terminologies are Allport's (1955) event-structure theory and J. G. Miller's (1956) general behavior systems theory, both of which will require long intensive study to become proficient with and simply to master the terms with any facility. And even after the new terminology is mastered, there still remains the problem of relating the new contributions to existing knowledge to discover whether or not the new formulation makes any distinctive contribution. There is great need for the profession to adopt a standard nomenclature with a universal index of factors to be measured. The most promising beginnings in this direction have been made by the factor analysts who are working towards standard methods for labelling and mapping new factors in their space-time dimensions, and we have personally adopted standard terminology in our approach to psychological examining. Semantic chaos will result from the multiplication of new theories and systems unless standard nomenclature is uniformly adopted to relate new developments to existing coordinates. In our own editorial work, we uniformly reject papers introducing new and esoteric terminology unless it can be clearly shown that such refinements are needed to describe genuinely new developments. As matters now stand, students entering the field must spend entirely unreasonable amounts of time trying to master the babel of conflicting terminologies.

PREDICTIONS FOR THE FUTURE

The most urgent theoretical question in personality counseling and, indeed, all psychotherapy, is the matter of the relation of diagnosis to valid therapy. Currently, it is fashionable in some circles to ignore problems of diagnosis or to categorize such interests as authoritarian (Shoben, 1956b, p. 43). It is a basic postulate of all scientific method to attempt to discover the nature and etiology of all variables determining a natural occurrence, i.e., to identify causes and effects. Without in any way attempting to defend the inadequacies of current diagnostic methods and systems, we cannot see how any progress can be made in understanding causation or rationally manipulating determinants unless a diagnosis is made of all antecedents leading to consequences. Our opinion is that advances in psychotherapy must depend on more valid diagnosis and to this end we have evolved a systematic method (Thorne, 1955) for evaluating all factors known to organize personality integration. We emphatically reject the hypothesis that psychotherapy is in any way different from other clinical science in the sense of it being possible to dispense with diagnosis in scientific case handling.

This has nothing to do with any philosophic bias but is a tenet of scientific method.

Within this general basic science orientation, we may predict future developments in the issues which are now so controversial. We predict that the current heavy investment of time and energy in speculative theorizing and system-building will be supplanted by a consistent effort to relate all knowledge and new developments in terms of a standard nomenclature and universal index of factors and results. We predict that exclusive preoccupation with special operational approaches such as perception or learning theory will be replaced by a broader eclectic utilization of all available operational approaches according to the indications and contraindications of time and place. We predict that nondirectivism (and all other special therapies) will be demoted from their current status as mutually exclusive systems to take their proper places as limited technical advances integrated into a broad diagnostic-therapeutic armamentarium applied eclectically, without special bias or preference for specific tools. We predict that much of psychoanalytic speculation and dialectics will be abandoned, either because ultimately proven to be unvalidatable or more parsimoniously explained in terms of basic science concepts, and leaving a residual of fact which can be integrated into basic science knowledge in the proper places. We predict that all clinicians will accept ultimately the absolute essentiality of diagnostic thinking and will cease to seek short-cuts motivated by current deficiencies. In other words, we reaffirm our belief in the ultimate victory of scientific methodology in proving its capability of dealing with all psychological problems without recourse to less rigorous philosophizing and speculation.

We cannot escape the fact that all natural phenomena reflect the operation of laws which determine causes and effects. If we are to understand and manipulate these causes and effects with maximum efficiency, then we must recognize the various categories of action imperatives involved in the concept of "ought". Elsewhere (Thorne, 1953b), we have explored the implications of the psychology of "ought" for social planning in general, and individual efficiency in particular, with special reference to what can be accomplished in diagnosis and therapy. We insist that all this can be accomplished within the orientation of eclecticism. We hope that adherents of various special positions will cease projecting various characterizations upon each other and will work in common to discover and control the actual etiologic factors which must be operating.

REFERENCES

Allport, F. H. Theories of perception and the concept of structure. New York: Wiley, 1955.

Combs, A. W. Counseling as a learning process. J. counsel. Psychol., 1954, 1: 31-36.

Miller, J. G. General behavior systems theory and summary. J. counsel. Psychol., 1956, 3: 120-124.

Rogers, C. R. Counseling and psychotherapy. Boston: Houghton Mifflin, 1942.

Rogers, C. R. Persons or science? A philosophical question. Amer. Psychol., 1955, 10: 267-278.

Shaw, F. J. Counseling from the standpoint of an "Interactive Conceptualist." J. counsel. Psychol., 1954, 1:36-42.

Shoben, E. J., Jr. Introduction: Behavior theories and a counseling case. J. counsel. Psychol., 1956a, 3:107-108.

Shoben, E. J., Jr. The mosaic for psychotherapy. Contemporary Psychol., 1956b, 1: 42-44.

Snyder, W. U. Comment. J. counsel. Psychol., 1956, 3: 91-92.

Thorne, F. C. A critique of nondirective methods of psychotherapy. J. abn. soc. Psychol., 1944, 39: 459-470.

Thorne, F.C. Principles of directive counseling and psychotherapy. Amer. Psychologist, 1948, 3: 160-166.

Thorne, F. C. Principles of personality counseling. Brandon, Vt.: Journal of Clinical Psychology, 1950.

Thorne, F. C. Operational concepts in clinical psychology and medicine. J. clin. Psychol., 1953a, 9: 137-142.

Thorne, F. C. Directive psychotherapy: Theory, practice and social implications. J. clin. Psychol. 1953b, 9: 267-280.

Thorne, F. C. Principles of psychological examining. Brandon, Vt.: Journal of Clinical Psychology, 1955.

Walker, D. E. Carl Rogers and the nature of man. J. counsel. Psychol., 1956, 3: 89-91.

Williamson, E. G. and Foley, J. D. Counseling and discipline. New York: McGraw-Hill, 1949.

III

THEORETICAL PRINCIPLES UNDERLYING
THE COUNSELING PROCESS

Leona E. Tyler

Counseling is serious business. Across a counselor's desk
come the aspirations and anxieties, the convictions and the difficult choices that have generated all the theories about human personality. Because this is so, a counselor needs the kind of organization that some theory of his own gives to his thinking. A theory
about anything is simply a way of organizing what is known with
regard to it, and a psychological theory is a way of organizing
present knowledge about human nature. A counselor can scarcely
avoid thinking theoretically about the human situations he encounters.

Persons in most kinds of psychological and educational work
find it quite feasible to adopt a general theory that seems reasonable and stick with it, rather than to devote a large part of their
own time and energy to thinking about theory. Since a laboratory
scientist cannot do all possible kinds of experiments anyway, he
might as well do those suggested by one theory and let someone
else tackle those which an alternative theory suggests. A classroom teacher has no difficulty in setting up adequate conditions for
learning on the basis of whatever learning theory she was exposed
to in the course of her professional training.

THE COUNSELOR'S PERSONAL THEORY

But, for a counselor, the situation is more complex. His
first responsibility is to <u>understand</u> the individuals with whom he

Reprinted by permission of the author and the *Journal of Counseling Psychology*, 1958, 5:3–10.

works. Every personality has many facets. Different theories of personality are like spotlights focused on the individual from different directions. The same facets do not show up when one turns on the light labeled Freud that appear clearly when one throws the Rogers switch. And while Freudian concepts may enable a counselor to understand and to help Bill Amory, they may hinder him from seeing what is really the dominant factor in the life of Sarah Peele.

The counselor thus needs many different varieties of theoretical concept, but for his own confidence and peace of mind he needs to have them organized in some way. Such an organization, one's own individual personality theory, can be a dynamic, growing thing with the kind of unity that maintains itself in spite of constant modification. The cultivation of such a theory is, of course, a lifetime undertaking. Every book one reads, every client one comes to know well, adds to the complexity of its pattern.

This, then, is one counselor's selection from the dominant personality theories of our time of a few of the concepts she has found essential to her understanding of the people with whom she works, and her attempt to bring them together into an organized whole. I am not recommending this particular synthesis for anyone else because I am convinced that each person needs to produce his own. My purpose is to point the way to a sort of theorizing counselors can employ rather than to a sort of theory they should adopt.

SOURCES OF PERSONALITY THEORY

Our basic concepts about personality have come to us from many sources. We will encounter most of the essential ones if we examine what we have received from the physiological and psychological laboratories, from the psychiatric consulting room, from the field of practical activities, and from whatever place it is that the ideas of philosophers and religious leaders emanate.

The Laboratory. First let us turn to the laboratory work. Physiologists who have studied the complex organ systems of the body have had a great influence on theories of personality. A concept that has permeated all of recent psychological thinking is what is called homeostasis, meaning the maintenance of constant inner states—temperature, blood sugar, etc.—even in the face of drastic changes in the external environment. In the last few years, Selye and his co-workers have been sketching the outlines of a still more complicated picture that they call the <u>general adaptation syndrome,</u> meaning the body's reaction to <u>stress</u> of any kind. We are learning to think in terms of complicated dynamic structures, equilibria that maintain themselves by a constant series of delicately balanced changes. In our thinking about emotion we must consider both this complex physiological state and the mental content. They occur together. One is not prior to the other. Familiarity with these ideas makes us less prone to try to change one part of a personality, to remove a single neurotic symptom, for example, without being concerned with what happens to the rest of it.

From the psychological laboratories has come work on many research problems. Of these, learning and perception have turned out to be most relevant to counseling. If we are not too fussy about details, we can classify the theories about learning from which experiments have been generated into the <u>stimulus-response</u> theories and the <u>cognitive</u> theories.

The workers in the stimulus-response group have been most interested in the relationship of the observable end-product—what the subject does—to a variety of stimulating conditions. But attitudes, emotions, and social behavior can all be included as varieties of end-product or response. Thus it has been possible to think about personality as well as specific kinds of behavior within a stimulus-response framework. The basic problem, from this theoretical point of view, is how <u>habits</u>, or tendencies to respond in certain ways, are strengthened or weakened. The essential concepts are <u>reinforcement</u>, of both positive and negative varieties, <u>extinction</u>, and the <u>generalization</u> of responses to new stimulating situations.

The cognitive learning theorist is more likely to focus his attention on the internal <u>relationships</u> or organization of experience, rather than on the responses. He holds that it is the way the person sees things, consciously or unconsciously, that changes as learning proceeds, and that it is the central patterning of experience, rather than any automatic tendency, that leads to a response. Evidence for such changes in some inner structure comes most frequently in problem-solving situations when a person suddenly sees the way to a solution. The key concept is <u>insight</u>. Because counseling can be thought of as a problem-solving situation, this kind of theory has had much to contribute to our thinking.

Laboratory work on perception is closer to the work of the cognitive learning theorists than to those of the stimulus-response school. Perception <u>is</u> this process of inner organization. Experimental work in many specific areas—on illusions and on size and color constancy, for example—has shown how pervasive and universal this organizing process is. There has been recent work showing the relationships between motivational states and what is perceived in ambiguous situations, and between personality traits and general perceptual characteristics. This has made us aware of the fact that each person's world is to some extent an individual creation. I cannot look at a landscape or listen to a symphony and assume that my companion is seeing or hearing the same thing as I am. I cannot analyze a client's relationship to his family and assume that he sees it as I do. It is these concepts of the organized and individual quality of perception that counselors must incorporate in their theories.

Psychonalysis. From the consulting room have come theories centering around the difficulties and abnormalities that arise in the course of human life. The dominant theoretical system has been Freudian psychoanalysis. It would obviously be impossible in a paper of this length even to list all the Freudian concepts that influence present-day thinking about conseling and most other things. In making a selection, I would give first place to the concept of unconscious processes. While many psychologists do not like the notion of the unconscious as a part of the personality and while some have been able to dispense with the whole notion, most of us who are doing counseling constantly encounter what seems to be evidence for processes that occur without the subject's awareness. Somehow our system must take these into account. The second theoretical concept I find indispensable is what Freud called instinct, but most psychologists would rather consider simply as motivation. The assumption that life is basically a dynamic process, with wishing and striving woven into its very fiber, has deeply penetrated our thinking, whether we call ourselves Freudian or not. Another concept or habit of thinking we employ constantly is that of anxiety and defenses against it. We can hardly avoid becoming very sensitive to factors that raise a person's level of anxiety and to the individual ways each person has of defending himself against such threats. Finally, the idea of the special significance for personality development of the first few years of life has become a basic principle in almost all personality theories, a principle we apply over and over again in our thinking about people's lives.

The tremendous influence of the Freudian viewpoint has perhaps led us to underestimate the theoretical contributions of non-Freudian analysts. I have found the idea of creative, constructive unconscious processes, emphasized by both Jung and Adler, very useful in my own thinking. The social emphasis in Adler and the neo-Freudians has much to contribute to a counselor's theory, the assumption that man is basically a social creature and that the socialization process does not proceed against nature but with it. Rank's emphasis on the will, his insistence that a person's own free choices have some effect on his personality, and that there is a need for separation and independence, represents a point of view we often take in counseling, even when it conflicts with other aspects of the general theory under which we operate.

The Social Disciplines. Next let us look at research from the field rather than the laboratory or clinic. The thinking about personality that has been done in cultural anthropology has the advantage that it is based on objective observations of people in natural settings. Under the impact of such work we have been modifying our concept of a person as a biological system affected by a social environment. We have been learning to think in terms of a larger system in which biological and social aspects are inextricably bound together. From anthropology and sociology we have also taken over the very useful concept of social role and the part it plays in personality and behavior.

Another kind of field work that has given us concepts we use constantly in counseling activities is the development of mental tests and their application to all sorts of problems in the selection and classification of personnel. Here the central concept that has permeated our theoretical thinking is that of personality trait. It implies that one aspect of personality at a time—such as intelligence, sociability, ego strength—can be considered apart from the rest and measured along some scale. The concept of quantitative differences in personality traits common to all has been very influential.

Philosophy and Religion. The fourth major source of theoretical ideas has been philosophical thinking. No survey of theoretical concepts we need in thinking about personality would be complete without the ideas of the great philosophers and religious leaders of all time. I would select for special comment from this great stream of thought the emphasis on the significance of the individual soul. We find this showing up among psychologists as emphasis on the self in personality organization and as a concern with choice and freedom and responsibility. As counselors we must somehow come to terms with these issues, since so much of our work has to do with the choices and decisions of our clients.

THE BASIC PRINCIPLE IS DEVELOPMENT
—ONE COUNSELOR'S THEORY

   With this all-too-brief survey of essential theoretical concepts, I turn to the attempt at a synthesis. For me, the basic
principle out of which such a synthesis grows is that of development. At each moment of life, any person is in process of changing into something a little different from what he now is. The
whole pattern is changing, and it is important to keep in mind at
one time both the fact of pattern and the fact of change. What the
pattern at any stage will be depends upon the previous pattern and
upon the influences being brought to bear upon the individual from
his present surroundings. But it depends also on his own response,
both to what has gone on before and to the influences that are acting
upon him now. A person to some extent shapes the pattern of his
life by the choices and decisions he makes at successive stages.
Once a choice has been made and its effects built into the developing structure, it can never be eradicated. Development is a one-
way street.
   Stages. Like other continuous processes, development can be
split up into separate parts to facilitate its study. We can think of
life as a series of stages of development. While these could be delimited in various ways, the division that seems now to be of most
value to educators and counselors is based on the concept of developmental tasks. At each stage, certain special tasks or challenges
face a person. The choices that matter most to his future are
those centered around these particular tasks. With our increasing
concern for the adjustment of the aged, we have come to realize
that development is a lifelong process and that the later stages,
like the earlier, can be marked off from one another by the developmental tasks they bring. One of the reasons I have come to prefer the term "development" to the term "growth" is because it
more obviously fits all the periods of life.
   Because it provides for complex, multiple causation of whatever happens in a human life, this general framework has a place
for all of the separate concepts that have been stressed by the various personality theories—learning and motivation, cultural influences, individual differences, and self-determination. If a counselor adopts this general orientation, he sees his task as a process
of working with nature in each individual case. He sees sensitivity
as the most important asset he can have—the ability to grasp the
complex pattern of each developing life and the nature of the

changes that are occurring or that can occur in it. He finds a general attitude of acceptance very important also, since there is nothing to be done with the fixed aspects of any present pattern, determined as they are by factors in the unrecoverable past, except to accept them.

Learning-in-General. It has always seemed to me that so far as learning is concerned, the detailed propositions that have come from the experimentalists of either the stimulus-response or the cognitive schools are less applicable in counseling than just the general ideas. There is one thing laboratory workers do in setting up experiments that we can hardly ever do. It is to fix outcomes in advance. The first step in planning an experiment is to decide what the experimental task or problem is to be. This is the very step we cannot usually take in the counseling setting. We know that the client needs to learn something and that a learning process will certainly occur, but we have no way of knowing at the outset what it is that this person really needs to learn. Our concern has to be with the setting up of conditions favorable to learning in general, so that the amount contributed by this learning experience to the total developmental process may be as large as possible.

Development of Personal Identity. The over-all concept of development, with its application to all of life, is somewhat too broad for our purposes. All kinds of people have a part in promoting development as a whole—parents, teachers, physicians, playground supervisors, and many others. But there is one kind of development that seems to me to be the special province of counselors, although even this is certainly not their exclusive responsibility. I am thinking of the process by means of which a sense of personal identity grows and is maintained. Many personality theorists are talking about the self-concept. What I am calling "identity" means pretty much the same thing. I have a slight preference for it because it has a social as well as a personal reference. Identity covers what and whom one belongs to as well as what one is.

Psychologists have concerned themselves mostly with the problem of what kind of a self-concept each person has. They have asked him to sort cards or check adjectives in order to show what characteristics he sees himself as possessing. An increasing number of literary and philosophical writers are concerned with another question—how firm or certain is the individual's grasp of his own identity. As counselors, our methods and techniques are more suitable for helping with the first kind of question than with the second. We know how to give tests and to collect ratings and records of previous achievement and to use the information in a way that enables a person to see the pattern of his own individual personality more clearly than he did before. But how do we proceed with the person who feels lost, unattached, uncommitted—who does not know who he is? There are many such. Our theory should be able to account for such failure to grasp one's own identity, and our skills should enable us to help such people.

Limitations of Development. As I have considered this matter, the orientation I have found most helpful is to consider the whole developmental process as the actualization of potentialities. Counseling should help each person with his personal task of making potentialities into realities. But what we must recognize is that there are far fewer realities than potentialities, and that the process of self-actualization requires drastic self-limitation of some sort. This is true from the moment of conception on. The genetic potentialities in thousands of sperm cells are wasted when only one of them fertilizes an egg. At a later stage, all sorts of possibilities for personality development are ruled out by the fact that the individual spends his earliest, most formative years in a certain kind of family, in a certain geographical location, belonging to a certain kind of subculture. At still later stages, each choice that the person himself makes actualizes some possibilities but rules out many others. Thus if he commits himself to an attempt to make a career in music, and really takes it seriously, he will probably never be an athlete, although his neuromuscular structures would originally have made either line of specialization possible.

In our time, the wealth of opportunities and the many channels of communication, by means of which people are made aware of them, tend to make self-limitation especially difficult. It is true that in some cases a physical disability rules out many possibilities and determines which potentialities are to be actualized. In other cases, financial circumstances or family responsibilities delimit the area of choice. But for most adolescents or young adults, self-actualization involves a real problem of renunciation of parts of the self that can never come to fruition. It is out of this real dilemma that identity problems can easily grow.

At first glance, this may seem like a pessimistic view of development, bleaker and less appealing than many discussions of human potentialities that we hear. In practice it does not turn out to be this way. It is the richness and depth of the life that is lived within a person's distinctive pattern of internal and external limitations that really matters. And the counselor's most important job is to help each person locate his special areas of strength, the most promising process growth potentialities. The developmental process counseling should try to facilitate includes acceptance of limitations, exploration of strengths, and finally choice, decision, or commitment. Just what counseling can contribute will vary from person to person. In some cases it may help define limitations, in others it may locate or help the person to develop assets. In still others a little extra courage to make a commitment and live by it is what should come out of the counseling relationship.

DEVELOPING IDENTITY VERSUS THERAPY

During the last few minutes I have been focusing on only some parts of a general developmental theory which would incorporate concepts from many theoretical sources. I have selected the parts that seem to me to apply particulary to counseling. In doing this I have limited the meaning of counseling to one kind of process—that of helping a person attain a clear sense of personal identity. Such a concept of what counseling is departs from some current usage in that it distinguishes it from psychotherapy. Therapy is aimed essentially at change in developmental structures rather than at fulfillment. It should be obvious that these two things cannot always be separated in practice. But it seems to me to add clarity to our thinking about our task when we make such a distinction on a conceptual level.

Our job, as counselors, is not to remove physical and mental handicaps or to get rid of limitations, but to find sturdy shoots that can grow and flourish even though some of the branches of the plant are defective. Our acceptance of limitations and our respect for strengths go together. When we play our other roles as therapists or as educators, we may relate ourselves to the development of the individual in other ways. We may take action designed to repair damage done to him in the past, to stimulate inadequate development of some stunted aspect of his personality, or to bring into his life new kinds of knowledge and skill. I make a distinction between counseling and these other activities, not because I would restrict anyone's job to one of them but to enable us to decide, as we go about our helping activities, what it is we are trying to do in each case. It can be very confusing to a client if at the same time we try to cure him, remodel him, educate him, and still encourage him to "be himself."

To summarize, this general personality theory is centered around the concept of a complex, patterned developmental process which, for convenience, can be divided into several successive stages. Counseling is one kind of psychological helping activity, the kind that concentrates on the growth of a clear sense of ego-identity and the willingness to make choices and commitments in accordance with it. Remember that I am not selling this theoretical product, but rather am trying to promote do-it-yourself activity. It is out of the interchange of theoretical formulations based on unique experience that deeper, more richly patterned personality theories will come into existence.

Counseling and Psychotherapy Theories

IV

A THEORY OF THERAPY
AS DEVELOPED IN THE CLIENT-CENTERED FRAMEWORK

Carl R. Rogers

No theory can be adequately understood without some knowledge of the cultural and personal soil from which it springs. This means that I must take the reader through some autobiographical material since, although the client-centered orientation has become very much of a group enterprise in every respect, I, as an individual, carry a considerable responsibility for its initiation and for the beginning formulation of its theories. I shall, therefore, mention briefly some cultural influences and personal experiences which may or may not have relevance to the theory itself. I shall not attempt to evaluate these influences, since I am probably a poor judge of the part they have played.

I lived my childhood as a middle child in a large, close-knit family, where hard work and a highly conservative (almost fundamentalist) Protestant Christianity were about equally revered. When the family moved to a farm at the time I was twelve, I became deeply interested and involved in scientific agriculture. The heavy research volumes I read on my own initiative in the next few years regarding feeds and feeding, soils, animal husbandry, and the like, instilled in me a deep and abiding respect for the scientific method as a means of solving problems and creating new advances in knowledge. This respect was reinforced by my first years in college, where I was fond of the physical and biological sciences. In my work in history I also realized something of the satisfactions of scholarly work.

Having rejected the family views of religion, I became interested in a more modern religious viewpoint and spent two profitable years in Union Theological Seminary, which at that time was

Reprinted and abridged, by permission of the author and the publisher, from Sigmund Koch (Ed.), *Psychology: A Study of a Science*, Vol. 3. New York: McGraw-Hill, 1959. Pp. 184–256.

deeply committed to a freedom of philosophical thought which respected any honest attempt to resolve significant problems,
whether this led into or away from the church. My own thinking
led me in the latter direction, and I moved "across the street" to
Teachers College, Columbia University. Here I was exposed to
the views of John Dewey, not directly, but through William H.
Kilpatrick. I also had my first introduction to clinical psychology
in the warmly human and common-sense approach of Leta Holling-
worth. There followed a year of internship at the Institute for
Child Guidance, then in its chaotic but dynamic first year of existence. Here I gained much from the highly Freudian orientation of
most of its psychiatric staff, which included David Levy and
Lawson Lowrey. My first attempts at therapy were carried on at
the Institute. Because I was still completing my doctorate at
Teachers College, the sharp incompatibility of the highly speculative Freudian thinking of the Institute with the highly statistical
and Thorndikean views at Teachers College was keenly felt.

There followed twelve years in what was essentially a community child guidance clinic in Rochester, New York. This was
a period of comparative isolation from the thinking of others. The
psychology department of the University of Rochester was uninter-
ested in what we were doing because our work was not, in its opinion, in the field of psychology. Our colleagues in the social agencies, schools, and courts knew little and cared less about psychological ideologies. The only element which carried weight with
them was the ability to get results in working with maladjusted
individuals. The staff was eclectic, of diverse background, and
our frequent and continuing discussion of treatment methods was
based on our practical everyday working experience with the children, adolescents, and adults who were our clients. It was the
beginning of an effort, which has had meaning for me ever since,
to discover the order which exists in our experience of working
with people. The volume on the Clinical Treatment of the Problem
Child (Rogers, 1939) was one outcome of this effort.

During the second half of this period there were several individuals who brought into our group the controversial therapeutic
views of Otto Rank and the Philadelphia group of social workers
and psychiatrists whom he had influenced. Personal contact with
Rank was limited to a three-day institute we arranged; nevertheless his thinking had a very decided impact on our staff and helped
me to crystallize some of the therapeutic methods we were groping
toward. For by this time I was becoming more competent as a
therapist, and beginning to sense a discoverable orderliness in

this experience, an orderliness which was inherent in the experience, and (unlike some of the Freudian theories which had grown so far from their original soil) did not have to be imposed on the experience.

Though I had carried on some part-time university teaching throughout the Rochester years, the shift to a faculty position at Ohio State University was a sharp one. I found that the emerging principles of therapy, which I had experienced largely on an implicit basis, were by no means clear to well-trained, critically minded graduate students. I began to sense that what I was doing and thinking in the clinical field was perhaps more of a new pathway than I had recognized. The paper I presented to the Minnesota chapter of Psi Chi in December, 1940, which later became chapter 2 of Counseling and Psychotherapy (1942), was the first conscious attempt to develop a relatively new line of thought. Up to that time I had felt that my writings were essentially attempts to distill out more clearly the principles which "all clinicians" were using.

The new influence at Ohio State, which continued to be felt in my years at Chicago, was the impact of young men and women—intellectually curious, often theoretically oriented, eager to learn from experience and to contribute through research and theory to the development of a field of knowledge. Through their mistakes as well as their successes in therapy, through their research studies, their critical contributions, and through our shared thinking, have come many of the recent developments in this orientation.

In the decade at the University of Chicago the new elements which stand out most sharply are the opportunity for and the encouragement of research, the inclusion of graduate students from education, theology, human development, sociology, industrial relations, as well as psychology, in the ramified activities of the Counseling Center, and the creative thinking of my faculty colleagues, especially those connected with the Center.

The persistent influence which might not be fully recognized, because it is largely implicit in the preceding paragraphs, is the continuing clinical experience with individuals who perceive themselves, or are perceived by others to be, in need of personal help. Since 1928, for a period now approaching thirty-five years, I have spent probably an average of 15 to 20 hours per week, except during vacation periods, in endeavoring to understand and be of therapeutic help to these individuals. To me, they seem to be the major stimulus to my psychological thinking. From these hours, and from my relationships with these people, I have drawn most of whatever insight I possess into the meaning of therapy, the dynamics of interpersonal relationships, and the structure and functioning of personality.

SOME BASIC ATTITUDES

Out of this cultural and personal soil have grown certain basic convictions and attitudes which have undoubtedly influenced the theoretical formulation which will be presented. I will endeavor to list some of these views which seem to me relevant:

1. I have come to see both research and theory as being aimed toward the inward ordering of significant experience. This research is not something esoteric, nor an activity in which one engages to gain professional kudos. It is the persistent, disciplined effort to make sense and order out of the phenomena of subjective experience. Such effort is justified because it is satisfying to perceive the world as having order and because rewarding results often ensue when one understands the orderly relationships which appear to exist in nature. One of these rewarding results is that the ordering of one segment of experience in a theory immediately opens up new vistas of inquiry, research, and thought, thus leading one continually forward.

Thus the primary reason for research and systematic theory in the field of therapy is that it is personally dissatisfying to permit the cumulating experiences of therapeutic hours to remain as a conglomeration of more or less isolated events. It feels as though there is an order in these events. What could it be? And of any hunch regarding the inherent order, it is necessary to ask the question, is this really true, or am I deceiving myself? Thus slowly there is assembled a body of facts, and systematic constructs to explain those facts, which have as their basic function the satisfaction of a need for order which exists in me.

(I have, at times, carried on research for purposes other than the above to satisfy others, to convince opponents and sceptics, to gain prestige, and for other unsavory reasons. These errors in judgment and activity have only deepened the above positive conviction.)

2. It is my opinion that the type of understanding which we call science can begin anywhere, at any level of sophistication. To observe acutely, to think carefully and creatively—these activities, not the accumulation of laboratory instruments, are the beginnings of science. To observe that a given crop grows better on the rocky hill than in the lush bottom land, and to think about this observation, is the start of science. To notice that most sailors

get scurvy but not those who have stopped at islands to pick up
fresh fruit is a similar start. To recognize that, when a person's
views of himself change, his behavior changes accordingly, and to
puzzle over this, is again the beginning of both theory and science.
I voice this conviction in protest against the attitude, which seems
too common in American psychology, that science starts in the
laboratory or at the calculating machine.

3. A closely related belief is that there is a natural history
of science—that science, in any given field, goes through a patterned course of growth and development. For example, it seems
to me right and natural that in any new field of scientific endeavor
the observations are gross, the hypotheses speculative and full of
errors, the measurements crude. More important, I hold the
opinion that this is just as truly science as the use of the most re-
fined hypotheses and measurements in a more fully developed field
of study. The crucial question in either case is not the degree of
refinement but the direction of movement. If in either instance
the movement is toward more exact measurement, toward more
clear-cut and rigorous theory and hypotheses, toward findings
which have greater validity and generality, then this is a healthy
and growing science. If not, then it is a sterile psuedo-science,
no matter how exact its methods. Science is a _developing_ mode
of inquiry, or it is of no particular importance.

4. I have been asked to cast our theoretical thinking in the
terminology of the independent-intervening-dependent variable, in
so far as this is feasible. I regret that I find this terminology
somehow uncongenial. I cannot justify my negative reaction very
adequately, and perhaps it is an irrational one, for the logic behind these terms seems unassailable. But to me the terms seem
static—they seem to deny the restless, dynamic, searching, changing aspects of scientific movement. There is a tendency to suppose that a variable thus labeled, remains so, which is certainly
not true. The terms also seem to me to smack too much of the
laboratory, where one undertakes an experiment de _novo_ with
everything under control, rather than of a science which is endeavoring to wrest from the phenomena of experience the inherent
order which they contain. Such terms seem to be more applicable
to the advanced stages of scientific endeavor than to the beginning
stages.

Please do not misunderstand. I quite realize that _after the
fact_ any research investigation, or any theory constructed to relate the discovered facts, should be translatable into the language
of independent and dependent variables or there is something

wrong with the research or theory. But the terms seem to me better adapted to such autopsies than to the living physiology of scientific work in a new field.

5. It should be quite clear from the foregoing that the model of science which I find most helpful is not taken from the advanced stages of theoretical physics. In a field such as psychotherapy or personality the model which seems more congenial to me would be taken from the much earlier stages of the physical sciences. I like to think of the discovery of radioactivity by the Curies. They had left some pitchblende ore, which they were using for some purpose or other, in a room where they stored photographic plates. They discovered that the plates had been spoiled. In other words, first there was the observation of a dynamic event. This event might have been due to a multitude of causes. It might have been a flaw in the manufacture of the plates. It might have been the humidity, the temperature, or any of a dozen other things. But acute observation and creative thinking fastened on a hunch regarding the pitchblende, and this became a tentative hypothesis. Crude experiments began to confirm the hypothesis. Only slowly was it discovered that it was not the pitchblende, but a strange element in the pitchblende which was related to the observed effect. Meanwhile a theory had to be constructed to bring this strange phenomenon into orderly relationship with other knowledge. And although the theory in its most modest form had to do with the effect of radium on photographic plates, in its wider and more speculative reaches it was concerned with the nature of matter and the composition of the universe. By present-day standards in the physical sciences, this is an example of a primitive stage of investigation and theory construction. But in the fields in which I am most deeply interested I can only hope that we are approaching such a stage. I feel sure that we are not beyond it.

6. Another deep-seated opinion has to do with theory. I believe that there is only one statement which can accurately apply to all theories—from the phlogiston theory to the theory of relativity, from the theory I will present to the one which I hope will replace it in a decade—and that is that at the time of its formulation every theory contains an unknown (and perhaps at that point an unknowable) amount of error and mistaken inference. The degree of error may be very great, as in the phlogiston theory, or small, as I imagine it may be in the theory of relativity, but unless we regard the discovery of truth as a closed and finished book, then there will be new discoveries which will contradict the best theories which we can now construct.

To me this attitude is very important, for I am distressed at the manner in which small-caliber minds immediately accept a theory—almost any theory—as a dogma of truth. If theory could be seen for what it is—a fallible, changing attempt to construct a network of gossamer threads which will contain the solid facts—then a theory would serve as it should, as a stimulus to further creative thinking.

I am sure that the stress I place on this grows in part out of my regret at the history of Freudian theory. For Freud, it seems quite clear that his highly creative theories were never more than that. He kept changing, altering, revising, giving new meaning to old terms—always with more respect for the facts he observed than for the theories he had built. But at the hands of insecure disciples (so it seems to me), the gossamer threads became iron chains of dogma from which dynamic psychology is only recently beginning to free itself. I feel that every formulation of a theory contains this same risk and that, at the time a theory is constructed, some precautions should be taken to prevent it from becoming dogma.

7. I share with many others the belief that truth is unitary, even though we will never be able to know this unity. Hence any theory, derived from almost any segment of experience, if it were complete and completely accurate, could be extended indefinitely to provide meaning for other very remote areas of experience. Tennyson expressed this in sentimental fashion in his "Flower in the Crannied Wall." I too believe that a complete theory of the individual plant would show us "what God and man is."

The corollary, however, is of equal importance and is not so often stated. A slight error in a thoery may make little difference in providing an explanation of the observed facts out of which the theory grew. But when the theory is projected to explain more remote phenomena, the error may be magnified, and the inferences from the theory may be completely false. A very slight error in the understanding of Tennyson's flower may give a grossly false understanding of man. Thus every theory deserves the greatest respect in the area in which it was drawn from the facts and a decreasing degree of respect as it makes predictions in areas more and more remote from its origin. This is true of the theories developed in our own group.

8. There is one other attitude which I hold, which I believe has relevance for the proper evaluation of any theory I might present. It is my belief in the fundamental predominance of the subjective. Man lives essentially in his own personal and subjective

50

world and even his most objective functioning, in science, math-
ematics, and the like, is the result of subjective purpose and subjective choice. In relation to research and theory, for example,
it is my subjective perception that the machinery of science as we
know it—operational definitions, experimental method, mathematical proof—is the best way of avoiding self-deception. But I cannot
escape the fact that this is the way it appears to me, and that had
I lived two centuries ago, or if I were to live two centuries in the
future, some other pathway to truth might seem equally or more
valid. To put it more briefly, it appears to me that though there
may be such a thing as objective truth, I can never know it; all I
can know is that some statements appear to me subjectively to
have the qualifications of objective truth. Thus there is no such
thing as Scientific Knowledge; there are only individual perceptions of what appears to each person to be such knowledge.

Since this is a large and philosophical issue, not too closely
related to what follows, I shall not endeavor to state it more fully
here but refer any who are interested to an article in which I have
tried to expound this view somewhat more fully (Rogers & Dymond,
1954, chapter 13). I mention it here only because it is a part of
the context in which my theoretical thinking has developed.

THE GENERAL STRUCTURE OF
OUR SYSTEMATIC THINKING

Before proceeding to the detailed statement of some of our theoretical views, I believe it may be helpful to describe some of the
interrelationships between various portions of our theoretical
formulations.

The earliest portion, most closely related to observed fact,
most heavily supported by evidence, is the theory of psychotherapy and personality change which was constructed to give order to
the phenomena of therapy as we experienced it. In this theory
there were certain hypotheses regarding the nature of personality
and the dynamics of behavior. Some of these were explicit, some
implicit. These have been developed more fully into a theory of
personality. The purpose has been to provide ourselves with a
tentative understanding of the human organism and its developing
dynamics—an attempt to make sense of this person who comes to
us in therapy.

Implicit in the theories of therapy and of personality are certain hypotheses regarding the outcomes of therapy—hence, hypotheses regarding a more socially constructive or creative individual.

In the last few years we have endeavored to spell out the picture of the theoretical end point of therapy, the maximally creative, self-actualizing, or fully functioning person.

In another direction, our understanding of the therapeutic relationship has led us to formulate theoretical statements regarding all interpersonal relationships, seeing the therapeutic relationship simply as one special case. This is a very new and tentative development, which we believe has promise.

Finally, it has seemed that if our views of therapy have any validity they have application in all those fields of human experience and endeavor which involve (a) interpersonal relationships and (b) the aim or potentiality of development or change in personality and behavior. Consequently, a cluster of partially developed theories exists in relation to such fields as family life, education, group leadership, and situations of group tension and conflict.

Before proceeding to set forth something of the theories themselves, I should like gratefully to stress the extent to which this is basically a group enterprise. I have drawn upon specific written contributions to theory made by Victor Raimy, Richard Hogan, Stanley Standal, John Butler, and Thomas Gordon. Many others have contributed to my thinking in ways known and unknown, but I would particularly like to mention the valuable influence of Oliver Bown, Desmond Cartwright, Arthur Combs, Eugene Gendlin, A. H. Maslow, Julius Seeman, John Shlien, and Donald Snygg on the theories which I am about to present. Yet these individuals are by no means to be held responsible for what follows, for their own attempts to order experience have often led them into somewhat different channels of thinking.

DEFINITIONS OF CONSTRUCTS

In the development of our theories various systematic constructs have emerged, gradually acquiring sharper and more specific meaning. Also terms in common usage have gradually acquired somewhat specialized meanings in our theoretical statements. In this section I have endeavored to define, as rigorously as I am able, these constructs and terms. These definitions supply the means by which the theory may be more accurately understood.

In this section one will find all of the constructs defined, grouped in related clusters. There are eleven of these clusters, each with a focal concept. If these focal concepts are understood, the understanding of each of the related terms should not be diffi-

cult, since each of the constructs within a group has a close and
meaningful relationship to the others.

It is quite possible that such a section, devoted entirely to
definitions, will prove dull reading. The reader may prefer to go
at once to the theory of therapy in the following section, where he
will find each defined term underlined. He may then refer back to
this section for the exact meaning of each such term.

1. Actualizing tendency. This is the inherent tendency of the
organism to develop all its capacities in ways which serve to maintain or enhance the organism. It involves not only the tendency to
meet what Maslow (1954) terms "deficiency needs" for air, food,
water, and the like, but also more generalized activities. It involves development toward the differentiation of organs and of
functions, expansion in terms of growth, expansion of effectiveness
through the use of tools, expansion and enhancement through reproduction. It is development toward autonomy and away from heter-
onomy, or control by external forces. Angyal's (1941) statement
could be used as a synonym for this term: "Life is an autonomous
event which takes place between the organism and the environment.
Life processes do not merely tend to preserve life but transcend
the momentary status quo of the organism, expanding itself continually and imposing its autonomous determination upon an ever
increasing realm of events."

It should be noted that this basic actualizing tendency is the
only motive which is postulated in this theoretical system. It
should also be noted that it is the organism as a whole, and only
the organism as a whole, which exhibits this tendency. There are
no homunculi, no other sources of energy or action in the system.
The self, for example, is an important construct in our theory, but
the self does not "do" anything. It is only one expression of the
general tendency of the organism to behave in those ways which
maintain and enhance itself.

It might also be mentioned that such concepts of motivation as
are termed need-reduction, tension-reduction, drive-reduction,
are included in this concept. It also includes, however, the growth
motivations which appear to go beyond these terms: the seeking of
pleasurable tensions, the tendency to be creative, the tendency to
learn painfully to walk when crawling would meet the same needs
more comfortably.

2. Tendency toward self-actualization. Following the development of the self-structure, this general tendency toward actualization expresses itself also in the actualization of that portion of the
experience of the organism which is symbolized in the self. If the

self and the total experience of the organism are relatively congruent, then the actualizing tendency remains relatively unified. If self and experience are incongruent, then the general tendency to actualize the organism may work at cross purposes with the subsystem of that motive, the tendency to actualize the self.

This definition will be better understood when various of its terms—self, incongruence, etc.—are defined. It is given here because it is a subaspect of motivation. It should perhaps be reread after the other terms are more accurately understood.

3. Experience (noun). This term is used to include all that is going on within the envelope of the organism at any given moment which is potentially available to awareness. It includes events of which the individual is unaware, as well as all the phenomena which are in consciousness. Thus it includes the psychological aspects of hunger, even though the individual may be so fascinated by his work or play that he is completely unaware of the hunger; it includes the impact of sights and sounds and smells on the organism, even though these are not in the focus of attention. It includes the influence of memory and past experience, as these are active in the moment, in restricting or broadening the meaning given to various stimuli. It also includes all that is present in immediate awareness or consciousness. It does not include such events as neuron discharges or changes in blood sugar, because these are not directly available to awareness. It is thus a psychological, not a physiological, definition.

Synonyms are "experiential field," or the term "phenomenal field" as used by Snygg and Combs, which also covers more than the phenomena of consciousness. I have in the past used such phrases as "sensory and visceral experiences" and "organic experiences" in the attempt to convey something of the total quality of this concept.

It is to be noted that experience refers to the given moment, not to some accumulation of past experience. It is believed that this makes the operational definition of experience, or of an experience, which is a given segment of the field, more possible.

4. Experience (verb). To experience means simply to receive in the organism the impact of the sensory or physiological events which are happening at the moment.

Often this process term is used in the phrase "to experience in awareness" which means to symbolize in some accurate form at the conscious level the above sensory or visceral events. Since there are varying degrees of completeness in symbolization, the phrase is often "to experience more fully in awareness," thus indicating that it is the extension of this process toward more complete and accurate symbolization to which reference is being made.

5. <u>Feeling, Experiencing a feeling</u>. This is a term which has been heavily used in writings on client-centered therapy and theory. It denotes an emotionally tinged experience, together with its personal meaning. Thus it includes the emotion but also the cognitive content of the meaning of that emotion in its experiential context. It thus refers to the unity of emotion and cognition as they are experienced inseparably in the moment. It is perhaps best thought of as a brief theme of experience, carrying with it the emotional coloring and the perceived meaning to the individual. Examples would include "I feel angry at myself," "I feel ashamed of my desires when I am with her," "For the first time, right now, I feel that you like me." This last is an example of another phenomenon which is relevant to our theory, and which has been called <u>experiencing a feeling fully</u>, in the immediate present. The individual is then congruent in his experience (of the feeling), his awareness (of it), and his expression (of it).

6. <u>Awareness, Symbolization, Consciousness</u>. These three terms are defined as synonymous. To use Angyal's expression, consciousness (or awareness) is the symbolization of some of our experience. Awareness is thus seen as the symbolic representation (not necessarily in verbal symbols) of some portion of our experience. This representation may have varying degrees of sharpness or vividness, from a dim awareness of something existing as ground, to a sharp awareness of something which is in focus as figure.

7. <u>Availability to awareness</u>. When an experience can be symbolized freely, without defensive denial and distortion, then it is available to awareness.

8. <u>Accurate symbolization</u>. The symbols which constitute our awareness do not necessarily match, or correspond to, the "real" experience, or to "reality." Thus the psychotic is aware of (symbolizes) electrical impulses in his body which do not seem in actuality to exist. I glance up quickly and perceive a plane in the distance, but it turns out to be a gnat close to my eye. It seems important to distinguish between those awarenesses which, in common-sense terms, are real or accurate and those which are not. But how can this be conceptualized if we are trying to think rigorously?

The most adequate way of handling this predicament seems to me to be to take the position of those who recognize that all perception (and I would add, all awareness) is transactional in nature, that it is a construction from our past experience and a hypothesis or prognosis for the future. Thus the examples given are both hypotheses which can be checked. If I brush at the gnat and it disappears, it increases the probability that what I was aware of was a gnat and not a plane. If the psychotic were able to permit himself to check the electric currents in his body, and to see whether they have the same characteristics as other electric currents, he would be checking the hypothesis implicit in his awareness. Hence when we speak of accurate symbolization in awareness, we mean that the hypotheses implicit in the awareness will be borne out if tested by acting on them.

We are, however, well over the border line of simple awareness and into the realm which is usually classified as perception, so let us proceed to a consideration of that concept.

9. Perceive, Perception. So much has the meaning of this term changed that one definition has been given as follows: "Perception is that which comes into consciousness when stimuli, principally light or sound, impinge on the organism from the outside" (Kelly, 1955, p. 250). Although this seems a bit too general, it does take account of the work of Hebb, Riesen, and others, which indicates that the impingement of the stimuli and the meaning given to the stimuli are inseparable parts of a single experience.

For our own definition we might say that a perception is a hypothesis or prognosis for action which comes into being in awareness when stimuli impinge on the organism. When we perceive "this is a triangle," "that is a tree," "this person is my mother," it means that we are making a prediction that the objects from which the stimuli are received would, if checked in other ways, exhibit properties we have come to regard from our past experience as being characteristic of triangles, trees, mother.

Thus we might say that perception and awareness are synonymous, perception being the narrower term, usually used when we wish to emphasize the importance of the stimulus in the process, and awareness the broader term, covering symbolizations and meanings which arise from such purely internal stimuli as memory traces, visceral changes, and the like, as well as from external stimuli.

To define perception in this purely psychological fashion is not meant to deny that it can be defined in physiological fashion by referring to the impact of a pattern of light rays upon certain nerve cells, for example. For our purpose, however, the psychological definition seems more fruitful, and it is in this sense that the term will be used in our formulations.

10. <u>Subceive, Subception</u>. McCleary and Lazarus (1949) formulated this construct to signify discrimination without awareness. They state that "even when a subject is unable to report a visual discrimination he is still able to make a stimulus discrimination at some level below that required for conscious recognition." Thus it appears that the organism can discriminate a stimulus and its meaning for the organism without utilizing the higher nerve centers involved in awareness. It is this capacity which, in our theory, permits the individual to discriminate an experience as threatening, without symbolization in awareness of this threat.

11. <u>Self-experience</u>. This is a term coined by Standal (1954), and defined as being any event or entity in the phenomenal field discriminated by the individual which is also discriminated as "self," "me," "I," or related thereto. In general, self-experiences are the raw material of which the organized self-concept is formed.

12. <u>Self, Concept of self, Self-structure</u>. These terms refer to the organized, consistent conceptual gestalt composed of perceptions of the characteristics of the "I" or "me" and the perceptions of the relationships of the "I" or "me" to others and to various aspects of life, together with the values attached to these perceptions. It is a gestalt which is available to awareness though not necessarily in awareness. It is a fluid and changing gestalt, a process, but at any given moment it is a specific entity which is at least partially definable in operational terms by means of a Q sort or other instrument or measure. The term self or self-concept is more likely to be used when we are talking of the person's view of himself, self-structure when we are looking at this gestalt from an external frame of reference.

13. <u>Ideal self.</u> Ideal self (or self-ideal) is the term used to denote the self-concept which the individual would most like to possess, upon which he places the highest value for himself. In all other respects it is defined in the same way as the self-concept.

14. <u>Incongruence between self and experience</u>. In a manner which will be described in the theory of personality a discrepancy frequently develops between the self as perceived, and the actual experience of the organism. Thus the individual may perceive himself as having characteristics $\underline{a}$, $\underline{b}$, and $\underline{c}$, and experiencing feelings $\underline{x}$, $\underline{y}$, and $\underline{z}$. An accurate symbolization of his experience would, however, indicate characteristics $\underline{c}$, $\underline{d}$, and $\underline{e}$, and feelings $\underline{v}$, $\underline{w}$, $\underline{x}$. When such a discrepancy exists, the state is one of incongruence between self and experience. This state is one of tension and internal confusion, since in some respects the individual's behavior will be regulated by the actualizing tendency, and in other

respects by the self-actualizing tendency, thus producing discordant or incomprehensible behaviors. What is commonly called neurotic behavior is one example, the neurotic behavior being the product of the actualizing tendency, whereas in other respects the individual is actualizing the self. Thus the neurotic behavior is incomprehensible to the individual himself, since it is at variance with what he consciously "wants" to do, which is to actualize a self no longer congruent with experience.

15. Vulnerability. Vulnerability is the term used to refer to the state of incongruence between self and experience, when it is desired to emphasize the potentialities of this state for creating psychological disorganization. When incongruence exists, and the individual is unaware of it, then he is potentially vulnerable to anxiety, threat, and disorganization. If a significant new experience demonstrates the discrepancy so clearly that it must be consciously perceived, then the individual will be threatened, and his concept of self disorganized by this contradictory and unassimilable experience.

16. Anxiety. Anxiety is phenomenologically a state of uneasiness or tension whose cause is unknown. From an external frame of reference, anxiety is a state in which the incongruence between the concept of self and the total experience of the individual is approaching symbolization in awareness. When experience is obviously discrepant from the self-concept, a defensive response to threat becomes increasingly difficult. Anxiety is the response of the organism to the "subception" that such discrepancy may enter awareness, thus forcing a change in the self-concept.

17. Threat. Threat is the state which exists when an experience is preceived or anticipated (subceived) as incongruent with the structure of the self. It may be regarded as an external view of the same phenomenon which, from the internal frame of reference, is anxiety.

18. Psychological maladjustment. Psychological maladjustment exists when the organism denies to awareness, or distorts in awareness, significant experiences, which consequently are not accurately symbolized and organized into the gestalt of the self-structure, thus creating an incongruence between self and experience.

It may help to clarify this basic concept of incongruence if we recognize that several of the terms we are defining are simply different vantage points for viewing this phenomenon. If an individual is in a state of incongruence between self and experience and we are looking at him from an external point of view we see him as vulnerable (if he is unaware of the discrepancy), or threatened (if he has some awareness of it). If we are viewing him from a social point of view, then this incongruence is psychological maladjustment. If the individual is viewing himself, he may even see himself as adjusted (if he has no awareness of the discrepancy) or anxious (if he dimly subceives it) or threatened or disorganized (if the discrepancy has forced itself upon his awareness).

19. Defense, Defensiveness. Defense is the behavioral response of the organism to threat, the goal of which is the maintenance of the current structure of the self. This goal is achieved by the perceptual distortion of the experience in awareness, in such a way as to reduce the incongruity between the experience and the structure of the self, or by the denial to awareness of an experience, thus denying any threat to the self. Defensiveness is the term denoting a state in which the behaviors are of the sort described.

20. Distortion in awareness, Denial to awareness. It is an observed phenomenon that material which is significantly inconsistent with the concept of self cannot be directly and freely admitted to awareness. To explain this the construct of denial or distortion has been developed. When an experience is dimly perceived (or "subceived" is perhaps the better term) as being incongruent with the self-structure, the organism appears to react with a distortion of the meaning of the experience, (making it consistent with the self) or with a denial of the existence of the experience, in order to preserve the self-structure from threat. It is perhaps most vividly illustrated in those occasional moments in therapy when the therapist's response, correctly heard and understood, would mean that the client would necessarily perceive openly a serious inconsistency between his self-concept and a given experience. In such a case, the client may respond, "I can hear the words you say, and I know I should understand them, but I just can't make them convey any meaning to me." Here the relationship is too good for the meaning to be distorted by rationalization, the meaning too threatening to be received. Hence the organism denies that there is meaning in the communication. Such outright denial of experience is much less common than the phenomenon of distortion. Thus if the concept of self includes the characteristic "I am a poor student" the experience of receiving a high grade can be easily distorted to make it congruent with the self by perceiving in it such meanings as, "That professor is a fool"; "It was just luck"; etc.

21. Intensionality. This term is taken from general semantics. If the person is reacting or perceiving in an intensional fash-

ion he tends to see experience in absolute and unconditional terms, to overgeneralize, to be dominated by concept or belief, to fail to anchor his reactions in space and time, to confuse fact and evaluation, to rely upon abstractions rather than upon reality-testing. This term covers the frequently used concept of rigidity but includes perhaps a wider variety of behaviors than are generally thought of as constituting rigidity.

It will perhaps be evident that this cluster of definitions all have to do with the organism's response to threat. Defense is the most general term: distortion and denial are the mechanisms of defense; intensionality is a term which covers the characteristics of the behavior of the individual who is in a defensive state.

22. Congruence, Congruence of self and experience. This is a basic concept which has grown out of therapeutic experience, in which the individual appears to be revising his concept of self to bring it into congruence with his experience, accurately symbolized. Thus he discovers that one aspect of his experience if accurately symbolized, would be hatred for his father; another would be strong homosexual desires. He reorganizes the concept he holds of himself to include these characteristics, which would previously have been inconsistent with self.

Thus when self-experiences are accurately symbolized and are included in the self-concept in this accurately symbolized form, then the state is one of congruence of self and experience. If this were completely true of all self-experiences, the individual would be a fully functioning person, as will be made more clear in the section devoted to this aspect of our theory. If it is true of some specific aspect of experience, such as the individual's experience in a given relationship or in a given moment of time, then we can say that the individual is to this degree in a state of congruence. Other terms which are in a general way synonymous are these: integrated, whole, genuine.

23. Openness to experience. When the individual is in no way threatened, then he is open to his experience. To be open to experience is the polar opposite of defensiveness. The term may be used in regard to some area of experience or in regard to the total experience of the organism. It signifies that every stimulus, whether originating within the organism or in the environment, is freely relayed through the nervous system without being distorted or channeled off by any defensive mechanism. There is no need of the mechanism of "subception" whereby the organism is forewarned of experiences threatening to the self. On the contrary, whether the stimulus is the impact of a configuration of form, color, or sound in the environment on the sensory nerves, or a

memory trace from the past, or a visceral sensation of fear, pleasure, or disgust, it is completely available to the individual's awareness. In the hypothetical person who is completely open to his experience, his concept of self would be a symbolization in awareness which would be completely congruent with his experience. There would, therefore, be no possibility of threat.

24. Psychological adjustment. Optimal psychological adjustment exists when the concept of the self is such that all experiences are or may be assimilated on a symbolic level into the gestalt of the self-structure. Optimal psychological adjustment is thus synonymous with complete congruence of self and experience, or complete openness to experience. On the practical level, improvement in psychological adjustment is equivalent to progress toward this end point.

25. Extensionality. This term is taken from general semantics. If the person is reacting or perceiving in an extensional manner he tends to see experience in limited, differentiated terms, to be aware of the space-time anchorage of facts, to be dominated by facts, not by concepts, to evaluate in multiple ways, to be aware of different levels of abstraction, to test his inferences and abstractions against reality.

26. Mature, Maturity. The individual exhibits mature behavior when he perceives realistically and in an extensional manner, is not defensive, accepts the responsibility for his own behavior, evaluates experience in terms of the evidence coming from his own senses, changes his evaluation of experience only on the basis of new evidence, accepts others as unique individuals different from himself, prizes himself, prizes others. (If his behavior has these characteristics, then there will automatically follow all the types of behavior which are more popularly thought of as constituting psychological maturity.)

These last five definitions form a cluster which grows out of the concept of congruence. Congruence is the term which defines the state. Openness to experience is the way an internally congruent individual meets new experience. Psychological adjustment is congruence as viewed from a social point of view. Extensional is the term which describes the specific types of behavior of a congruent individual. Maturity is a broader term describing the personality characteristics and behavior of a person who is, in general, congruent.

The concepts in the group of definitions which follow have all been developed and formulated by Standal (1954), and have taken the place of a number of less satisfactory and less rigorously defined constructs. Essentially this group has to do with the concept of positive regard, but since all transactions relative to this construct take place in relationships, a definition of psychological contact, or minimal relationship, is set down first.

27. Contact. Two persons are in psychological contact, or have the minimum essential of a relationship, when each makes a perceived or subceived difference in the experiential field of the other.

This construct was first given the label of "relationship," but it was found that this led to much misunderstanding, for it was often understood to represent the depth and quality of a good relationship, or a therapeutic relationship. The present term has been chosen to signify more clearly that this is the least or minimum experience which could be called a relationship. If more than this simple contact between two persons is intended, then the additional characteristics of that contact are specified in the theory.

28. Positive regard. If the perception by me of some self-experience in another makes a positive difference in my experiential field, then I am experiencing positive regard for that individual. In general, positive regard is defined as including such attitudes as warmth, liking, respect, sympathy, acceptance. To perceive oneself as receiving positive regard is to experience oneself as making a positive difference in the experiential field of another.

29. Need for positive regard. It is postulated by Standal that a basic need for positive regard, as defined above, is a secondary or learned need, commonly developed in early infancy. Some writers have looked upon the infant's need for love and affection as an inherent or instinctive need. Standal is probably on safer ground in regarding it as a learned need. By terming it the need for positive regard, he has, it is believed, selected out the significant psychological variable from the broader terms usually used.

30. Unconditional positive regard. Here is one of the key constructs of the theory, which may be defined in these terms: If the self-experiences of another are perceived by me in such a way that no self-experience can be discriminated as more or less worthy of positive regard than any other, then I am experiencing unconditional positive regard for this individual. To perceive oneself as receiving unconditional positive regard is to perceive that of one's self-experiences none can be discriminated by the other individual as more or less worthy of positive regard.

Putting this in simpler terms, to feel unconditional positive regard toward another is to "prize" him (to use Dewey's term, recently used in this sense by Butler). This means to value the person, irrespective of the differential values which one might place on his specific behaviors. A parent "prizes" his child, though he may not value equally all of his behaviors. Acceptance is another term which has been frequently used to convey this meaning, but it perhaps carries more misleading connotations than the phrase which Standal has coined. In general, however, acceptance and prizing are synonymous with unconditional positive regard.

This construct has been developed out of the experiences of therapy, where it appears that one of the potent elements in the relationship is that the therapist "prizes" the whole person of the client. It is the fact that he feels and shows an unconditional positive regard toward the experiences of which the client is frightened or ashamed, as well as toward the experiences with which the client is pleased or satisfied, that seems effective in bringing about change. Gradually the client can feel more acceptance of all of his own experiences, and this makes him again more of a whole or congruent person, able to function effectively. This clinical explanation will, it is hoped, help to illuminate the meaning contained in the rigorous definition.

31. Regard complex. The regard complex is a construct defined by Standal as all those self-experiences, together with their interrelationships, which the individual discriminates as being related to the positive regard of a particular social other.

This construct is intended to emphasize the gestalt nature of transactions involving positive or negative regard, and their potency. Thus, for example, if a parent shows positive regard to a child in relationship to a specific behavior, this tends to strengthen the whole pattern of positive regard which has previously been experienced as coming from that parent. Likewise specific negative regard from this parent tends to weaken the whole configuration of positive regard.

32. Positive self-regard. This term is used to denote a positive regard satisfaction which has become associated with a particular self-experience or a group of self-experiences, in which this satisfaction is independent of positive regard transactions with social others. Though it appears that positive regard must first be experienced from others, this results in a positive attitude toward self which is no longer directly dependent on the attitudes

of others. The individual, in effect, becomes his own significant
social other.

33. Need for self-regard. It is postulated that a need for
positive self-regard is a secondary or learned need, related to
the satisfaction of the need for positive regard by others.

34. Unconditional self-regard. When the individual perceives
himself in such a way that no self-experience can be discriminated
as more or less worthy of positive regard than any other, then he
is experiencing unconditional positive self-regard.

35. Conditions of worth. The self-structure is characterized
by a condition of worth when a self-experience or set of related
self-experiences is either avoided or sought solely because the
individual discriminates it as being less or more worthy of self-
regard.

This important construct has been developed by Standal to take
the place of "introjected value," which was a less exact concept
used in earlier formulations. A condition of worth arises when the
positive regard of a significant other is conditional, when the individual feels that in some respects he is prized and in others not.
Gradually this same attitude is assimilated into his own self-regard
complex, and he values an experience positively or negatively
solely because of these conditions of worth which he has taken over
from others, not because the experience enhances or fails to enhance his organism.

It is this last phrase which deserves special note. When the
individual has experienced unconditional positive regard, then a
new experience is valued or not, depending on its effectiveness in
maintaining or enhancing the organism. But if a value is "introjected" from a significant other, then this condition of worth is
applied to an experience quite without reference to the extent to
which it maintains or enhances the organism. It is an important
specific instance of inaccurate symbolization, the individual
valuing an experience positively or negatively, as if in relation to
the criterion of the actualizing tendency, but not actually in relation to it. An experience may be perceived as organismically
satisfying, when in fact this is not true. Thus a condition of worth,
because it disturbs the valuing process, prevents the individual
from functioning freely and with maximum effectiveness.

36. Locus of evaluation. This term is used to indicate the
source of evidence as to values. Thus an internal locus of evaluation, within the individual himself, means that he is the center of
the valuing process, the evidence being supplied by his own senses.

When the locus of evaluation resides in others, their judgment as to the value of an object or experience becomes the criterion of value for the individual.

37. <u>Organismic valuing process</u>. This concept describes an ongoing process in which values are never fixed or rigid, but experiences are being accurately symbolized and continually and freshly valued in terms of the satisfactions organismically experienced; the organism experiences satisfaction in those stimuli or behaviors which maintain and enhance the organism and the self, both in the immediate present and in the long range. The actualizing tendency is thus the criterion. The simplest example is the infant who at one moment values food, and when satiated, is disgusted with it; at one moment values stimulation, and soon after, values only rest; who finds satisfying that diet which in the long run most enhances his development.

38. <u>Internal frame of reference</u>. This is all of the realm of experience which is available to the awareness of the individual at a given moment. It includes the full range of sensations, perceptions, meanings, and memories, which are available to consciousness.

The internal frame of reference is the subjective world of the individual. Only he knows it fully. It can never be known to another except through empathic inference and then can never be perfectly known.

39. <u>Empathy</u>. The state of empathy, or being empathic, is to perceive the internal frame of reference of another with accuracy, and with the emotional components and meanings which pertain thereto, as if one were the other person, but without ever losing the "as if" condition. Thus it means to sense the hurt or the pleasure of another as he senses it, and to perceive the causes thereof as he perceives them, but without ever losing the recognition that it is <u>as if</u> I were hurt or pleased, etc. If this "as if" quality is lost, then the state is one of identification.

40. <u>External frame of reference</u>. To perceive solely from one's own subjective internal frame of reference without empathizing with the observed person or object, is to perceive from an external frame of reference. The "empty organism" school of thought in psychology is an example of this. Thus the observer says that an animal has been stimulated when the animal has been exposed to a condition which, in the observer's subjective frame of reference, is a stimulus. There is no attempt to understand, empathically, whether this is a stimulus in the animal's experiential field. Likewise the observer reports that the animal emits a

response when a phenomenon occurs which, in the observer's subjective field, is a response.

We generally regard all "objects" (stones, trees, or abstractions) from this external frame of reference since we assume that
they have no "experience" with which we can empathize. The
other side of this coin is that anything perceived from an external
frame of reference (whether an inanimate thing, an animal, or a
person) becomes for us an "object" because no empathic inferences
are made.

This cluster of three ways of knowing deserves some further
comment. In so far as we are considering knowledge of human
beings we might say that these ways of knowing exist on a continuum. They range from one's own complete subjectivity in one's
own internal frame of reference to one's own complete subjectivity
about another (the external frame of reference). In between lies
the range of empathic inference regarding the subjective field of
another.

Each of these ways of knowing is essentially a formulation of
hypotheses. The differences lie in the way the hypotheses are
checked. In my own internal frame of reference if I experience
love or hate, enjoyment or dislike, interest or boredom, belief or
disbelief, the only way I can check these hypotheses of experience
is by further focusing on my experience. Do I really love him?
Am I really enjoying this? Do I really believe this?—all are questions which can only be answered by checking with my own organism. (If I try to find out whether I really love him by checking
with others, then I am observing myself as an object, am viewing
myself from an external frame of reference.)

Although in the last analysis each individual lives in and by his
own subjective knowledge, this is not regarded socially as "knowledge" and certainly not as scientific knowledge.

Knowledge which has "certainty," in the social sense, involves
the use of empathic inference as a means of checking, but the direction of that empathy differs. When the experience of empathic
understanding is used as a source of knowledge, one checks one's
empathic inferences with the subject, thus verifying or disproving
the inferences and hypotheses implicit in such empathy. It is this
way of knowing which we have found so fruitful in therapy. Utilizing empathic inference to the fullest, the knowledge thus gained of
the client's subjective world has led to understanding the basis of
his behavior and the process of personality change.

In knowing a person or an object from the external frame of
reference, our implicit hypotheses are checked with other people

but <u>not</u> with the subject of our concern. Thus a rigorous behaviorist believes that S is a stimulus for his experimental animal and R is a response, because his colleagues and even the man in the street agree with him and regard S and R in the same way. His empathic inferences are made in regard to the internal frame of reference of his colleagues, rather than in regard to the internal frame of reference of the animal.

Science involves taking an external frame of reference, in which we check our hypotheses basically through empathic inferences as to the internal frame of reference of our colleagues. They perform the same operations we have (either actually or through symbolic representation), and if they perceive the same events and meanings, then we regard our hypotheses as confirmed.

The reason for thus elaborating the different ways of knowing is that it seems to us that all ways of knowing have their usefulness, and that confusion arises only when one is not clear as to the type of knowledge which is being specified. Thus in the theory of therapy which follows one will find certain conditions of therapy specified as subjective experiencing states, another as empathic knowledge of the client, and yet the scientific checking of the hypotheses of the theory can only be done from an external frame of reference.

A THEORY OF THERAPY AND PERSONALITY CHANGE

This theory is of the if-then variety. If certain conditions exist (independent variables), then a process (dependent variable) will occur which includes certain characteristic elements. If this process (now the independent variable) occurs, then certain personality and behavioral changes (dependent variables) will occur. This will be made specific.

In this and the following sections the formal statement of the theory is given briefly. The underlined terms or phrases in these formal statements have been defined in the previous section and are to be understood as defined. The remaining paragraphs are explanatory and do not follow the rigorous pattern of the formal statements.

A. <u>Conditions</u> <u>of</u> <u>the</u> <u>Therapeutic</u> <u>Process</u>

For therapy to occur it is necessary that these conditions exist:

    1. That two persons are in <u>contact</u>.

2. That the first person, whom we shall term the client, is in a state of <u>incongruence</u>, being <u>vulnerable</u> or <u>anxious</u>.

3. That the second person, whom we shall term the therapist, is <u>congruent</u> in the <u>relationship</u>.

4. That the therapist is <u>experiencing unconditional positive regard</u> toward the client.

5. That the therapist is <u>experiencing</u> an <u>empathic</u> understanding of the client's <u>internal frame of reference.</u>

6. That the client <u>perceives,</u> at least to a minimal degree, conditions 4 and 5, the <u>unconditional positive regard</u> of the therapist for him, and the <u>empathic</u> understanding of the therapist.

<u>Comment</u>. These seem to be the necessary conditions of therapy, though other elements are often or usually present. The process is more likely to get under way if the client is anxious, rather than merely vulnerable. Often it is necessary for the contact or relationship to be of some duration before the therapeutic process begins. Usually the empathic understanding is to some degree expressed verbally, as well as experienced. But the process often commences with only these minimal conditions, and it is hypothesized that it never commences <u>without</u> these conditions being met.

The point which is most likely to be misunderstood is the omission of any statement that the therapist <u>communicates</u> his empathic understanding and his unconditional positive regard to the client. Such a statement has been omitted only after much consideration, for these reasons. It is not enough for the therapist to communicate, since the communication must be received, as pointed out in condition 6, to be effective. It is not essential that the therapist <u>intend</u> such communication, since often it is by some casual remark, or involuntary facial expression, that the communication is actually achieved. However, if one wishes to stress the communicative aspect which is certainly a vital part of the living experience, then condition 6 might be worded in this fashion:

6. That communication to the client of the therapist's empathic understanding and unconditional positive regard is, at least to a minimal degree, achieved.

The element which will be most surprising to conventional therapists is that the same conditions are regarded as sufficient for therapy, regardless of the particular characteristics of the client. It has been our experience to date that although the therapeutic relationship is used differently by different clients, it is not necessary nor helpful to manipulate the relationship in specific ways for specific kinds of clients. To do this damages, it seems to us, the most helpful and significant aspect of the experience, that it is a genuine relationship between two persons, each of whom is endeavoring, to the best of his ability, to be himself in the interaction.

The "growing edge" of this portion of the theory has to do with point 3, the congruence or genuineness of the therapist in the relationship. This means that the therapist's symbolization of his own experience in the relationship must be accurate, if therapy is to be most effective. Thus if he is experiencing threat and discomfort in the relationship and is aware only of acceptance and understanding, then he is not congruent in the relationship and therapy will suffer. It seems important that he should accurately "be himself" in the relationship, whatever the self of that moment may be.

Should he also express or communicate to the client the accurate symbolization of his own experience? The answer to this question is still in an uncertain state. At present we would say that such feelings should be expressed, if the therapist finds himself persistently focused on his own feelings rather than those of the client, thus greatly reducing or eliminating any experience of empathic understanding, or if he finds himself persistently experiencing some feeling other than unconditional positive regard. To know whether this answer is correct demands further testing of the hypothesis it contains, and this is not simple since the courage to do this is often lacking, even in experienced therapists. When the therapist's real feelings are of this order: "I find myself fearful that you are slipping into a psychosis," or "I find myself frightened because you are touching on feelings I have never been able to resolve," then it is difficult to test the hypothesis, for it is very difficult for the therapist to express such feelings.

Another question which arises is this: is it the congruence, the wholeness, the integration of the therapist in the relationship which is important, or are the specific attitudes of empathic understanding and unconditional positive regard vital? Again the final answer is unknown, but a conservative answer, the one we have embodied in the theory, is that for therapy to occur the wholeness of the therapist in the relationship is primary, but a part of the congruence of the therapist must be the experience of unconditional positive regard and the experience of empathic understanding.

Another point worth noting is that the stress is upon the experience in the relationship. It is not to be expected that the therapist is a completely congruent person at all times. Indeed if this were a necessary condition there would be no therapy. But it is enough if in this particular moment of this immediate relationship with this specific person he is completely and fully himself, with his experience of the moment being accurately symbolized and integrated into the picture he holds of himself. Thus it is that imperfect human beings can be of therapeutic assistance to other imperfect human beings.

The greatest flaw in the statement of these conditions is that they are stated as if they were all-or-none elements, whereas conditions 2 to 6 all exist on continua. At some later date we may be able to say that the therapist must be genuine or congruent to such and such a degree in the relationship, and similarly for the other items. At the present we can only point out that the more marked the presence of conditions 2 to 6, the more certain it is that the process of therapy will get under way, and the greater the degree of reorganization which will take place. This function can only be stated qualitatively at the present time.

B. The Process of Therapy

When the preceding conditions exist and continue, a process is set in motion which has these characteristic directions:

1. The client is increasingly free in expressing his feelings, through verbal and/or motor channels.

2. His expressed feelings increasingly have reference to the self, rather than nonself.

3. He increasingly differentiates and discriminates the objects of his feelings and perceptions, including his environment, other persons, his self, his experiences, and the interrelationships of these. He becomes less intensional and more extensional in his perceptions, or to put it in other terms, his experiences are more accurately symbolized.

4. His expressed feelings increasingly have reference to the incongruity between certain of his experiences and his concept of self.

5. He comes to experience in awareness the threat of such incongruence.

    a. This experience of threat is possible only because of the continued unconditional positive regard of the therapist, which is extended to <u>incongruence</u> as much as to <u>congruence</u>, to <u>anxiety</u> as much as to absence of <u>anxiety</u>.

6. He <u>experiences</u> fully, in <u>awareness</u>, feelings which have in the past been <u>denied to awareness</u> or <u>distorted in awareness</u>.

7. His <u>concept of self</u> becomes reorganized to assimilate and include these <u>experiences</u> which have previously been <u>distorted in</u>, or <u>denied to</u>, <u>awareness</u>.

8. As this reorganization of the <u>self-structure</u> continues, his <u>concept of self</u> becomes increasingly <u>congruent</u> with his <u>experience</u>, the <u>self</u> now including <u>experiences</u> which previously would have been too <u>threatening</u> to be in <u>awareness</u>.

   a. A corollary tendency is toward fewer perceptual <u>distortions in awareness</u> or <u>denials to awareness</u> since there are fewer <u>experiences</u> which can be <u>threatening</u>. In other words, <u>defensiveness</u> is decreased.

9. He becomes increasingly able to <u>experience</u>, without a feeling of <u>threat</u>, the therapist's <u>unconditional positive regard</u>.

10. He increasingly feels an <u>unconditional positive self-regard</u>.

11. He increasingly experiences himself as the <u>locus of evaluation</u>.

12. He reacts to experience less in terms of his <u>conditions of worth</u> and more in terms of an organismic valuing process.

<u>Comment</u>. It cannot be stated with certainty that all of these are <u>necessary</u> elements of the process, though they are all characteristic. Both from the point of view of experience and from the logic of the theory, items 3, 6, 7, 8, 10 and 12 are necessary elements in the process. Item 5a is not a logical step in the theory but is put in as an explanatory note.

The element which will doubtless be most puzzling to the reader is the absence of explanatory mechanisms. It may be well to restate our scientific purpose in terms of an example. <u>If</u> one strokes a piece of steel with a magnet, and <u>if</u> one places the piece of steel so that it can rotate freely, <u>then</u> it will point to the north. This statement of the if-then variety has been proved thousands of times. Why does it happen? There have been various theoretical answers, and one would hesitate to say, even now, that we know with certitude why this occurs.

In the same way I have been saying in regard to therapy, "If these conditions exist, then these subsequent events will occur." Of course we have speculations as to why this relationship appears to exist, but the most basic element of our theory is that if the described conditions exist, then the process of therapy occurs, and the events which are called outcomes will be observed. We may be quite wrong as to why this sequence occurs. I believe there is an increasing body of evidence to show that it does occur.

C. Outcomes in Personality and Behavior

There is no clear distinction between process and outcome. Items of process are simply differentiated aspects of outcome. Hence the statements which follow could have been included under process. For reasons of convenience in understanding, there have been grouped here those changes which are customarily associated with the terms "outcomes" or "results," or are observed outside of the therapeutic relationship. These are the changes which are hypothesized as being relatively permanent:

1. The client is more congruent, more open to his experience, less defensive.

2. He is consequently more realistic, objective, extensional in his perceptions.

3. He is consequently more effective in problem-solving.

4. His psychological adjustment is improved, being closer to the optimum.

    a. This is owing to, and a continuation of, the changes in self-structure described in B7 and B8.

5. As a result of the increased congruence of self and experience (C4 above) his vulnerability to threat is reduced.

6. As a consequence of C2 above, his perception of his ideal self is more realistic, more achievable.

7. As a consequence of the changes in C4 and C5 his self is more congruent with his ideal self.

8. As a consequence of the increased congruence of self and ideal self (C6) and the greater congruence of self and experience, tension of all types is reduced—physiological tension, psychological tension, and the specific type of psychological tension defined as anxiety.

9. He has an increased degree of positive self-regard.

10. He perceives the locus of evaluation and the locus of choice as residing within himself.

    a. As a consequence of C9 and C10 he feels more confident and more self-directing.

    b. As a consequence of C1 and C10, his values are determined by an organismic valuing process.

11. As a consequence of C1 and C2, he <u>perceives</u> others more realistically and accurately.

12. He <u>experiences</u> more <u>acceptance</u> of others, as a consequence of less need for distortion of his perceptions of them.

13. His behavior changes in various ways.

    a. Since the proportion of <u>experience</u> assimilated into the <u>self-structure</u> is increased, the proportion of behaviors which can be "owned" as belonging to the <u>self</u> is increased.

    b. Conversely, the proportion of behaviors which are disowned as <u>self-experiences,</u> felt to be "not myself," is decreased.

    c. Hence his behavior is <u>perceived</u> as being more within his control.

14. His behavior is perceived by others as more socialized, more <u>mature</u>.

15. As a consequence of C1, 2, 3, his behavior is more creative, more uniquely adaptive to each new situation, and each new problem, more fully expressive of his own purposes and values.

<u>Comment.</u> The statement in part C which is essential is statement C1. Items 2 through 15 are actually a more explicit spelling out of the theoretical implications of statement 1. The only reason for including them is that though such implications follow readily enough from the logic of the theory, they are often not perceived unless they are pointed out.

<u>Comments on the theory of therapy</u>. It is to be noted that this theory of therapy involves, basically, no intervening variables. The conditions of therapy, given in A, are all operationally definable, and some have already been given rather crude operational definitions in research already conducted. The theory states that if A exists, then B and C will follow. B and C are measurable events, predicted by A.

It should also be pointed out that the logic of the theory is such that: if A, then B; if A, then B and C; if A, then C (omitting consideration of B); if B, then C (omitting consideration of A).

<u>Specification of functional relationships.</u> At this point, the functional relationships can only be stated in general and qualitative form. The greater the degree of the conditions specified in A, the more marked or more extensive will be the process changes in B, and the greater or more extensive the outcome changes specified in C. Putting this in more general terms, the greater the degree of anxiety in the client, congruence in the therapist in the relationship, acceptance and empathy experienced by the therapist,

and recognition by the client of these elements, the deeper will be the process of therapy, and the greater the extent of personality and behavioral change. To revert now to the theoretical logic, all we can say at present is that

$$B=(f)A \qquad C=(f)A \qquad B+C=(f)A \qquad C=(f)B$$

Obviously there are many functional interrelationships not yet specified by the theory. For example, if anxiety is high, is congruence on the part of the therapist less necessary? There is much work to be done in investigating the functional relationships more fully.

D. Some Conclusions Regarding the Nature of the Individual

From the theory of therapy as stated above, certain conclusions are implicit regarding the nature of man. To make them explicit involves little more than looking at the same hypotheses from a somewhat different vantage point. It is well to state them explicitly, however, since they constitute an important explanatory link of a kind which gives this theory whatever uniqueness it may possess. They also constitute the impelling reason for developing a theory of personality. If the individual is what he is revealed to be in therapy, then what theory would account for such an individual? We present these conclusions about the characteristics of the human organism:

1. The individual possesses the capacity to experience in awareness the factors in his psychological adjustment, namely, the incongruences between his self-concept and the totality of his experience.

2. The individual possesses the capacity and has the tendency to reorganize his self-concept in such a way as to make it more congruent with the totality of his experience, thus moving himself away from a state of psychological maladjustment, and toward a state of psychological adjustment.

3. These capacities and this tendency, when latent rather than evident, will be released in any interpersonal relationship in which the other person is congruent in the relationship, experiences unconditional positive regard toward, and empathic understanding of the individual, and achieves some communication of these attitudes to the individual. (These are, of course, the characteristics already given under IA3, 4, 5, 6.)

It is this tendency which is elaborated into the tendency toward actualization.

I believe it is obvious that the basic capacity which is hypothesized is of very decided importance in its psychological and philosophical implications. It means that psychotherapy is the releasing of an already existing capacity in a potentially competent individual, not the expert manipulation of a more or less passive personality. Philosophically it means that the individual has the capacity to guide, regulate, and control himself, providing only that certain definable conditions exist. Only in the absence of these conditions, and not in any basic sense, is it necessary to provide external control and regulation of the individual.

REFERENCES

Angyal, A. Foundations for a science of personality. New York: Commonwealth Fund, 1941.

Kelley, E. C. Education in communication. ETC, Summer, 1955, 12: 248-256.

Maslow, A. H. Motivation and personality. New York: Harper, 1954.

McCleary, R. A., & Lazarus, R. S. Autonomic discrimination without awareness. J. Pers., 1949, 18: 171-179.

Rogers, C. R. Clinical treatment of the problem child. Boston: Houghton Mifflin, 1939.

Rogers, C. R. Counseling and psychotherapy. Boston: Houghton Mifflin, 1942.

Rogers, C. R., & Dymond, R. F. (Eds.) Psychotherapy and personality change. Chicago: Univer. Chicago Press, 1954.

Standal, S. The need for positive regard: a contribution to client-centered theory. Unpublished doctoral dissertation, Univer. of Chicago, 1954.

SUGGESTED READINGS

Rogers, C. R. Client-centered therapy. Boston: Houghton Mifflin, 1951.

Rogers, C. R. On becoming a person. Boston: Houghton Mifflin, 1961.

V

PRINCIPLES OF DIRECTIVE COUNSELING
AND PSYCHOTHERAPY

Frederick C. Thorne

Clinical psychology has emerged from the prescientific into the scientific era of development. There is urgent need for a comprehensive integration of all scientific data into a "system" of practice which would be genuinely eclectic and provide a basis for the standardization of practice throughout the world. Such a system would be based upon the most modern scientific principles and methods, and would attempt to relate the most recent discoveries with the great mass of information accumulated during the history of the profession. An example of this phase of development in the medical field was the work of Sir William Osler who wrote the first systematic text on the practice of medicine and laid the foundations of the great medical center at Johns Hopkins University. Characteristic of the newer theory of professional education has been the insistence that the orientation must be genuinely eclectic with every student being required to familiarize himself with the latest developments in every clinical specialty.

Prior to World War II, uniform training was non-existent in clinical psychology and every student operated more or less on his own with whatever tools and qualifications he had been able to acquire informally. This situation is being rapidly remedied during the post-war period through the efforts of the APA committees on graduate training in cooperation with the universities, but in spite of this desirable trend clinical psychology in America is still characterized by a primitive state of organization in which the leaders in the field operate more or less independently. Until the recent popularity of nondirective methods, there was no general agreement on any theoretical viewpoint with the result that there

Condensed from a paper presented at a symposium under the auspices of the Division of Consulting Psychology at the Detroit meeting of the American Psychological Association, September 10, 1947. Reprinted by permission of the author and *American Psychologist*, 1948, 3:160–65.

were almost as many brands of clinical psychology as there were clinical psychologists. Lacking any formally systemized viewpoint, the theoretical biases of clinical psychologists literally represented all the permutations and combinations of behaviorism, experimentalism, Gestalt psychology, Freudianism, Adlerian individual psychology, Jungian analytic psychology, purposivism and many other minor schools. Most of the leaders in clinical psychology were represented by groups of adherents who were well-trained only in the methods of their teachers. So divergent were the different ideologies and terminologies that proponents of the various schools were frequently unable to communicate with each other. In view of these theoretical differences, it is easy to understand why clinical psychologists have been viewed with suspicion by their experimental colleagues to say nothing of psychiatrists and psychoanalysts who have theoretical biases all their own.

ORIGINS OF DIRECTIVE PSYCHOTHERAPY

The purpose of this paper is to review the basic principles of the comprehensive system of directive psychotherapy described in the series of papers appearing in the Journal of Clinical Psychology beginning in 1945, and to make a definitive statement concerning the eclectic orientation which is the basis for the proposed system of practice. The primary motivation was to formulate a comprehensive system of counseling and psychotherapy which would integrate and relate the positive values of newer viewpoints with traditional methods. This system would be more than a compilation of isolated facts, and would be based primarily on the objective foundations of experimental psychology. Its basic orientation would be determined by a detailed system of psychopathology derived from a more comprehensive method of personality analysis than had ever been attempted before. Modifying the classical psychiatric methods involving (a) Kraepelinian descriptive classifications, (b) psychobiological longitudinal studies, and (c) psychoanalytic depth analysis, the new method would seek to systematically evaluate and, if indicated, to modify all known important personality traits by the eclectic utilization of all available methods according to their indications and contraindications.

Although recognizing the undesirability of designating a system of psychotherapy by the term "directive," the choice was partially determined by our apprehension that the sudden popularity of Rogerian nondirective methods to the exclusion of traditional methods was a dangerous development both for the profession and for the student. This critical attitude was directed not so much toward nondirective methods which are admitted to have great value in their place, but toward the attitude of uncritical enthusiasm and cultism associated with the new development. It appeared that there was definite need for a comprehensive system which would relate directive and nondirective methods in their proper perspective and emphasize the values of eclecticism in clinical science.

TERMINOLOGICAL CONSIDERATIONS

The term <u>directive</u> seemed particularly appropriate to designate a system of therapy which is based upon a formal plan for the identification and modification of etiologic factors in maladjustment. Based upon the historical study of the evolution of clinical methods in science which have been outlined elsewhere (Thorne, 1947), it was our opinion that any valid therapeutic system must be oriented about a comprehensive knowledge of psychopathology and the uses and limitations of <u>all</u> known clinical methods. It is presupposed that persons representing themselves as clinical psychologists should have training and experience to enable them to adequately utilize all known methods according to the standards of time and place. Possession of such training and experience beyond that which might be expected of the most intelligent and best-informed layman implies that the basic responsibility for the <u>direction</u> of all stages of case handling lies with the therapist even though he may choose to delegate some portion of this responsibility to other persons including the client himself. In our opinion the possibility of a completely nondirective method is nonexistent since by the very nature of the therapist-client relationship (a) the client comes to a therapist considered to be of superior experience and training which thereby establishes a relationship of dominance through prestige, (b) the therapist determines the method to be used, and (c) what happens in the therapeutic relationship must be evaluated not only in terms of what the therapist thinks he is doing but also in terms of what the therapy means to the patient. Rather than involving a dichotomy of either-or directive or nondirective, we are dealing with a continuum involving various degrees of directiveness of which nondirective methods may be regarded as being at one extreme along with other "passive" techniques. We are in disagreement with Rogers' contention that any lapse from complete nondirectiveness is a grave therapeutic error, since our experience indicates that all degrees of directiveness may be used with a single case according to the indications of each individual situation.

The concepts of <u>directive</u> and <u>direction</u> also imply straightforwardness, i.e. straight, leading by the shortest way to a point or end. <u>Directed</u> movements of an organism are those which are observed to be related to a specific stimulus or goal. <u>Direction</u> is an attribute of behavior indicative of specific function and variously expressed in terms of needs, drives, goals, purposes and other concepts descriptive of integrated behavior. One of the principal characteristics of the maladjusted or disordered person is the inability to resolve problems unaided. Although self-direction is the highest democratic goal and evidence of integration, the maladjusted person either asks for help spontaneously or is induced to do so for his own good. Until such time as the person demonstrates his ability to regulate his behavior within the limits of what is socially acceptable, he is subjected to varying degrees of direction or regulation from the environment. The general rule may be stated that the need for direction is inversely correlated with the person's potentialities for effective self-regulation, i.e., the healthier the personality, the less the need for direction; the sicker the personality, the more the need for direction. It is to be assumed that the well-trained psychological scientist is the person best equipped to provide whatever degree of direction may be necessary to catalyze therapeutic processes by the shortest route. Judiciously utilized, psychological knowledge may have specific action in facilitating curative processes in much shorter time than might be accomplished by the client working by trial and error even assuming that homeostatic resources would be sufficient. While recognizing the dangers of over-regulation and over-interpretation in cases of mild personality disorder, it is our opinion that failure to institute the indicated degrees of direction in more serious cases may constitute malpractice since the therapist has the obligation to protect the interests of the client when the client is unable to do so himself.

The significance of these facts is that the therapist is supposed to <u>direct</u> the overall details of case handling according to tested scientific procedures whether he is utilizing nondirective methods or authoritarian methods in an institution. It is assumed that training and experience will provide the therapist with the knowledge concerning when to be directive or relatively nondirective. The validity of the results will be determined by the skill with which any method is used with reference to etiological diagnosis and the indications of each individual case. The critical factor is not what method is used but rather the skill with which it is used. We are not in agreement with the ideological bias of many nondirective therapists to the effect that all which is directive is bad, while all that is nondirective is good. In his basic text, Rogers (1942) attacks directive methods by setting up the straw man of criticizing the most crude and unacceptable forms of directive methods and implying that all directive techniques are subject to the same handicaps. Directive methods can only be fairly judged when they are employed with maximum skill; it is unrepresentative to base criticisms on atypical examples which would be condemned by all experienced directive therapists. Long before the development of nondirective methods, psychoanalysis had demonstrated the errors of over-interpretation, too much leading, crude interference and other pitfalls of the beginning counselor. The nondirective viewpoint appears to have gone to the extreme of rejecting direction in any form simply because it has frequently been misused. Hahn and Kendall (1947) and others have recently pointed out the logical inconsistencies involved in many of the theoretical criticisms made by Rogers and his pupils against directive methods. Perhaps most important is it to emphasize that all valid therapy is client-centered and that nondirective therapy has no monopoly on methods which are to the best interests of the client. As pointed out by Blain (1947), effective therapy frequently involves a compromise between what a patient sincerely believes he wants and what he needs according to the most objective judgment of the experienced therapist. Although it is theoretically desirable to place major dependence upon the growth principle and homeostatic processes as emphasized by Rogers and many others before him, there are many cases in which the client's resources and growth potentialities are so deficient or damaged that adjustment without outside help and direction is impossible.

A further application of the concept of directness is illustrated in our attempt toward a systematic application of the Law of Parsimony (Lloyd Morgan's canon). In contrast with the current popularity of psychoanalytically oriented approaches which seek to discover latent meanings, symbolism, unconscious complexes and other depth processes in personality, our viewpoint is that primary weight should be assigned to direct interpretations of manifest behavior according to the principles of scientific psychology and particularly the laws of learning. Much is lost by failing to make the simplest possible interpretations and also by proceeding in the most direct manner consistent with the needs of the client. In our own practice, we systematically avoid complex psychoanalytic interpretations, preferring to communicate whatever minimum amount seems indicated in the simplest of terms. It is an axiom of directive therapy, as well as nondirective, that the less said by the therapist the better.

Finally, we would specifically refute the implication made by Snyder (1947) and apparently accepted by others, that the term "directive psychotherapy" was coined by us simply to refer to traditional methods of therapy and involving little which is new. While it is true that many of the methods included under directive therapy have long been utilized, there has not been any systematic attempt known to us in the English literature to reevaluate them in terms of modern psychopathology with the objectives of determining their nature, indications and contraindications. Traditionally, these methods have been described and utilized as isolated units with no attempt being made to construct an integrated system about a central theory of personality.

THE BASIC METHOD

The theoretical foundations for directive psychotherapy are derived from a survey of the historical development of clinical science carrying over the principles and methods which appear to be valid for clinical psychology. As pointed out elsewhere (Thorne, 1947), clinical psychology has a medico-psychological heritage dating back to ancient Egypt and one must be familiar with the evolution of medical psychology in order to evaluate any development in proper perspective. Utilizing standard techniques of description, classification, statistical evaluation and integrative interpretation, directive psychotherapy attempts to discover the causal conditions resulting in maladaptation and then to utilize treatments specific for each pathological condition. Unless comprehensive etiologic studies are carried out with every case, it is difficult to understand how any objective evaluation in case handling may be made. However, this unending search for the causation of morbidity must never be allowed to conceal the basic objective of satisfying the needs of the client.

The basic pattern of directive therapy in which the therapist, though client-centered, assumes responsibility for the conduct of all details of case handling according to the highest ethical and professional standards of time and place is given in another paper (Thorne, 1947).

Gregg (1947) states a cardinal axiom that the human organism involves such a complex relationship of constituent parts that one cannot be modified without affecting all others; that, therefore, a given result comes usually not from one cause but from a combination of causes, sometimes a sequence, sometimes a constellation or pattern; and similarly, that a given cause has not one but many results, sometimes in sequence, sometimes in pattern. With such a complex situation, it is inevitable that a wide armamentarium of therapeutic tools will be needed, each used as skillfully as possible based on a valid knowledge of what each tool can be expected to accomplish.

PSYCHOPATHOLOGICAL RATIONALE

One of the most important contributions of Adolf Meyer's psychobiological approach to personality was his recognition that pathological processes of different types may involve personality functions as a whole or in parts. By careful appraisal of all the known functions of personality, it becomes possible to identify areas of dysfunction, to postulate etiologic factors, and to outline specific plans of treatment. The psychobiologic approach is genuinely eclectic in the sense that it seeks to assess all known functions with proper weight being assigned to dysfunctions of each in the longitudinal study of personality. In this respect, the psychobiologic viewpoint may be contrasted with that of psychoanalysis in its various forms. In our opinion, psychoanalytic theory is one-sided in that it overemphasizes latent, unconscious, affective-impulsive components of personality while almost disregarding the direct, manifest, rational intellectual components characteristic of the higher mental functions and which are best understood by the psychology of learning and thinking. When the psychoanalytic viewpoint is carried to its logical conclusions as in nondirective therapy, the main emphasis is placed on affective-impulsive components which are regarded as involving the principal etiologic factors in maladjustment. Snyder (1947) even defines the objective of psychotherapeutic counseling as to "modify emotional attitudes that are socially maladjusted" and omits any reference to intellectual factors which may also be productive of maladjustment.

The system of directive psychotherapy which has been outlined in our published series of papers is theoretically oriented upon psychobiological approaches to the whole organism with perhaps more emphasis on rational intellectual components than on affective-impulsive since we believe that the highest potentialities for adaptation are related to the maturation and effective utilization of the higher cortical functions. The developmental phenomena associated with the maturation of the cerebral cortex are now well known and may be summarized in the statement that although the biologically more primitive affective-impulsive components of personality are constantly operative throughout life, the maturation of the cortex with the development of the higher mental functions results in the achievement of rational intellectual control through cerebral inhibition of lower functions and the acquisition of tremendously enhanced powers of learning. The dominance of the cerebrum over mid and hind-brain functions is achieved very slowly and only incompletely in the average person so that learning self-regulation, making the most of one's resources, and achieving insight into the meanings of behavior and life in general is a very gradual process.

In outlining the theoretical foundations of directive psychotherapy, we have attempted to integrate the principal contributions of the main schools of psychology. From behaviorism comes a major emphasis on the role of learning and of environmental stimulation in the development of acquired patterns of behavior. Experimental psychology of the traditional type contributes important information concerning sensation, memory, association, physiological reactions, and other relatively elemental phenomena. Gestalt psychology is important because of its emphasis on wholes, and its detailed studies of the perceptual process. Psychoanalysis gives most important emphasis to depth psychology, with its developmental studies of the affective-impulsive life. Finally, hormic psychology contributes the stimulating viewpoint that organic phenomena are largely determined by purposive factors as yet not clearly understood. Following the psychobiological approach which assumes that the psychologist will have detailed and extensive training and experience in the basic sciences of anatomy, biochemistry, physiology, pathology, as well as in normal psychology, directive psychotherapy depends for its validity upon the psychological sophistication and broadness of the person who attempts to utilize it. The better oriented is the clinician to the psychological sciences and to life in general, the more able is he to avoid the pitfalls which are recognized as inherent in any active (directive) method. Any method is no better than the skill of the person who makes it. We have come to regard psychotherapy as involving the hardest kind of work for both therapist and client, since deviant personality patterns become chronic over the years and can hardly be expected to be unlearned and relearned with startling rapidity.

Directive psychotherapy accepts the concept of distributive analysis and treatment developed by Meyer and described by Diethelm (1936). The distributive principle assumes that it is most effective to budget time and energy during the treatment process giving major emphasis to trends which appear to be most etiologically important. Instead of spending hundreds of hours more or less passively exploring the channels taken by the client, considerable saving may be accomplished without violence to the client-centered principle by directing the course of treatment along what may seem to be the most profitable lines. In addition to etiologic studies exploring the developmental history of the person, it seems important also to assess learning ability and accomplishment in all areas of activity. Directive psychotherapy is particularly concerned with maximizing the self-regulatory functions of personality with particular emphasis on self-control and conative life. It seems important to deal with certain phenomena usually denied or ignored in traditional psychology including the study of the nature of consciousness, nonconscious mental functions, volition, suggestion, hypnosis, deviant personalities of all types, and other phenomena which have important significance for psychopathology.

The directive principle that intellectual resources constitute the highest potentialities for adaptation in the organism and that therapy must be realistically distributed to deal with both affective-impulsive and rational-intellectual factors as they are encountered in the individual case, is based on the important distinction concerning primary and secondary etiologic factors in maladaptation. Etiologic factors may be identified as precipitating, predisposing or perpetuating. To explain our conception of the relative psychopathological importance of affective vs. intellectual factors in personality would require much more time than is here available. In summary, it seems important to reevaluate the entire etiologic role of affective factors in maladjustment with particular reference to the distinction between (a) reactive affective disorders, and (b) deeper habitual affective reactions based on constitutional or acquired personality complexes. In our opinion, affective disorders of reactive type have a much higher incidence and have most hopeful prognosis with or without treatment (although perhaps more quickly with treatment) when the stimulating factors are modified. In these cases, affective disorders are recognized to be symptomatic and therapy is primarily directed toward the intellectual failure to react adaptively. It may be necessary to treat affective-impulsive disorders first in order to prepare the stage for rational problem-solving activity but it should clearly be recognized that treatment of such reactive affective disorders results in only transient alleviation of symptoms which are prone to recur unless effective intellectual solutions are achieved. A basic diagnostic question therefore becomes: "Is the client maladjusted because he is emotionally disturbed, or is he emotionally disturbed because he is maladjusted?" The solution to this hen-egg problem is not always easily achieved, since reactive affective states may be of long duration. The degree of directiveness indicated in the individual case will be determined by the client's demonstrated ability to solve the problem alone.

Recognition of the need for maximally potentiating intellectual resources of personality in problem solving behavior has important implications in both theoretical orientation and practical application. If human behavior is determined by unconscious, instinctual, affective-impulsive components in personality, it follows that maladjustment is caused by mechanistic, physiological factors over which a person can exert little conscious, voluntary control unless his growth resources or homeostatic tendencies are sufficiently strong to fortunately effect a cure. On the other hand, if it is accepted that rational-intellectual factors may supersede and control impulsive behavior, then the normal person may be expected to achieve some success in solving problems by conscious use of intellectual resources. This viewpoint does not necessarily involve the postulation of such mental functions as will or volition. On the contrary, the acquisition of self-regulatory abilities is regarded as a function of past training, usually by directive methods since few individuals are gifted enough to work out optimal methods by themselves, nor would such a trial and error process be economically desirable even if possible. Important areas of maladjustment are regarded as being caused by failure to learn to solve such problems using intellectual resources. This learning would normally take place in early life, thus normally preventing maladaptation. Since the basic factor in most psychotherapy is commonly recognized to be reeducation, it follows that the treatment process is essentially a training situation. It is occasionally necessary to resolve emotional attitudes before training can be begun, but this is not inevitable, since training may proceed even in unfavorable conditions. If latent, subconscious, unverbalized affective-impulsive reactions are important determiners of behavior, so are acquired intellectual traits and attitudes operating on manifest conscious levels. The goal of therapy is to replace emotional-compulsive behavior with deliberate rational-adaptive behavior based on the highest utilization of intellectual resources. To accomplish this may require the use of many directive techniques over and above the simple nondirective handling of emotional reactions which may be understood as simply the first step in therapy.

STATUS OF DIRECTIVE METHODS

Unfortunately, the traditional discussions of directive methods have dealt primarily with theoretical considerations with very little detail concerning the actual mechanics of case handling. Since each clinician has largely been forced to develop techniques by himself, it is understandable that the actual execution of these techniques ranged from literal perfection in the hands of the masters to the crudest bungling in the hands of amateurs. The situation is further complicated by the fact that the practical details have been taught by the apprenticeship method and only rarely described objectively. One of the purposes of the medical internship is to teach many small details of case handling which have never appeared in print, and which can only be learned by actually doing. No matter how rigidly and experimentally the treatment process may be controlled, the actual success is largely a function of the skill and intuitiveness of the individual practitioner in making the patient comfortable while attempting to treat the basic condition.

Before any extensive research program could be planned or undertaken, it has been necessary to achieve a theoretical formulation of the principles and methods of directive therapy and this has been attempted in the series of papers appearing in the Journal of Clinical Psychology. The failure to produce more quantitative evidence in support of the validity of directive psychotherapy is a function of its youth. Experimental work with any of the traditional methods has been almost completely lacking. Directive methods are only now being formally described and related to a system of therapy, and it will take many years to accumulate objective validation as evidenced by the fact that the basic outlines of psychoanalysis have still not been confirmed after almost fifty years of research. Although slightly more objective research has been accomplished with nondirective methods, it is insufficient either to establish the rather optimistic claims of its proponents or, conversely, to offer objective evidence that directive methods are invalid.

The status of all methods of psychotherapy is in such an elementary stage of evolution that clinical psychologists find themselves in the position of the chemists who having discovered some of the rarer elements did not know what to do with them. Some of the neglected methods such as suggestion, hypnosis, reconditioning or reassurance may well turn out to have such startling possibilities when properly used as did uranium in relation to the atom bomb. When psychologists devote as much time and energy to training themselves in the use of any of these methods as do professional athletes or craftsmen, much of the crudeness which is now so much in evidence will inevitably disappear. In our experience, nondirective methods constitute just a beginning with respect to what the clinical psychologist may be expected to do. Some cases will show some improvement with the use of any superficial method, but others become progressively more maladjusted and constitute a challenge which will require the most effective use of all resources if the problem is to be solved. Directive psychotherapy requires that the therapist will be trained and able to make use of every known method in his field as indication may arise.

REFERENCES

Alexander, F., French, T. M., et al. Psychoanalytic therapy. New York: Ronald, 1946.

Blain, D. The psychiatrist and the psychologist. J. clin. Psychol., 1947, 3: 4-9.

Diethelm, O. Treatment in psychiatry. New York: Macmillan, 1936.

Gregg, A. Transition in medical education. J. Assoc. Med. Coll., 1947, 22: 226-232.

Hahn, M. E., and Kendall, W. E. Some comments in defense of "non-directive" counseling. J. consult. Psychol, 1947, 11: 74-81.

Rogers, C. R. Counseling and psychotherapy. Boston: Houghton Mifflin, 1942.

Rogers, C. R. Significant aspects of client-centered therapy. Amer. Psychologist, 1946, 1: 415-422.

Snyder, W. U. The present status of psychotherapeutic counseling. Psychol. Bull., 1947, 44: 297-386.

Thorne, F. C. The clinical method in science. Amer. Psychologist, 1947, 2: 159-166.

Thorne, F. C. Theoretical foundations of directive psychotherapy. Annals N. Y. Acad. Sci., 1948, 49: 869-877.

VI

MINIMUM CHANGE THERAPY

Leona E. Tyler

I have some misgivings about the problem we are considering
today. Any attempt we make to limit the duration of counseling,
though we may think of it as a purely quantitative change, may turn
out to have large qualitative effects. One of our ground rules, so
basic that we seldom even state it explicitly, is that a person is
worth whatever amount of time and trouble it takes to help him.
We do not measure concern and kindness in hours or dollars. It
would be as though a mother should say to herself: "Let's see. I
can afford to devote 10 years of my life primarily to the nurture of
these children. That means that the total amount of time that each
of them can claim is 10,000 hours." Instead of thinking in this
fashion, a mother naturally assumes that she must give whatever
the task demands, without rationing it. An increasing mass of evidence is showing that the optimal growth of a human being requires
just this kind of unlimited commitment on somebody's part. Under
favorable circumstances, a person has had enormous amounts of
love and care devoted to him by the time he reaches maturity.

The experience of having someone really care about him is
such an indispensable part of what counseling means for a client
that we must be especially careful never to jeopardize it. It is for
this reason that I am inclined to doubt the wisdom of setting arbitrary time limits. If what the client understands by the arrangements we make is: "You are worth spending 10 hours on, but no
more," an experience he might otherwise have had simply will not
occur. It has always seemed to me that there is a big difference
psychologically, between limits that are inevitable and obviously

Reprinted from the *Personnel and Guidance Journal*, 1960, 38:475–479, with
the permission of the author and the American Personnel and Guidance Association.

necessary, such as those resulting from the end of a school term or the illness of the therapist and those that are arbitrary or unexplained.

However, after all this has been said, the fact remains that to prolong counseling contacts unnecessarily does not do a client any good and may even hamper his further development. And our own full schedules make it imperative that we try to avoid this type of error. Thus we do need to give some thought to the matter of how this can best be done.

CHANGE OR UTILIZATION

My approach to this and other counseling problems has been to attempt to clarify the nature of the task itself. Elsewhere during the last year I have tried to distinguish between two kinds of helping process. Therapy generally has as its goal personality change; counseling attempts to bring about the best possible utilization of what the person already has. It is a distinction similar to the one Tolman years ago introduced into learning theory, the difference between learning and performance.

The only trouble with simple, clear-cut classifications like this is that they don't seem to fit a lot of the tasks and situations with which we are confronted. Certainly most of the work we do in facilitating occupational choices and educational decisions can be classified as utilization rather than as change. But what of the client with major or minor personality problems? Is the treatment we offer in such cases therapy or counseling? Is it perhaps really therapy, but called counseling in order to make it more palatable to him or to the community? It would not be so important what label we used, except that the ambiguity spreads out over our own thinking about what we call therapeutic counseling. And because we are not at all sure what we are trying to accomplish, we never know just when we are through.

What I have been questioning in my own mind more and more is the assumption that therapy should attempt to bring about as much personality change as possible. Could it be largely because of the enormous prestige psychoanalysis has acquired that we tend to assume that personality reorganization is the goal toward which we should strive? Is it really true that the therapy that produces the most changes is the best therapy? Would it not be possible to make the opposite assumption and deliberately set as our goal "minimum-change" therapy? This would be a kind of undertaking that would fit in well with the rest of the activities that go on under the name of counseling. We would try in each case to help the person discover some unblocked path in which he could move forward, develop his unique personality, and thus transcend rather than delve into the anxieties and conflicts in which he is now enmeshed.

I picture this process in terms of a change of direction rather than in terms of distances or amounts. The difficulties a client is experiencing can be thought of as indications that he is headed in a direction that is wrong for him or that he has at some former time made a wrong turn into a blind alley. All of this may have occurred without conscious awareness, of course. Counseling can create a situation in which a person may become aware of the directional shifts that are possible for him and in which he can be sure someone will see him through what may be a difficult "rotation of his axis." In pursuing the implications of this geometric analogy a little further I calculated that a directional shift of only 10 degrees makes a difference of 170 miles in where one comes out if his journey is 1,000 miles long—enough to make a considerable difference in terrain and landscape. Similarly, a relatively minor shift in the psychological direction in which a person is moving may well change his life considerably over a long period of years.

This is what I mean by "minimum-change therapy." It has made it possible for me to see how in principle therapeutic counseling could be shortened considerably without making it any less valuable. It involves no great change in the procedures we use, but some aspects of the complex counseling situation need to be emphasized or even modified to some extent.

EMPHASIS ON STRENGTH

In the first place, it implies that more emphasis than one ordinarily finds be placed on positive diagnosis. By and large, our diagnostic thinking rests on concepts taken over from psychopathology. We try to ascertain where a person's weak spots are. Many psychologists, especially in recent years, have criticized this approach and advocated the diagnosis of strengths. In minimum-change therapy we pay no attention to personality weaknesses that are adequately controlled or neutralized. We all have areas like this. It is only the difficulties that are actually blocking the person's forward movement that we must attempt to deal with. And as suggested in the previous section, it is quite possible that these may be by-passed rather than attacked. A person who knows his real strengths and is clear about his basic values may be able to turn away from anxieties about aspects of his life that would be very difficult to change.

Though there is a widespread current interest in ego processes and positive personality traits, we do not as yet have tests we can count on for this sort of diagnostic task. We are more likely to become aware of a person's strengths by observing things he does than by asking him questions. Some of this meaningful behavior occurs in the interview situation itself. For example, when Mary Hart flashes a sudden smile as she is struck with the amusing aspects of a particularly humiliating social experience she is recounting, we know that she possesses an asset that may be of considerable use to her. Call it a defense if you will, but in social situations and in personal emotional adaptation to the vicissitudes of life her ability to laugh at her own predicament will be a valuable asset. Other assets frequently showing up even in interviews where hostility, doubt, guilt, and anxiety are the main themes include moral principles of which the person is absolutely certain, demonstrated courage in the face of adversities, loyalty to those he loves. Whether or not it is advisable for the counselor to reflect or interpret such expressions at the time they occur is another question. But he can make a mental note of them.

We are more likely to become aware of a client's personality assets if we have some knowledge of his life outside the counseling room. In small or moderate-sized colleges, the counselor is likely to encounter his clients here or there—on the street, in the student union, at concerts, plays, or games. The growing practice of placing psychologists on the wards in mental hospitals serves the same purpose of permitting the kind of observation that positive diagnosis is based on. Conversations with a client's family or friends is another resource, but I am strongly of the opinion that it should not be used without the person's knowledge or permission. It is the characteristics he knows you have had a chance to observe—the things you can talk over together—that are grist for counseling's mill. In the last analysis, it is the client himself who must make the positive diagnosis we have been talking about if it is to be effective in his life.

COUNSELING STRUCTURE

A second point of emphasis in minimum-change therapy is the way in which the situation is structured for the client. We must take into account <u>his</u> expectations and goals as well as our own.

To a person profoundly dissatisfied with the way his life has been going, the only thing that really looks good is change—complete change. What he may have read about psychotherapy in popular magazines or seen in movies leads him to expect or at least hope that some fundamental change will occur. True, the experience of countless therapists has shown that such a person will hang on to his unconscious defenses and fight every sort of change at every step of the way. But if anyone tells him at the beginning that small shifts of direction rather than larger changes in total pattern are to be expected he is likely to reject the whole undertaking. He thinks he wants to be made over.

It is in this connection that some explicit verbal distinction between counseling and therapy may be useful. Instead of trying to fight the person's wishful dreams about miraculous effects of therapy, I can simply explain that I am a counselor rather than a psychoanalyst and that my job is to help a person find out what his personality is like and decide how he can use the assets he has and get rid of the obstacles that are blocking his progress. If he accepts the situation on these terms, therapeutic counseling can proceed within the framework of the very broad general question "What kind of person are you?" Anything the person wishes to bring up can be considered, but we have not committed ourselves to an analysis of all his problems and innumerable childhood experiences out of which they may have arisen.

NECESSARY SUPPORT

A third essential feature of minimum-change therapy is the use of the counseling relationship to reduce the client's anxiety enough to allow him freedom to consider new possibilities. This, of course, is nothing new or at all peculiar to therapy of this type. It seems to be the one common denominator linking together all sorts of diverse procedures. I suppose many workers in the psychotherapeutic vineyard would classify the approach I have been presenting as just another variety of supportive therapy. I would have no quarrel at all with that idea were it not that we are so prone to discredit support and to think of it as a superficial palliative measure to be used when more powerful methods are impractical. The idea of support should not be devalued in this way. Obviously by support I do not mean inspirational pep talks, shallow reassurance, or the encouragement of dependence. What I do mean is the act of lending one's own strength to the client for the period during which he needs it, so that he can be certain that his

world is not going to fall apart if he moves. I have an idea that
this is by far the most important thing we do for our clients, whatever our special theoretical predilections are. It is the crucial
factor that enables his own development processes to operate.

I suspect that it would be possible in many cases to furnish
this firm support much more economically than we now do if we
were willing to use it without working for insight or drastic re-
structuring of self-concepts. Once a client has established new
direction for himself, it may well be that regularly scheduled
interview hours a month apart may be enough to maintain his
courage and confidence. It is the quality of the relationship rather
than the amount of time spent in the counselor's presence that
constitutes support.

THE CLOSING PHASE

This brings us to the last point I wish to make about minimum-
change therapy. Its intensive phase is brought to a close as soon
as a clear direction has been established in the client's life, even
though there are many emotional complexes still unexplored, many
interpersonal problems still unsolved. Here again, as in the preliminary diagnosis, evidence from outside the interview room can
be combined with what comes up during therapy sessions in judging
whether a change of direction has been stabilized. A client may
mention casually, without apparently attaching any importance to
the remark, something that marks such a significant movement.
Mr. Eldridge, for example, may speak of having had a long talk
with his wife the night before, an action unprecedented in his previous experience. Gwen Riley, who has always been an anxious,
perfectionistic procrastinator, may say that she has handed in, on
time, an assigned paper for a course she is taking. Or the counselor may note the change in the incidental observation we discussed earlier. When he sees Bill Laraway having a coke with a
girl, he knows that Bill has taken the first step toward overcoming
the paralyzing shyness of which he has been complaining. A newspaper item stating that Mr. Bellingham has given a talk before the
Active Club indicates to the counselor that this client's inferiority
feelings are being surmounted. I know that, taken alone, such examples sound trivial. But remember, it is these ten-degree or
even five-degree changes in direction that we are trying to facilitate. A small change in the direction of closer emotional ties with
one's family or greater willingness to assume responsibility is the
kind of shift that has a profound effect on later development. When

it is clear that this shift has occurred it is time to think about the termination of formal therapy interviews.

One way of characterizing this kind of therapeutic counseling is to say that its basic premises come from the psychology of development and individual differences rather than from the psychology of adjustment. Its most fundamental assumption is that there are many different ways of living an individual life richly and well, and that it is natural for a person to continue to develop throughout his life in his own unique way. We work with nature instead of fighting or ignoring it.

I have often been struck by the fact that almost any personality trait one can think of may be either an asset or a liability, depending on how it is used. Touchy oversensitiveness to slights and insults is not really basically different from tact and social awareness. Aggression can lead to high achievement as well as murderous rage. Timidity and reasonable caution, compulsiveness and constructive orderliness are opposite sides of the same coins. Instead of bewailing our heredity and the mistakes that were made in bringing us up, perhaps we can learn to turn what we have to good account.

I have been thinking a good deal about the way in which therapeutic counseling of this sort might be evaluated. It is an intriguing thought that the very failure to obtain clear evidence for personality change as a result of therapy may be construed as success rather than failure if we reverse our basic assumption—namely, that maximum change is what we are after. It may even be that Eysenck is right and that no kind of therapy produces change that is greater than that which time and the processes of nature would ultimately have brought about by themselves. The therapist may make a contribution only to the extent that he facilitates or speeds up this natural process. The kind of evaluation I should like to see would be designed to show whether our therapeutic efforts do in fact accomplish this facilitation, so that individuals find their way with less suffering and wasted time with therapy than without. And if so, we need to know what aspects of the help we give contribute most toward this end.

To come back at the end to the topic of this symposium, the point I have been trying to make is that we can best control the duration of counseling contacts by adopting consistently an attitude of respect for what each individual client now is and lending him support and understanding while he comes to terms with this unique self of his. Whether it takes him two hours or two hundred, if he succeeds the effort will have been very much worth while.

VII

THE ESSENCE OF RATIONAL THERAPY

Albert Ellis

It is the central theme of this volume [Reason and Emotion in Psychotherapy] that the kinds of basic irrational ideas listed in the previous chapter (Chapter 3), and the many corollaries to which they normally lead, are the basic causes of most emotional disturbances.[1] For once a human being believes the kind of nonsense included in these notions, he will inevitably tend to become inhibited, hostile, defensive, guilty, anxious, ineffective, inert, uncontrolled, or unhappy. If, on the other hand, he could become thoroughly released from all these fundamental kinds of illogical thinking, it would be exceptionally difficult for him to become intensely emotionally upset, or at least to sustain his disturbance for any extended period.

Does this mean that all the other so-called basic causes of neurosis, such as the Oedipus complex or severe maternal rejection in childhood, are invalid and that the Freudian and other psychodynamic thinkers of the last sixty years have been barking up the wrong tree? Not necessarily. It only means, if the main hypotheses of this book are correct, that these psychodynamic thinkers have been emphasizing secondary causes or results of emotional disturbances rather than truly prime causes.

Let us take, for example, an individual who acquires, when he is young, a full-blown Oedipus complex: that is to say, he lusts

Reprinted by permission of the author and publisher from Albert Ellis. *Reason and Emotion in Psychotherapy*. New York: Lyle Stuart, 1962.

[1]Editor's note: Ellis lists eleven irrational ideas; for example, "The idea that it is a dire necessity for an adult human being to be loved by virtually every significant other person in his community," or "that it is easier to avoid than to face certain life difficulties and self-responsibilities."

after his mother, hates his father, is guilty about his sex desires
for his mother, and is afraid his father is going to castrate him.
This person, when he is a child, will certainly be disturbed. But,
if he is reared so that he acquires none of the basic illogical ideas
we have been discussing in the last chapter, it will be impossible
for him to remain disturbed.

For we must remember that this individual's disturbance,
when he is a child, does not consist of the _facts_ of his Oedipal attachment to his mother but of his attitudes—his guilt and his fear—
about these facts. He is not guilty, moreover, because he lusts
after his mother, but because he thinks it is criminal for him to
lust after her. And he is not fearful because his father disap-
proves his sexual attachment to his mother, but because he thinks
it is horrible to be disapproved by his father.

It may be very "natural"—meaning quite common—for a child
to think himself a criminal when he lusts after his mother; but
there is no evidence that he is born with this idea or that he has to
acquire it. In fact, considerable autobiographical and clinical evidence regarding individuals reared even in our own very anti-
incestuous society shows that many boys are able to lust after their
mothers quite consciously and openly without becoming guilty about
their lusting or terribly fearful of their father's opposition.

So it should be clear that Oedipal attachments do not have to
result in Oedipal complexes. Even if, in a given case, a boy does
become disturbed about his sexual feelings for his mother, he does
not, as the Freudians stoutly and erroneously contend, have to
remain neurotic in his adult life. For if he is reared (as, alas,
he rarely is in our society) to be a truly rational person, he will
not, as an adult, be too concerned if his parents or others do not
approve all his actions, since he will be more interested in his
own self-respect than in their approval. He will not believe that
his lust for his mother (even should it continue to his adolescent
and adult years) is wicked or villainous, but will accept it as a
normal part of being a fallible human whose sex desires may
easily be indiscriminate. He will realize that the actual danger of
his father castrating him is exceptionally slight, and will have no
fears on that account. And he will not feel that because he was
once afraid of his Oedipal attachment he need forever remain so.

If this individual, when he is adult, still believes that it would
be improper for him to have sex relations with his mother, instead of castigating himself for even thinking of having such relations, he will merely resolve not to carry his desires into practice
and will stick determinedly to his resolve. If (by any chance) he

weakens and actually has incestuous relations, he will again refuse to castigate himself mercilessly for being weak but will keep
showing himself how self-defeating his behavior is and will actively work and practice at changing it.

Under these circumstances, if this individual has a truly logical and rational approach to life in general, he will take an equally
sane approach to Oedipal feelings in particular. How, then, can
he possibly remain disturbed about any Oedipal attachment that he
may have?

Take, by way of further illustration, the case of a person who,
as a child, is continually criticized by his parents, who consequently feels himself loathesome and inadequate, who refuses to
take chances at trying and possibly failing at difficult tasks, and
who comes to hate himself more because he knows that he is eva-
sive and cowardly. Such a person, during his childhood, would
of course be seriously neurotic. But how would it be possible for
him to sustain his neurosis if he began to think, later in life, in a
truly logical manner?

For if this person does begin to be consistently rational, he
will quickly stop being overconcerned about what others think of
him and will begin to care primarily about what _he_ wants to do in
life and what he thinks of himself. Consequently, he will stop
avoiding difficult tasks and, instead of blaming himself for making
mistakes, he will say to himself something like: "Now this is not
the right way to do things; let me stop and figure out a better way."
Or: "There's no doubt that I made a mistake this time; now let me
see how I can benefit from making it, so that my next performance
will be improved."

This person, if he is thinking straight in the present, will not
blame his defeats on external events, but will realize that he himself is causing them by his inadequate or incompetent behavior.
He will not believe that it is easier to avoid than to face difficult
life problems, but will see that the so-called easy way is invariably the harder and more idiotic procedure. He will not think that
he needs someone greater or stronger than himself on whom to
rely, but will independently buckle down to hard tasks without outside help. He will not feel, because he once defeated himself by
avoiding doing things the hard way, that he must always continue
to act in this self-defeating manner.

How, with this kind of logical thinking, could an originally disturbed person possibly maintain and continually revivify his neurosis? He just couldn't. Similarly, the spoiled brat, the worry-
wart, the egomaniac, the autistic stay-at-home—all these disturbed

individuals would have the devil of a time indefinitely prolonging their neuroses if they did not continue to believe utter nonsense: namely, the kinds of basic irrational postulates listed in the previous chapter.

Will not the individual's experiences during his early childhood frequently make him think illogically, and thereby cause his neurosis? No, not exactly. For even during his childhood, the human being has to accept the ideas that are pounded into his head, and need not (at least technically speaking) automatically take them over.

Thus, it is statistically probable that the great majority of children, if taught that they are monstrous if they do not behave well, will get the idea that this is true, and will come to despise themselves for their misdeeds. But all children need not accept this belief; and a few, at least, do not seem to do so. These few, apparently, can and do challenge the notion that they are worthless, and somehow manage to grow up thinking of themselves as being worthwhile, even though their parents or others teach them the contrary.

Moreover, even when young children tend to accept their parent-inculcated irrational thinking, they are quite able, in many instances, to challenge and contradict these views during their adolescence and adulthood, and to think otherwise—just as they are able to give up the religious views of their parents at this time. It is certainly difficult for an adolescent or young adult to disbelieve the nonsense about himself (or about religion) that his parents raise him to believe; but it is not impossible for him to do so. Childhood training, then, is an exceptionally strong influence in causing an individual to think illogically or neurotically. But it is not a fatal or irrevocable influence.

Neurosis, in sum, seems to originate in and be perpetuated by some fundamentally unsound, irrational ideas. The individual comes to believe in unrealistic, impossible, often perfectionistic goals—especially the goals that he should be approved by everyone who is important to him, should do many things perfectly, and should never be frustrated in any of his major desires. Then, in spite of considerable contradictory evidence, he refuses to surrender his original illogical beliefs.

Why do so many millions of intelligent, well-educated, potentially rational people act in such an illogical, neurotic manner today? A full answer to this question can only—and will eventually —be given in a volume of its own. Part of this answer is summarized in the final chapter of the present book [Reason and Emotion in Psychotherapy, Chapter 20]. Suffice it to say here that even the most intelligent and capable persons in our society tend also to be, because of their biological inheritance, amazingly suggestible, unthinking, overgeneralizing, and strongly bound to the low-level kinds of ideation which it is so easy for them to become addicted to as children; and, perhaps more importantly, we bring up our citizens so that, instead of counteracting their normal biological tendencies toward irrationality, we deliberately and forcefully encourage them to keep thinking in childish, nonsensical ways.

By innate predisposition, therefore, as well as by powerful social propaganda (especially that promulgated by our families, schools, churches, and governmental institutions), even the brightest human beings often tend to become and to remain neurotic—that is, to behave stupidly and self-defeatingly when they are potentially able to behave more sanely and constructively.

Some of the neurotic's basic philosophies, such as the idea that he should be approved or loved by all the significant people in his life, are not entirely inappropriate to his childhood state; but they are decidedly inappropriate to adulthood. Since most of his irrational ideas are specifically taught him by his parents and other social agencies, and since these same irrational notions are held by the great majority of others in his community, we must acknowledge that the neurotic individual we are considering tends to be statistically normal. In many respects, he has what may be called a cultural or philosophic rather than a psychiatric disturbance (Paul Meehl and William Schofield, personal communications).

Ours, in other words, is a generally neuroticizing civilization, in which most people are more or less emotionally disturbed because they are brought up to believe, and then to internalize and to keep reinfecting themselves with, arrant nonsense which must inevitably lead them to become ineffective, self-defeating, and unhappy. Nonetheless, it is not absolutely necessary that human beings believe the irrational notions which, in point of fact, most of them seem to believe today; and the task of psychotherapy is to get them to disbelieve their illogical ideas, to change their self-sabotaging attitudes.

This, precisely, is the task the rational-emotive therapist sets himself. Like other therapists, he frequently resorts to some of the usual techniques of therapy which I have outlined elsewhere (Ellis, 1955a, 1955b)—including the techniques of relationship, expressive-emotive, supportive, and insight-interpretative therapy. But he views these techniques, as they are commonly employed, largely as preliminary strategies, designed to gain rapport with the patient, to let him express himself fully, to show him that he has the ability to change, and to demonstrate how he originally became disturbed.

Most therapeutic techniques, in other words, wittingly or unwittingly show the patient that he is illogical and how he originally became so. But they usually fail to show him how he is presently maintaining his illogical thinking and precisely what he must do to change it and replace it with more rational philosophies of life. And where most therapists rather passively or indirectly show the patient that he is behaving illogically, the rational therapist goes beyond this point to make a forthright, unequivocal attack on his general and specific irrational ideas and to try to induce him to adopt more rational views.

Rational-emotive psychotherapy makes a concerted attack on the disturbed person's illogical positions in two main ways: (a) The therapist serves as a frank counter-propagandist who directly contradicts and denies the self-defeating propaganda and superstitions which the patient has originally learned and which he is now self-instilling. (b) The therapist encourages, persuades, cajoles, and occasionally even insists that the patient engage in some activity (such as his doing something he is afraid of doing) which itself will serve as a forceful counter-propaganda agency against the nonsense he believes.

Both these main therapeutic activities are consciously performed with one main goal in mind: namely, that of finally inducing the patient to internalize a rational philosophy of life just as he originally learned and internalized the irrational views of his parents and his community.

The rational therapist, then, assumes that the patient somehow imbibed irrational modes of thinking and that, through his illogical thoughts, he literally made himself disturbed. It is the therapist's function not merely to show the patient that he has these low-level thinking processes but to persuade him to change and substitute for them more efficient cognitions.

If, because the patient is exceptionally upset when he comes to therapy, he must first be approached in a cautious, supportive, permissive, and warm manner, and must sometimes be allowed to ventilate his feeling in free association, abreaction, role playing, and other expressive techniques, that may be a necessary part of effective therapy. But the rational therapist does not delude himself that these relationship-building and expressive-emotive methods are likely to really get to the core of the patient's illogical thinking and induce him to cogitate more rationally.

Occasionally, this is true: since the patient may, through experiencing relationship and emotive-expressive aspects of therapy, come to see that he is acting illogically; and he may therefore resolve to change and actually work at doing so. More often than not, however, his illogical thinking will be so ingrained from constant self-repetitions and will be so inculcated in motor pathways (or habit patterns) by the time he comes for therapy, that simply showing him, even by direct interpretation, that he is illogical will not greatly help. He will often, for example, say to the therapist: "All right: now I understand that I have castration fears and that they are illogical. But I still feel afraid of my father."

The therapist, therefore, must usually keep pounding away, time and time again, at the illogical ideas which underlie that patient's fears and hostilities. He must show the patient that he is afraid, really, not of his father, but of being blamed, of being disapproved, of being unloved, of being imperfect, of being a failure. And he must convincingly demonstrate to the patient how and why such fears (for some of the reasons explained in the previous chapter) are irrational and must lead to dreadful results.

If the therapist, moreover, merely tackles the individual's castration fears, and shows how ridiculous they are, what is to prevent this person's showing up, a year or two later, with some other illogical fear—such as the horror of his being sexually impotent? But if the therapist tackles the patient's basic irrational thinking processes, which underlie all kinds of fear that he may have, it is going to be most difficult for this patient to turn up with a new neurotic symptom some months or years hence. For once an individual truly surrenders ideas of perfectionism, of the horror of failing at something, of the dire need to be approved by others, of the world's owing him a living, and so on, what else is there for him to be fearful of or disturbed about?

To give some idea of precisely how the rational therapist works, a good many excerpts from therapeutic sessions will be given in some of the remaining chapters of this book [Reason and Emotion in Psychotherapy, Chapters 5-20]. Before this is done, however, it might be well to outline an illustrative case.

Mervin Snodds, a 23 year old male, came into his therapeutic session a few weeks after he had begun therapy and said that he was very depressed but did not know why. A little questioning showed that this severely neurotic patient, whose main presenting problem was that he had been doing too much drinking during the last two years, had been putting off the inventory-keeping he was required to do as part of his job as an apprentice glass-staining

artist. "I know," he reported, "that I should do the inventory before it keeps piling up to enormous proportions, but I just keep
putting it off and off. To be honest, I guess it's because I resent
doing it so much."

"But why do you resent it so much?"

"It's boring. I just don't like it."

"So it's boring. That's a good reason for disliking this work,
but is it an equally good reason for resenting it?"

"Aren't the two the same thing?"

"By no means. Dislike equals the sentence, 'I don't enjoy
doing this thing and therefore I don't want to do it.' And that's a
perfectly sane sentence in most instances. But resentment is the
sentence, 'Because I dislike doing this thing, I shouldn't have to
do it.' And that's invariably a very crazy sentence."

"Why is it so crazy to resent something that you don't like to
do?"

"For several reasons. First of all, from a purely logical
standpoint, it just makes no sense at all to say to yourself, 'Because I dislike doing this thing, I shouldn't have to do it.' The
second part of this sentence just doesn't follow in any way from the
first part. For the full sentence that you are saying actually goes
something like this: 'Because I dislike doing this thing, other
people and the universe should be so considerate of me that they
should never make me do what I dislike.' But, of course, this
sentence doesn't make any sense: for why should other people and
the universe be that considerate of you? It might be nice if they
were. But why the devil should they be? In order for your sentence to be true, the entire universe, and all the people in it,
would really have to revolve around and be uniquely considerate
of you."

"Am I really asking that much? It seems to me that all I'm
asking, in my present job, is that I don't have to do the inventory-
keeping. Is that too much to ask?"

"Yes, from what you've told me, it certainly is. For the
inventory-keeping is an integral part of your job, isn't it? You
do have to do it, in order to keep working at your present place,
don't you?"

"Yes. I guess I do."

"And you do, from what you told me previously, want to keep
working at this place, for your own reasons, do you not?"

"Yes. As I told you before, in my field I must have an apprenticeship for at least a year. And they agreed to take me on as an
apprentice, if I'd work pretty long hours and do the work—"

"—including the inventory-keeping?—"

"Yes, including the inventory-keeping. If I did that and worked long hours, they'd take me on for the year I'd need toward the apprenticeship."

"All right, then. Because you wanted to learn the art of glass-staining and you can only learn it by having a year's apprentice-ship, you decided to take on this job, with all its onerous aspects, especially including the inventory-keeping. You had, in other words, a logical choice between graciously accepting this job, in spite of the onerous parts of it, or giving up trying to be a glass-stainer. But then, after presumably taking the first of these al-ternatives, you're now resentful because you can't get the second alternative without this onerous first part."

"Oh, but it isn't the work itself that I resent, in toto; but just the inventory-keeping part."

"But that still doesn't make sense. For the work, in toto, includes the inventory-keeping; and your choice of accepting the work in toto obviously includes accepting this part of it, too. So, again, instead of selecting one of two logical alternatives—doing the onerous work, including the inventory-keeping, or giving up trying to be a glass-stainer—you are resentfully and grandiosely refusing the first of these and yet insisting that you should not have to give up the second one, too. You are thereby actually in-sisting, as I said before, that the universe and the people in it should really revolve around your wishes rather than be what it and they actually are."

"It sounds, the way you're putting it, like I really haven't got a leg to stand on logically. But what about the fact that my boss could, if he wanted to be really fair to me—since I do quite a bit of work for him at a very low rate of pay—get someone else to do the inventory-keeping? After all, he knows perfectly well how I feel about it; and it is not work that is necessary for my glass-staining apprenticeship."

"True. Your boss could arrange matters differently and could let you off from this work that you so abhor. And let's even as-sume, for the moment, that he is wrong about not arranging things more this way and that any decent kind of boss would let you, say, do more glass-staining and less inventory-keeping work."

"Oh, that would be fine! Then I wouldn't gripe at all."

"No, probably you wouldn't. But even assuming that your boss is completely in the wrong about this inventory-keeping matter, your resenting him for being wrong still makes no sense."

"Oh? How come?"

"Because, no matter how wrong he is, every human being has the right to be wrong—and you're not giving him that right."

"But why does every human being have the right to be wrong?"

"Simply because he is human; and, because he is human, is fallible and error-prone. If your boss, for example, is wrong about making you do this inventory work—and let's assume that he is dead wrong about it—then his wrongdoing would obviously result from some combination of his being stupid, ignorant, or emotionally disturbed; and he, as a fallible human being, has every right to be stupid, ignorant, or disturbed—even though it would be much better, perhaps, if he weren't."

"He has a right, you say, to be as nutty or as vicious as he may be—even though I and others might very much like him to be less nutty or vicious?"

"Correct. And if you are blaming him for being the way he is, then you are denying his right to be human and you are expecting him—which is certainly silly, you'll have to admit!—to be super-human or angelic."

"You really think that that's what I'm doing?"

"Well, isn't it? Besides, look again at how illogical you are by being resentful. Whether your boss is right or wrong about this inventory deal, resenting him for being, in your eyes, wrong is hardly going to make him be any the righter, is it? And your resentment, surely, is not going to do you any good or make you feel better. Then what good is it—your resentment—doing?"

"No good, I guess. If I take the attitude that—well, it's too bad that inventory-keeping is part of my job, and that my boss sees it this way, but that's the way it is, and there's no point in resenting the way it is, I guess I'd feel a lot better about it, wouldn't I?"

"Yes, wouldn't you? On still another count, too, your resentful attitude doesn't make sense."

"On what ground is that?"

"The ground that no matter how annoying the inventory-keeping may be, there's no point in your making it still more irksome by your continually telling yourself how awful it is. As we consistently note in rational therapy, you're not merely being annoyed by the inventory-keeping job itself, but you're making yourself annoyed at being annoyed—and you're thereby creating at least two annoyances for the price of one. And the second, the one of your own creation, may well be much more deadly than the first, the one that is being created by the circumstances of your job."

"Because I'm refusing to gracefully accept the inherent annoyingness of doing the inventory, I'm giving myself an even harder time than it is giving me—is that right?"

"Quite right. Where the inventory-keeping is a real pain in the neck to you, you are a much bigger pain in the neck to yourself."

"Yeah. And since I have to do this kind of clerical work anyway, since I know darned well that the boss is not going to take it away from me, I would be doing myself much more good if I calmly and quickly got it out of the way, instead of making this terrible to-do about it."

"Right again. Can you see, then, the several points at which your resentment is thoroughly illogical in this situation, even though your dissatisfaction with doing the bookkeeping procedure may well be justified?"

"Let's see, now. First, I make a decision to take the job, in spite of its disadvantages, because I really want to be an apprentice, and then I try to go against my own decision by refusing to accept these disadvantages that I had first presumably accepted."

"Yes, that's illogical point number one."

"Then, second, I go to work for a human being, my boss, and then I refuse to accept him as human, and insist that he be a goddam angel."

"Exactly. That's illogical point number two."

"Third—let's see—I get quite wrapped up in my resentment, and give myself a start on an ulcer, when it's not likely at all to get my boss to change his mind or do me any good."

"Right."

"And fourth. Now, what was the fourth? I don't seem to remember."

"Fourth: you make yourself annoyed at being annoyed and put off doing work that you'll have to do, sooner or later, anyway, and with your annoyed-at-being-annoyed attitude, almost certainly make that work become considerably more onerous than it otherwise doubtless would be."

"Oh, yes. To my real annoyance I add to and imagine up a fake annoyance. And I make an unpleasant job more unpleasant than ever."

"Yes. Now can you see, not just in this case, but in every case of this kind, how your resenting someone is highly irrational?"

"Hm. I think so. But how can I stop being resentful? Just by seeing that it doesn't pay for me to be so?"

"No, not exactly. That's too vague. And too easy. More concretely, you must track down the exact sentences which you are saying to yourself to cause your resentment; and then question and challenge these sentences, until you specifically see how silly they are and are prepared to substitute much saner sentences for them."

At this point, I helped this patient to see that he must be telling himself sentences like these in order to be upsetting himself: My boss makes me do inventory-keeping . . . I do not like to do this . . . There is no reason why I have to do it . . . He is therefore a black-guard for making me do this kind of boring, unartistic work. So I'll fool him and avoid doing it . . . And then I'll be happier."

But these sentences were so palpably foolish that Mervin could not really believe them, so he began to finish them off with sen-tences like this: "I'm not really fooling my boss, because he sees what I'm doing. So I'm not solving my problem this way . . . I really should stop this nonsense, therefore, and get the inventory-keeping done. . . . But I'll be damned if I'll do it for him! . . . How-ever, if I don't do it, I'll be fired. . . . But I still don't want to do it for him! . . . I guess I've got to, though. . . . Oh, why must I al-ways be persecuted like this? . . . And why must I keep getting my-self into such a mess? . . . I guess I'm just no good. . . . And people are against me. . . . Especially that son-of-a-bitch boss of mine. . . . Oh, what's the use?"

Employing these illogical kinds of sentences, Mervin soon be-came depressed, avoided doing the inventory-keeping, and then became still more resentful and depressed. Instead, I pointed out to him, he could tell himself quite different sentences, on this or-der: "Keeping inventory is a bore. . . . But it is presently an es-sential part of my job. . . . And I also may learn something useful by it. . . . Therefore, I'd better go about this task as best I may and thereby get what I want out of the job, and later what I want out of the profession of glass-staining."

I also emphasized that whenever Mervin found himself intensely angry, guilty, or depressed, he was thinking illogically and should immediately question himself as to what was the irrational element in his thinking, and set about replacing it with a more logical ele-ment or chain of sentences. I used his current dilemma—that of avoiding inventory-keeping—as an illustration of his general neuro-sis, which largely took the form of severe alcoholic tendencies. He was shown that his alcoholic trends, too, resulted from his trying to do things the easy way and from his resentment against people, such as his boss, who kept making him toe the line and blocking his easy-way-out patterns of response.

Several previous incidents of irrational thinking leading to emotional upheaval in Mervin's life were then reviewed, and some general principles of rational thought were discussed. Thus, the general principle of blame was raised and he was shown precisely why it is illogical for one person to blame anyone else (or himself) for anything.

The general principle of inevitability was brought up, and Mervin was shown that when a frustrating or unpleasant event is inevitable, it is only reasonable to accept it uncomplainingly instead of dwelling on its unpleasant aspects. The general principle of hostility was discussed, and he was shown that liking oneself and trying to do what one is truly interested in doing in life is far more important than being obsessed with others' behavior and resentfully trying to get back to them.

In this manner, by attempting to teach Mervin some of the general rules of rational living, I tried to go beyond his immediate problem and to help provide him with a generalized mode of thinking or problem-solving that would enable him to deal effectively with almost any future similar situation that might arise.

After 47 sessions of rational therapy, spread out over a two year period, Mervin was able to solve his work problems, to finish his apprenticeship, and to go on to high-level activity in his profession. More importantly, he cut out almost all drinking and restricted himself to a half dozen glasses of beer a week. His hostilities toward his bosses and his other associates became minimal, and for the first time in his life he became "popular." Today, three and a half years after the close of therapy, he is maintaining his gains and is reasonably unescapist and unhostile.

The rational therapist, then, is a frank propagandist who believes wholeheartedly in a most rigorous application of the rules of logic, of straight thinking, and of scientific method to everyday life. He ruthlessly uncovers the most important elements of irrational thinking in his patient's experience and energetically urges this patient into more reasonable channels of behaving. In so doing, the rational therapist does not ignore or eradicate the patient's emotions. On the contrary, he considers them most seriously and helps change them, when they are disordered and self-defeating, through the same means by which they commonly arise in the first place—that is, by thinking and acting. Through exerting consistent interpretive and philosophic pressure on the patient to change his thinking and his actions, the rational therapist gives him a specific impetus toward achieving mental health without which it is not impossible, but quite unlikely, that he will move very far.

Man is a uniquely suggestible as well as a uniquely rational

animal. Other animals are to some degree suggestible and reasoning, but man's better equipped cerebral cortex, which makes
possible his ability to talk to himself and others, gives him unusual opportunities to talk himself into and out of many difficulties.

The rational therapist hold that although man's possession of
a high degree of suggestibility and negative emotionality (such as
anxiety, guilt, and hostility) may possibly have been adequate or
advantageous for his primitive survival, he can get along with
himself and others much better today when he becomes more rational and less suggestible. Perhaps it would be more realistic to
say that since suggestibility seems to be an almost ineradicable
trait of human beings, we should not aim at destroying but at modifying it so that man becomes more intelligently suggestible.

In other words: people act in certain ways because they believe that they should or must act in these ways. If they are irrationally suggestible, they believe that they should act in intensely
emotional, self-defeating ways; and if they are more rationally
suggestible, they believe that they should act in less negatively
emotional, less neurotic ways. In either event, the deeds in
which they believe they tend to actualize. As Kelly (1955) has
noted, an individual's difficulty frequently "arises out of the intrinsic meaning of his personal constructs rather than out of the
general form which they have assumed. A person who believes
that punishment expunges guilt is likely to punish himself."

The main problem of effective living, then, would seem to be
not that of eradicating people's beliefs, but of changing them so
that they become more closely rooted to information and to reason.
This can be done, says the rational therapist, by getting people to
examine, to question, to think about their beliefs, and thereby to
develop a more consistent, fact-based, and workable set of constructs than they now may possess.

Rational-emotive psychotherapy is by no means entirely new,
since some of its main principles were propounded by Dubois
(1907) and many pre-Freudian therapists. Unfortunately, these
therapists for the most part did not understand the unconscious
roots of emotional disturbance, and it was Freud's great contribution to stress these roots. But although Freud, in his first book
with Josef Breuer (Studies on Hysteria, 1895), was willing to go
along with the notion that "a great number of hysterical phenomena,
probably more than we suspect today, are ideogenic," he later
often talked about emotional processes in such a vague way as to
imply that they exist in their own right, quite divorced from
thinking.

Because he came to believe that neurosis originates in and is perpetuated by unconscious "emotional" processes, and because he (and his leading followers) never defined the term "emotional" very accurately, Freud held that neurotic symptoms only could be thoroughly understood and eradicated through an intense emotional relationship, or transference relationship, between the patient and the therapist. He and his psychoanalytic followers have used cognitive, or interpretive, therapeutic techniques to a considerable degree. But they still mainly stress the importance of the transference encounter in therapy.

In this emphasis, the psychoanalysts are at least partly correct, since many borderline and psychotic individuals (whom Freud himself often mistakenly thought were hysterical neurotics) are so excitable and disorganized when they come for therapy that they can only be approached by highly emotionalized, supportive or abreactive methods.

Even those severely disturbed patients, however, are often surprisingly and quickly responsive to logical analysis of their problems and to philosophic reeducation if this is adequately and persuasively done with them. And the run-of-the-mill, less disturbed neurotics who come to therapy are usually quite reactive to rational therapeutic approaches and have little or no need of an intensely emotionalized transference relationship (including a transference neurosis) with the therapist.

That cognitive and rational processes can be most important in understanding and changing human behavior has become increasingly acknowledged in recent years. Thus, Robbins (1955) notes that "cure is change; cure is the development of rational consciousness." Sarnoff and Katz (1954), in listing four major modes of changing human attitudes, put first the attacking of the cognitive object and frame of reference in which it is perceived, or the rational approach. Cohen, Stotland and Wolfe (1955) point out that, in addition to the usual physical and emotional needs of the human organism, "a need for cognition may exist, and . . . it may be a measurable characteristic of the organism, and . . . it may operate independently of other needs."

Bruner, Goodnow and Austin (1956) note that "the past few years have witnessed a notable increase in interest in and investigation of the cognitive processes. . . . Partly, it has resulted from a recognition of the complex processes that mediate between the classical 'stimuli' and 'responses' out of which stimulus-response learning theories hoped to fashion a psychology that would bypass anything smacking of the 'mental.' The impeccable peripheralism of such theories could not last long. As 'S-R' theories came to be modified to take into account the subtle events that may occur between the input of a physical stimulus and the emission of an observable response, the old image of the 'stimulus-response bond' began to dissolve, its place being taken by a mediation model. As Edward Tolman so felicitously put it some years ago, in place of a telephone switchboard connecting stimuli and responses it might be more profitable to think of a map room where stimuli were sorted out and arranged before every response occurred, and one might do well to have a closer look at these intervening 'cognitive maps.'"

Mowrer (1960) even more strongly makes the point that the old S-R behaviorism has to be replaced by neobehaviorism which includes a liberalized view of perception. He notes that "the relevance of cognitive as well as affective processes is being recognized in systematic theory; and the solution to the problem of response selection and initiation hinges, quite specifically it seems, upon the reality of imagery (or memory), which is a cognitive phenomenon, pure and simple."

Even the Freudians have in recent years given much attention to "ego psychology," which is a distinct emphasis on the cognitive processes and how they make and can unmake human emotional disturbance. Freud himself noted, in The Future of an Illusion (1927): "We may insist as much as we like that the human intellect is weak. . . . But nevertheless there is something peculiar about this weakness. The voice of the intellect is a soft one, but it does not rest until it has gained a hearing. Ultimately, after endlessly repeated rebuffs, it succeeds." Modern psychoanalysts, such as Hartmann, Kris, and Loewenstein (1947, 1949), French (1952-1960), and Menninger (1958), have gone far beyond Freud, and beyond Anna Freud's (1937) pioneering work in ego psychology, and have helped make psychoanalytic technique radically different from its early ways and means.

In the field of modern psychology, Bartlett (1958), Berlyne (1960), Brown (1960), Brunswik (1952), Church (1961), Hovland and Janis (1959), Johnson (1955), Piaget (1952, 1954), in addition to the above-mentioned Bruner, Goodnow, and Austin (1956), have pioneered in the study of cognitive processes in recent years; and Leon Festinger (1957) has devised a theory of cognitive dissonance to explain much human normal and abnormal behavior. The work of these thinkers and experimentalists has sparked literally scores of recent studies that are adding to our knowledge in this area and showing how tremendously important cognitive and rational processes are in human affairs. As Arnold (1960) has appropriately noted in this connection, the emphasis of the orthodox Freudians on unconscious thinking and emotional affect may well have been an excellent corrective against the one-sided mentalistic views of the nineteenth century. But the fact remains that "in deliberate actions (and they comprise the large majority of our daily activities) we must depend on a judgment that is not intuitive to arouse an impulse to do something that may or may not be pleasant. Whatever may be the explanation for such rational judgments and deliberate actions, it is such judgments and actions that distinguish man from the brute."

It may also be glancingly noted that preoccupation with language and the cognitive processes has been most prevalent in recent years in many semi-psychological areas of knowledge, such as communication theory (Shannon, 1949; Wiener, 1948); the theory of games and economic behavior (Marschak, 1950; von Neumann and Morgenstern, 1944); philosophy (Ayer, 1947; Morris, 1946); and literature and semantics (Burke, 1950, 1954; Korzybski, 1933, 1951). In fact, it is difficult to think of any major social science where an absorbing interest in the cognitive-rational processes has not become pronounced in the last two decades.

Friedman (1955) contends that Pavlovian conditioning consists largely of laws of unconscious biological learning and does not by any means cover the whole field of human adaptability. Rather, there also exists "learning at a conscious level with little involvement of dominant biological activities" and this cognitive type of learning "may well follow principles that are quite different from those found by Pavlov." Fromm (1950) insists that "to help man discern truth from falsehood in himself is the basic aim of psychoanalysis, a therapeutic method which is an empirical application of the statement, 'The truth shall make you free.'" Flew (in Feigl and Scriven, 1956) contends "that the fundamental concepts of psychoanalysis are distinctly human because they can only be applied to creatures possessed of our unique capacity to employ a developed language; that these are precisely the notions which rational agents employ to give account of their own conduct and that of other rational agents qua rational agents; that their place in psychoanalysis necessarily makes this a peculiarly rational enterprise..."

Modern anthropological thinking, as Voget (1960) shows in an important recent paper, has also swung away from the concepts of the early 1900's which emphasized man's dependency upon and subservience to cultural processes or to his own unconscious emotions. Today, says Voget:

It is apparent that judgment in human action is admitted and the individual no longer is conceived to be a habituated social unit or subject wholly to unconscious feeling states. The trend moved cautiously in the direction of Grace de Laguna's (1949) assertion that:

". . . Man's rationality is not a higher faculty added to, or imposed upon, his animal nature. On the contrary, it pervades his whole being and manifests itself in all that he does well as in what he believes and thinks. Men may rationalize more often than they think objectively, but it is only because they are fundamentally rational beings that they are capable of rationalizing or feel the need of it. Man is rational in all his acts and attitudes, however unreasonable these may be; he is rational also in his feelings and aspirations, in his unconscious desires and motivations as well as in his conscious purposes, and his rationality shows itself in the very symbolism of his dreams. Men could not act and feel as they do if they could not form concepts and make judgments, but neither could they make use of concepts and engage in the ideal activity of thinking if they had not developed their innate capacity for the 'idealized' modes of behavior and feeling characteristic of human beings."

By direct statement and by implication, then, modern thinkers are tending to recognize the fact that logic and reason can, and in a sense must, play a most important role in overcoming human neurosis. Eventually, they may be able to catch up with Epictetus in this respect, who wrote—some nineteen centuries ago—that "the chief concern of a wise and good man is his own reason."

REFERENCES

Arnold, Magda. Emotion and personality. 2 vols. New York: Columbia Univer. Press, 1960.

Ayer, A. J. Language, truth and logic. New York: Dover, 1947.

Bartlett, F. Thinking. London: Allen & Unwin, 1958.

Berlyne, D. E. Conflict, arousal and curiosity. New York: McGraw-Hill, 1960.

Brown, R. W. Words and things. New York: Basic Books, 1960.

Bruner, J. S., Goodnow, Jacqueline J., & Austin, G. A study of thinking. New York: Wiley, 1956.

Brunswik, E. The conceptual framework of psychology. Chicago: Univer. of Chicago Press, 1952.

Burke, K. A rhetoric of motives. New York: Prentice-Hall, 1950.

Church, J. Language and the discovery of reality. New York: Random House, 1961.

Cohen, A. R., Stotland, E., & Wolfe, D. M. An experimental investigation of need for cognition. J. abnorm. soc. Psychol., 1955, 51:291-294.

Dubois, P. The psychic treatment of nervous disorders. New York: Funk & Wagnalls, 1907.

Ellis, A. New approaches to psychotherapy techniques. Brandon, Vt.: Journal of Clinical Psychology, 1955a.

Ellis, A. Psychotherapy techniques for use with psychotics. Amer. J. Psychother., 1955b, 9:452-476.

Feigl, H. & Scriven, M. (Eds.) Minnesota studies in the philosophy of science. Vol. 1. Minneapolis: Univer. of Minnesota Press, 1956.

Festinger, L. A theory of cognitive dissonance. Evanston, Ill.: Row, Peterson, 1957.

French, T. M. The integration of behavior. 4 vols. Chicago: Univer. of Chicago Press, 1952-1960.

Freud, Anna. The ego and the mechanisms of defense. London: Hogarth, 1937.

Freud, S. The future of an illusion. London: Hogarth, 1927.

Freud, S., & Breuer, J. Studies in hysteria, 1895. New York: Basic Books, 1957.

Friedman, I. Phenomenal, ideal and projected conceptions of self. J. abnorm. soc. Psychol., 1955, 51:611-615.

Fromm, E. Psychoanalysis and religion. New Haven: Yale Univer. Press, 1950.

Hartmann, H., Kris, E., & Loewenstein, R. M. Comments on the formation of psychic structure. Psychoanal. Stud. Child, 1947, 2:5-30.

Hartmann, H., Kris, E., & Loewenstein, R. M. Notes on the theory of aggression. Psychoanal. Stud. Child, 1949, 3:9-36.

Hovland, C. I., & Janis, I. L. Personality and persuasibility. New Haven: Yale Univer. Press, 1959.

Johnson, D. M. The psychology of thought and judgment. New York: Harper, 1955.

Kelly, G. The psychology of personal constructs. New York: Norton, 1955.

Korzybski, A. Science and sanity. Lancaster, Pa.: Lancaster Press, 1933.

Korzybski, A. The role of language in the perceptual process. In R. R. Blake & G. V. Ramsey (Eds.) Perception. New York: Ronald, 1951.

Laguna, Grace de. Culture and personality. Amer. Anthropol., 1949, 51:379-391.

Marschak, J. Rational behavior, uncertain prospects and measurable utility. Econometrica, 1950, 18:111-141.

Menninger, K. Theory of psychoanalytic technique. New York: Basic Books, 1958.

Morris, C. W. Signs, language, and behavior. New York: Prentice-Hall, 1946.

Mowrer, O. H. Learning theory and behavior. New York: Wiley, 1960.

Neumann, J. von, & Morgenstern, O. Theory of games and economic behavior. Princeton: Princeton Univer. Press, 1944.

Piaget, J. The language and thought of the child. New York: Humanities Press, 1952.

Piaget, J. The moral judgment of the child. Glencoe, Ill.: Free Press, 1954.

Robbins, B. S. The myth of latent emotion. Psychotherapy, 1955, 1:3-29.

Sarnoff, I., & Katz, D. The motivational bases of attitude change. J. abnorm. soc. Psychol., 1954, 49:115-124.

Shannon, C. E. The mathematical theory of communication. Urbana: Univer. of Illinois Press, 1949.

Voget, F. W. Man and culture. Amer. Anthropol., 1960, 62:943-965.

Wiener, N. Cybernetics. New York: Wiley, 1948.

VIII

REALITY THERAPY:
A REALISTIC APPROACH TO THE YOUNG OFFENDER

William Glasser

The first important step in correcting a young offender's behavior is to find out what it is you are trying to correct. Most of the theories contained in the literature on juvenile delinquency are psychoanalytic in nature (emphasizing unconscious intrapersonal conflict), sociological (stressing environmental difficulties), or some combination of both. To illustrate, let me present the case of a sixteen-year-old girl who has run away from home, indulged in heterosexual and homosexual activity, prostituted, experimented with narcotics, tatooed herself, and, in final custody, attempted suicide by slashing her wrists. If I stopped now and asked you the cause of her behavior I'm sure no one would venture an opinion. Rather, you would ask me to give more information than this brief description. From your training and experience, you would feel uncomfortable about committing yourself without some history, psychological tests, and background investigation of the girl. Very likely you would call on someone to make a psychiatric evaluation. Even with this information, many of you would still disagree, according to the way you have been taught, your experience, and the amount of introspection you have done.

One value of the theory [of reality therapy], and the therapy based upon it, is that it circumvents any disagreement over what caused the girl's behavior and it sharply reduces the need for the usual diagnostic procedures. Further, this theory, if clearly understood, can be used not only by trained psychotherapists but by everyone who comes in contact with the young offender, from the arresting officer to the parole officer. Only a consistent

Adapted from a speech presented to the British Columbia Correctional Association, Vancouver, Canada, Nov. 3, 1962. Reprinted by permission of the author and *Crime and Delinquency*, 1964, April: 135-144.

method of treatment, an approach that can be used to some extent by everyone in correction, will help young people in trouble.

THE THEORY

Personal Responsibility. The theory of "reality therapy" has been developed in the past seven years in consultation with a colleague, Dr. G. L. Harrington, who uses it exclusively with mental patients at the Los Angeles Veterans' Administration Center Neuropsychiatric Hospital and in his private practice. It is based on our belief that regardless of what he has done, how he feels, where he comes from, his size, shape, mental ability, physical condition, or heredity, the young offender suffers from a universal malady: he is unwilling to take responsibility for his behavior. We further believe that correctional problems are only a more dramatic expression of the lack of responsibility which is really a basic problem in all psychiatric work. The children and adults we deal with in correction express this irresponsibility directly by the act of breaking the law. Patients in mental hospitals express it by partially or completely withdrawing into a world of their own creation. The homosexual, for example, cannot take a responsible sex role although he may be perfectly responsible in other areas. The depressed patient is unable responsibly to express the intense anger he feels, so he turns it inward and becomes depressed. The obsessive-compulsive neurotic tries desperately to compensate for his basic lack of responsibility by becoming superresponsible—so much so that he can accomplish little because of his compulsive symptoms. Thus, all people who function badly in our society suffer from this difficulty, but none of them expresses it as clearly and as directly as the lawbreaker.

All the effort in the world to discover why a child is irresponsible and breaks the law won't change the fact that he is irresponsible. Neither will all the treatment we can muster, unless this treatment is from the start concerned with guiding the patient toward becoming a more responsible person right now. This is why we claim that diagnosis based on detailed studies is meaningless; however superficial or deep the explanation may be, the ultimate fact remains that the person involved is not acting or thinking in a responsible manner.

In the traditional process of looking for explanations and diagnoses, a reason for deviant behavior will often seem clear. For example, the psychotherapist may find out that a homosexual girl is afraid of men because her father was both brutal and seductive, so she turns toward women for gratification. When he understands this, and even when she understands this, he is in a poor position to help her because he has advanced a reasonable cause for her behavior. Dr. Harrington and I do not believe, as the traditional therapist does, that this understanding will allow her to relate to a man who is not her father. We believe that all she will understand is that the situation is just as she feared—men can be brutal and so it is much safer to remain homosexual. The psychotherapist's initial efforts have, in a sense, only made the girl's trouble more reasonable. She now has an excuse to stay the way she is. In fact, everyone is looking for an excuse for her behavior.

But our job is to make her behavior less reasonable, to help her take the responsibility she must take as a woman in order for her to turn away from this deviant approach to sex. Our job is not to discuss her father (who may or may not have been brutal) but to relate to her now so that she can feel that men are human beings with whom she can make emotional contact.

Therefore, if we want to face reality, we must admit that we can never rewrite a person's history. No matter how much we can understand about the cruel and unusual circumstances which led to his behavior, his neurosis, his ulcer, his depression, or his drug addiction, there is nothing this information can do for us or for him except reinforce the concept that indeed he has a reason to break the law and excuse this transgression on the ground that he is "sick." Therefore we emphasize what traditional therapy tries to ignore: No matter what happened to him, he still has the responsibility for what he does.

If we continue to accept the offender's irresponsibility because of his traumatic history, we become trapped from a therapeutic standpoint. With noncriminal psychiatric problems, we often avoid facing this trap directly. A man with a neurosis can come for traditional treatment indefinitely or a psychotic patient can be locked up for years in a mental hospital; neither exerts great pressure on anyone because his irresponsibility primarily hurts himself.

When a man breaks the law, however, we have to help him because, unless he becomes more responsible, he endangers us. Either we must help him to become more responsible or we must lock him up indefinitely. It is unrealistic to keep him locked up once he has demonstrated that he has gained responsibility. It is not up to us in correction to advance explanations for irresponsibility, but to recognize that individual responsibility must be the goal of our treatment.

<u>Treatment, Not Punishment</u>. At this point, many will think that I just want to return to the old Mosaic concept of "an eye for an eye" to punish the wrongdoer severely. Nothing could be further from my intention. What I advocate is treatment, not punishment. Until an offender can accept the fact that he is responsible for what he did, there can be no treatment in our field. If, as in the first example, the girl prostituted, both she and those who treat her must understand that she did it voluntarily and that better possibilities were open to her than prostitution. Until this is established, there is no treatment. I do not consider it punishment to confront her with her wrongdoing. She has to face both her lack of responsibility and the implication that this is not the way she has to be. She must see that we think she can do better.

From a treatment standpoint, exactly what a person did is of little importance. What matters is in how many areas of his present life he is responsible. The more we find, the easier he is to treat and the better his prognosis. (This is why in many cases it is easier to rehabilitate a murderer than any other criminal. Except for the single grossly irresponsible act, many murderers are fairly responsible people.) Thus, the crux of our theory of reality therapy is personal responsibility.

<u>Describing the Offender</u>. Under our concept, a helpful description of a young female offender might consist of a phrase such as "chronic runaway with minor sex delinquency but moderately responsible" and a brief outline of the areas in which she is responsible and those in which she is not. This description would give everyone working with her some basis for what to expect from her. It would indicate where we should work and where not too much of our effort is needed. It might further indicate, if she were a fairly responsible older girl, that she would be a good candidate for self-parole. We might, on the other hand, describe a narcotics addict as a young man who takes no responsibility for his behavior and lives only for the feeling that narcotics brings him. He can then be periodically reevaluated and treated until he can take more responsibility in important areas of his life.

The theory can be used by the judge, the probation or parole officer, and the psychiatrist, as well as by the nonprofessional correctional personnel because it can be easily understood without the use of such nebulous jargon as "insight," "conflict resolution," or "transference work-through."

<u>Happiness a Stumbling Block</u>. In addition to coming to grips with his irresponsible behavior, the offender must also face the question of that ill-defined term, happiness. From a treatment

standpoint, happiness can be a huge stumbling block. Most children who get into trouble do so in the pursuit of what they conceive to be happiness—"kicks" to escape boredom, to "feel high." The big obstacle in treatment is that upon inquiry into the life of the young offender, we generally find a wealth of material to indicate that he was unhappy. We then wrongly conclude that unhappiness leads to delinquency. When we find the mountains of misery that these children carry on their shoulders, our first human reaction is to do something to make them happy. So we try to change their environment, find them a good foster home, feed, clothe, and provide for their recreation. Then we wonder why they are not happier after we have done so much. After our good treatment why do they return to their old habits? We are puzzled because we haven't been taught that we can't make people happy, that unhappiness is the result, not the cause, of irresponsibility.

Therefore, in reality therapy, we ignore the unhappy past, but provide the offender with an opportunity to benefit himself in a responsible way. When a girl at Ventura comes to me and says she is unhappy, I won't sympathize. I'll listen, and then I'll suggest that she herself could do something about her problems. I'll further suggest what she might do. I'm a compassionate human being who wants to teach her better ways, but I'm not a crying towel. I don't promise to produce happiness or alleviate misery; it's not my job as a psychiatrist. That is up to her. In the same vein, I'll never do anything to keep her from taking responsibility, no matter how initially upsetting this may be. I'll never change the rules, no matter how much she begs, and I won't give her tranquilizers which promise her happiness without responsibility. Only when she becomes more responsible will she be in a position to find some lasting happiness.

Past Nonessential to Treatment. A final part of the theory is our belief that what happens to a person now is more important than anything which happened in the near or remote past. One has to assume that everything a person thinks and does in the present is a sum total of his past, that each present action carries with it roots from his whole existence. Although few psychiatrists will argue against this statement, most will nevertheless draw conclusions far different from the ones Dr. Harrington and I propose. The precept traditionally accepted and taught as essential to therapy is that a person cannot understand or change his present behavior unless he is able to tie it clearly to roots in the past. Logically, however, this view becomes redundant if one accepts the previous statement that the present is already a summation of the past. This redundancy, the crux of traditional therapy, is what causes the fruitless historical journeys, diagnostic studies, and unending psychotherapy which lead to excusing the offender's present actions as an unfortunate culmination of his history.

Our view of this assumption is much different. The present as the sum of the past is all that's really important. If a delinquent boy can understand that what he has been doing is irresponsible and can modify his present behavior, then his pathological past is effectively nullified. The object of our treatment is to replace his past experiences with what goes on between him and his various reality therapists. The boy will be willing and ready to accept reality therapy because he realizes it was his present behavior that resulted in his being locked up, and the indirect cause—his father's rejection of him, let us say—is forever beyond his or our control. In attempting to relate to the reality therapist, he must overcome the obstacles of reality, not run from them. Although this course is harder for both, he will readily accept it if it is presented in a firm but compassionate way. Reality therapy treats the youngster as a potentially responsible adult rather than as an unfortunate child. On the other hand, traditional psychiatry, by dragging him back into his forgotten past, blocks his progress and excuses his behavior, thereby leaving him exactly where he was before—or worse.

THE THERAPIST

All psychiatric theory is meaningless unless there is a therapist who knows how to use it to help the young offender. One therapist may know theory from A to Z and still be unable to provide the warmth and strength needed to make contact, while another who has these essential qualities may have no knowledge of theory whatever and still do some good. No one, delinquent or not, can become responsible without some warm human involvement with a strong mature person who cares about him. It takes human contact alone to initiate treatment. Books, movies, records, music, poetry, or lectures all will help make a responsible person more responsible, but he will be powerless to use these cultural advantages unless he has had good human relationships to start with.

The reality therapist has to assume that in the life of the young offender no one was close enough to enable him to feel worthwhile enough to take responsibility for himself. Unless we can provide this person, we will fail. The more people we can provide, the greater chance we have in succeeding. One caution, however: the delinquent youngster must be seen in a situation where his behavior can be controlled before a therapist can make progress. Merely sending the young offender to a psychiatrist while placing no control over the rest of his life is rarely successful. Without some external control, few therapists can provide enough firm contact in the brief time allotted to have a practical effect on their patient.

<u>Abiding by the Rules</u>. Expensive, well-designed, fully staffed institutions will have little effect unless each staff member takes a personal interest in the inmates. But "personal interest" does not mean condoning poor behavior. It means rigorous enforcement of the rules and realistic praise. No matter how bad his offense, we must show belief that the offender can become more responsible.

Never missing an opportunity to praise present responsible behavior, we must become as involved as possible with his strong points, his interests, his hopes, his fears—anything not tied up with his irresponsible past. If he wants to talk about his escapades, we should show little interest because he is testing us. If we are real friends, we should not be interested in his wrongdoing. If we are interested in it, then he has gained our attention through harming himself, and when he leaves will do so again. Our interest must emphasize the positive, never reinforce the negative aspect.

Just what do we, the reality therapists, do in an actual situation? Suppose, for example, the youngster runs away. What should be done with him once he's found? If the institution rules say he must be locked up securely for a few weeks, then the rules must be followed. This does not mean, however, that we reject him personally because of it. We're both sorry for the act but we go on from there. We do not ask him <u>why</u> he ran away, but we show him how his doing so has caused him to suffer.

Although this sort of treatment may sound rigid, we have so very little time that what we might overlook in more responsible people we have to be on guard for with the young people in our charge. Ventura School is one of the strictest institutions in California, yet most of the girls are happy and anyone is free to come in and talk with any girl at any time. No matter how strict we get, the girls always tell us we are too lenient, that we ought to tighten up.

Each person in an institution must function in his own framework. The cook is not a psychiatrist, the psychiatrist is not a cook. All persons in contact with the young offender must stick to their own skills and help in their areas of competence. The mechanics instructor should expect high standards of work performance from the young men assigned to him; he should not become their counselor because that would be false. The boys and girls have met many phonies in the world who feign deep interest in their problems but who, by their excessive willingness to listen to their tales of wrongdoing, are—at best—unwillingly evading their responsibility of guiding them toward a better life or—at worst—living vicariously through the children's misdeeds.

Too much listening to problems is one of the best ways of remaining detached and uninvolved because the young person knows that you can do nothing about his troubles. Listen for a short time, then offer him your skills. Accept him at your level, not his.

REALITY THERAPY IN PRACTICE

I would like to describe an ideal reality therapy situation—something we try very hard to approximate at Ventura School. But even what I describe as ideal for this institution has inherent shortcomings because when the young offender is apprehended it is usually late in his career. In many cases the school authorities, his parents, and others were aware of his delinquent potential well before he was arrested. With this in mind, let us look at realistic treatment of the young offender.

Let us suppose that tonight at 11 p.m. a police officer apprehended a sixteen-year-old boy who has just wrecked a stolen car in his effort to escape pursuit. In custody, he should first be given a careful physical examination and be checked to see whether he is under the influence of narcotics or alcohol. Police questions should be fair but brief. His parents should be notified and asked to cooperate, and he should be informed about his legal rights. The police should let him know the charge and ask him, in an unthreatening manner, whether he wants to make a statement. No attempt should be made to obtain a long statement that night. When questions are mandatory, they should concern the circumstances of, not the reasons for, his offenses. Open-end questions, such as "Why did you do it?" should be avoided. If he wishes, his story should be recorded without comment and he should be locked up, preferably alone, for the night. From a treatment standpoint, it's best, at first, to engage him in little conversation or questioning but to allow him time to think over his behavior.

Even if he is to be released in tne morning, he should spend one night by himself in custody because now, more than at any other time, he may begin to think that he has done something wrong and that he has some responsibility for it. Too much questioning, too much initial conversation, gives him the opportunity to make excuses, to feel antagonistic toward authority, to justify in his mind that what he did was not very wrong or, if wrong, not really his fault. As soon as possible and throughout reality therapy, we must hive him a chance to compare his values to his behavior, because ultimately the strength of this comparison will determine his future.

In the morning, assuming that he is to be kept, he should be taken to the detention home, where the rules should be carefully explained to him, whether or not he has been there before. We can never assume that the youngster already knows the rules, for, if he breaks one of them, this assumption allows him to blame us for not carefully explaining them.

An experienced staff member—a counselor, caseworker, or psychologist—should work with him until his case is decided in court. This counselor should see him as soon as possible and at regular intervals during his detention. In the interviews, he should put the boy at ease (allowing him to smoke if necessary), reread the charge along with the boy's statement, and ask him whether he wants to add or subtract anything. This should be done in a friendly, unaccusing way, but the situation should be reviewed so that the boy knows definitely what he is charged with.

Discussion should continue until the boy understands that he is being locked up because he broke the law. When this point has been reached (hopefully, during the first interview), the counselor should tell the boy that he would like to help him keep out of further trouble. If the boy is hostile or uncooperative, the counselor should tell him to think about it. The counselor should never return his hostility and never pressure him with "help." He should continue to see the boy regularly, but make no further issue over treatment.

The remainder of the counseling situation should be a discussion of the following three points:

1. Has the boy done anything else illegal or wrong? This is a short, factual discussion, not a case history. Hence the question of right and wrong will probably arise, as will the question of the boy's own values and standards. The counselor should ask the boy what his parents or relatives think of his offense. How do their values compare to his? Is he ashamed of what he has done?

Does he feel guilty? If he does, this is good; he should. (The counselor should never lighten the guilt; it is the most powerful weapon we have. This does not mean he should add to it, but he should not attempt to reduce it.) The therapist should also ask the boy what he has done that he considers responsible, something he can be proud of.

2. How is he getting along in the detention home right now? Does he feel that anything is unfair? If he has any complaints or he feels unjustly treated, the realities of life in a detention home should again be clarified.

3. Subsequent interviews should dwell more and more on his future plans. The counselor should review the various possibilities that will be decided in court—release to parent, probation, or training school. The therapist should be open with the boy, keep nothing secret from him. Both have to face the reality of the disposition. Does the boy have a home to go to? Does he want to go home? What does he think is the best place for him? Does he want to go to school, to work, to be trained for a vocation? A long discussion of his future will help him begin to feel responsibility for himself, the goal of reality therapy.

The counselor must never discuss causes—just or unjust—for the boy's actions or imply that he was emotionally disturbed. Our job is to help him, not convince him he's deeply maladjusted.

Further conversations can inquire about his friends. Whom would he like to visit him? The counselor should encourage the boy to write to the people he likes. The boy should not be made to feel that he would be better off without anyone he considers near or dear to him—even if the counselor feels these people are not a good influence. Attempts to sever close attachments will usually produce more trouble than benefits. Above all, the counselor should never imply that the boy's family or anyone is in any way responsible for his predicament. The boy's responsibility is to be a better person, and doing so may cause his parents and society to improve their attitudes toward him.

The counselor's report to the court should sum up the degree of responsibility and maturity found in the boy. Does he have a workable set of standards or values which he can use when not closely supervised? How much of what he says is just talk and how much does he really mean? Is he somewhat overwilling to admit irresponsibility (which is another way of saying, "I'm so mixed up I don't know what I'm doing")? Will someone enjoy working with him? What kind of person would work best with him? What is the best treatment for him in view of the material gathered?

When the report is completed and the recommendation made, it should be read and discussed with the boy so he knows where he stands and what will be brought up in court.

In court, the judge should again review the charges and the report. This repetition, though monotonous, is extremely important to the boy. It means we care. The boy's parents should be present and be given a chance to make a statement. If the judge, on the counselor's recommendation, decides to send the boy to a training school, he should state exactly where the boy will go, the approximate length of his stay, and what he can expect to do there. This means that the judge himself should have an accurate idea of the program at that school. The judge will also want to discuss how often the parents may visit and what responsibility they will take for their son while he is away. The judge then should take the boy aside, wish him luck, and perhaps tell him of other boys who have succeeded after going through training school. This extra personal touch from an authoritative power can often make a great impression on young people in trouble who, despite appearances, are as impressionable about good things as they are about the bad.

The boy leaves the court with the idea that a better future is up to him, not us, but that we'll help as much as we can. He arrives at the training school understanding that what was done has been done for him, not to him. Once there, he should be assigned a primary counselor trained in reality therapy who can continue what has been started, usually in group therapy. Here again, the charge is reviewed and the rules carefully explained. As soon as possible, he should participate in a training program conducted by staff who do not "counsel" but who point out what he is doing wrong and show him better ways.

What constitutes a good training program is, of course, another subject in itself. Briefly, I think it should be a program that teaches a youngster something useful for at least eight hours a day. Idleness and make-work are deadly.

A youngster's progress should be praised, but if he breaks the rules he should suffer reasonable consequences. Discipline for serious breaches should be complete isolation from the main program, followed by isolation from the recreational aspects of the program, and finally return to full program. This will be adequate punishment, however, only if the program is attractive enough to be missed. Corporal punishment is never justified.

Gradually, the youngster should be given more responsibility. He should be permitted week-end visits home in order to become acclimated to the place where he will live when he leaves the school. This is preferable to a sudden shift from school to parole.

The therapist who becomes involved with a boy's life cannot help feeling a little hurt and angry when the boy breaks the rules or gets into trouble in the school. If there is real feeling between them, the boy will always have the ability, in a sense, to hurt the therapist; but the therapist should always point out that when he is hurt, the boy is the real loser. The counselor who shows no emotion really isn't involved in treating this particular boy.

When the boy is discharged, treatment should be continued by the parole officer until a responsible adjustment at work, at school, or at home is made.

Reality therapy is much more than this brief introductory article can possibly explain. It is, in our opinion, the only kind of psychiatric treatment which works for behavior problems. When employed by everyone in the institution it works extremely well, and the positive results can be easily seen.

Young delinquents want the mature, responsible treatment that we offer and they are young and flexible enough to be helped quickly. Where this therapy is employed, there is no schism between treatment and custody.

Because reality therapy works so well in both large and small group therapy situations, it is especially suited for institutional practice. It does away with the need for expensive testing, record keeping, and numerous time-consuming speculative conferences. The only records needed are occasional notes about what has occurred that shows increased responsibility. If the boy fails, the reason is that we were not able to help him become responsible enough to live in society. We need no detailed record of this failure to explain why. The fact that the boy failed speaks for itself. We are human enough to admit that extenuating circumstances are of solace to us as therapists, but they are meaningless to the child whose parole is revoked. If all the time spent in keeping records and conferring about why we or our patients failed were devoted to doing reality therapy, there would be far fewer failures in correctional psychiatry.

IX

THE NECESSARY AND SUFFICIENT CONDITIONS OF THERAPEUTIC PERSONALITY CHANGE

Carl R. Rogers

For many years I have been engaged in psychotherapy with individuals in distress. In recent years I have found myself increasingly concerned with the process of abstracting from that experience the general principles which appear to be involved in it. I have endeavored to discover any orderliness, any unity which seems to inhere in the subtle, complex tissue of interpersonal relationship in which I have so constantly been immersed in therapeutic work. One of the current products of this concern is an attempt to state, in formal terms, a theory of psychotherapy, of personality, and of interpersonal relationships which will encompass and contain the phenomena of my experience. What I wish to do in this paper is to take one very small segment of that theory, spell it out more completely, and explore its meaning and usefulness.

THE PROBLEM

The question to which I wish to address myself is this: Is it possible to state, in terms which are clearly definable and measurable, the psychological conditions which are both necessary and sufficient to bring about constructive personality change? Do we, in other words, know with any precision those elements which are essential if psychotherapeutic change is to ensue?

Before proceeding to the major task let me dispose very briefly of the second portion of the question. What is meant by

Reprinted by permission of the author and *Journal of Consulting Psychology*, 1957, 21:95-103.

such phrases as "psychotherapeutic change," "constructive personality change"? This problem also deserves deep and serious consideration, but for the moment let me suggest a common-sense type of meaning upon which we can perhaps agree for purposes of this paper. By these phrases is meant: change in the personality structure of the individual, at both surface and deeper levels, in a direction which clinicians would agree means greater integration, less internal conflict, more energy utilizable for effective living; change in behavior away from behaviors generally regarded as immature and toward behaviors regarded as mature. This brief description may suffice to indicate the kind of change for which we are considering the preconditions. It may also suggest the ways in which this criterion of change may be determined.[1]

THE CONDITIONS

As I have considered my own clinical experience and that of my colleagues, together with the pertinent research which is available, I have drawn out several conditions which seem to me to be necessary to initiate constructive personality change, and which, taken together, appear to be sufficient to inaugurate that process. As I have worked on this problem I have found myself surprised at the simplicity of what has emerged. The statement which follows is not offered with any assurance as to its correctness, but with the expectation that it will have the value of any theory, namely that it states or implies a series of hypotheses which are open to proof or disproof, thereby clarifying and extending our knowledge of the field.

Since I am not, in this paper, trying to achieve suspense, I will state at once, in severely rigorous and summarized terms, the six conditions which I have come to feel are basic to the process of personality change. The meaning of a number of the terms is not immediately evident, but will be clarified in the explanatory sections which follow. It is hoped that this brief statement will have much more significance to the reader when he has completed the paper. Without further introduction let me state the basic theoretical position.

For constructive personality change to occur, it is necessary that these conditions exist and continue over a period of time:

    1. Two persons are in psychological contact.

[1]That this is a measurable and determinable criterion has been shown in research already completed. See Rogers & Dymond (1954), especially chapters 8, 13, and 17.

2. The first, whom we shall term the client, is in a state of incongruence, being vulnerable or anxious.

3. The second person, whom we shall term the therapist, is congruent or integrated in the relationship.

4. The therapist experiences unconditional positive regard for the client.

5. The therapist experiences an empathic understanding of the client's internal frame of reference and endeavors to communicate this experience to the client.

6. The communication to the client of the therapist's empathic understanding and unconditional positive regard is to a minimal degree achieved.

No other conditions are necessary. If these six conditions exist, and continue over a period of time, this is sufficient. The process of constructive personality change will follow.

A Relationship

The first condition specifies that a minimal relationship, a psychological contact, must exist. I am hypothesizing that significant positive personality change does not occur except in a relationship. This is of course an hypothesis, and it may be disproved.

Conditions 2 through 6 define the characteristics of the relationship which are regarded as essential by defining the necessary characteristics of each person in the relationship. All that is intended by this first condition is to specify that the two people are to some degree in contact, that each makes some perceived difference in the experiential field of the other. Probably it is sufficient if each makes some "subceived" difference, even though the individual may not be consciously aware of this impact. Thus it might be difficult to know whether a catatonic patient perceives a therapist's presence as making a difference to him—a difference of any kind—but it is almost certain that at some organic level he does sense this difference.

Except in such a difficult borderline situation as that just mentioned, it would be relatively easy to define this condition in operational terms and thus determine, from a hard-boiled research point of view, whether the condition does, or does not, exist. The simplest method of determination involves simply the awareness of both client and therapist. If each is aware of being in personal or psychological contact with the other, then this condition is met.

This first condition of therapeutic change is such a simple one that perhaps it should be labeled an assumption or a precondition in order to set it apart from those that follow. Without it, however, the remaining items would have no meaning, and that is the reason for including it.

The State of the Client

It was specified that it is necessary that the client be "in a state of incongruence, being vulnerable or anxious." What is the meaning of these terms?

Incongruence is a basic construct in the theory we have been developing. It refers to a discrepancy between the actual experience of the organism and the self picture of the individual insofar as it represents that experience. Thus a student may experience, at a total or organismic level, a fear of the university and of examinations which are given on the third floor of a certain building, since these may demonstrate a fundamental inadequacy in him. Since such a fear of his inadequacy is decidedly at odds with his concept of himself, this experience is represented (distortedly) in his awareness as an unreasonable fear of climbing stairs in this building, or any building, and soon an unreasonable fear of crossing the open campus. Thus there is a fundamental discrepancy between the experienced meaning of the situation as it registers in his organism and the symbolic representation of that experience in awareness in such a way that it does not conflict with the picture he has of himself. In this case to admit a fear of inadequacy would contradict the picture he holds of himself; to admit incomprehensible fears does not contradict his self concept.

Another instance would be the mother who develops vague illnesses whenever her only son makes plans to leave home. The actual desire is to hold on to her only source of satisfaction. To perceive this in awareness would be inconsistent with the picture she holds of herself as a good mother. Illness, however, is consistent with her self concept, and the experience is symbolized in this distorted fashion. Thus again there is a basic incongruence between the self as perceived (in this case as an ill mother needing attention) and the actual experience (in this case the desire to hold on to her son).

When the individual has no awareness of such incongruence in himself, then he is merely vulnerable to the possibility of anxiety and disorganization. Some experience might occur so suddenly or so obviously that the incongruence could not be denied. Therefore, the person is vulnerable to such a possibility.

If the individual dimly perceives such an incongruence in himself, then a tension state occurs which is known as anxiety. The incongruence need not be sharply perceived. It is enough that it is subceived—that is, discriminated as threatening to the self without any awareness of the content of that threat. Such anxiety is often seen in therapy as the individual approaches awareness of some element of his experience which is in sharp contradiction to his self concept.

It is not easy to give precise operational definition to this second of the six conditions, yet to some degree this has been achieved. Several research workers have defined the self concept by means of a Q sort by the individual of a list of self-referent items. This gives us an operational picture of the self. The total experiencing of the individual is more difficult to capture. Chodorkoff (1954) has defined it as a Q sort made by a clinician who sorts the same self-referent items independently, basing his sorting on the picture he has obtained of the individual from projective tests. His sort thus includes unconscious as well as conscious elements of the individual's experience, thus representing (in an admittedly imperfect way) the totality of the client's experience. The correlation between these two sortings gives a crude operational measure of incongruence between self and experience, low or negative correlation representing of course a high degree of incongruence.

The Therapist's Genuineness in the Relationship

The third condition is that the therapist should be, within the confines of this relationship, a congruent, genuine, integrated person. It means that within the relationship he is freely and deeply himself, with his actual experience accurately represented by his awareness of himself. It is the opposite of presenting a facade, either knowingly or unknowingly.

It is not necessary (nor is it possible) that the therapist be a paragon who exhibits this degree of integration, of wholeness, in every aspect of his life. It is sufficient that he is accurately himself in this hour of this relationship, that in this basic sense he is what he actually is, in this moment of time.

It should be clear that this includes being himself even in ways which are not regarded as ideal for psychotherapy. His experience may be "I am afraid of this client" or "My attention is so focused on my own problems that I can scarcely listen to him." If the therapist is not denying these feelings to awareness, but is able freely to be them (as well as being his other feelings), then the condition we have stated is met.

It would take us too far afield to consider the puzzling matter as to the degree to which the therapist overtly communicates this reality in himself to the client. Certainly the aim is not for the therapist to express or talk out his own feelings, but primarily that he should not be deceiving the client as to himself. At times he may need to talk out some of his own feelings (either to the client, or to a colleague or supervisor) if they are standing in the way of the two following conditions.

It is not too difficult to suggest an operational definition for this third condition. We resort again to Q technique. If the therapist sorts a series of items relevant to the relationship (using a list similar to the ones developed by Fiedler [1950, 1953] and Bown'[1954], this will give his perception of his experience in the relationship. If several judges who have observed the interview or listened to a recording of it (or observed a sound movie of it) now sort the same items to represent their perception of the relationship, this second sorting should catch those elements of the therapist's behavior and inferred attitudes of which he is unaware, as well as those of which he is aware. Thus a high correlation between the therapist's sort and the observer's sort would represent in crude form an operational definition of the therapist's congruence or integration in the relationship; and a low correlation, the opposite.

Unconditional Positive Regard

To the extent that the therapist finds himself experiencing a warm acceptance of each aspect of the client's experience as being a part of that client, he is experiencing unconditional positive regard. This concept has been developed by Standal (1954). It means that there are no conditions of acceptance, no feeling of "I like you only if you are thus and so." It means a "prizing" of the person, as Dewey has used that term. It is at the opposite pole from a selective evaluating attitude—"You are bad in these ways, good in those." It involves as much feeling of acceptance for the client's expression of negative, "bad," painful, fearful, defensive, abnormal feelings as for his expression of "good," positive, mature, confident, social feelings, as much acceptance of ways in which he is inconsistent as of ways in which he is consistent. It means a caring for the client, but not in a possessive way or in such a way as simply to satisfy the therapist's own needs. It means a caring for the client as a separate person, with permission to have his own feelings, his own experiences.

One client describes the therapist as "fostering my possession of my own experience . . . that [this] is <u>my</u> experience and that I am actually having it: thinking what I think, feeling what I feel, wanting what I want, fearing what I fear: no 'ifs,' 'buts,' or 'not really-lys.'" This is the type of acceptance which is hypothesized as being necessary if personality change is to occur.

Like the two previous conditions, this fourth condition is a matter of degree,[2] as immediately becomes apparent if we attempt to define it in terms of specific research operations. One such method of giving it definition would be to consider the Q sort for the relationship as described under Condition 3. To the extent that items expressive of unconditional positive regard are sorted as characteristic of the relationship by both the therapist and the observers, unconditional positive regard might be said to exist. Such items might include statements of this order: "I feel no revulsion at anything the client says"; "I feel neither approval nor disapproval of the client and his statements—simply acceptance"; "I feel warmly toward the client—toward his weaknesses and problems as well as his potentialities"; "I am not inclined to pass judgment on what the client tells me"; "I like the client." To the extent that both therapist and observers perceive these items as characteristic, or their opposites as uncharacteristic, Condition 4 might be said to be met.

<u>Empathy</u>

The fifth condition is that the therapist is experiencing an accurate, empathic understanding of the client's awareness of his own experience. To sense the client's private world as if it were your own, but without ever losing the "as if" quality—this is empathy, and this seems essential to therapy. To sense the client's anger, fear, or confusion as if it were your own, yet without your own anger, fear, or confusion getting bound up in it, is the condi-

---

[2]The phrase "unconditional positive regard" may be an unfortunate one, since it sounds like an absolute, an all or nothing dispositional concept. It is probably evident from the description that completely unconditional positive regard would never exist except in theory. From a clinical and experiential point of view I believe the most accurate statement is that the effective therapist experiences unconditional positive regard for the client during many moments of his contact with him, yet from time to time he experiences only a conditional positive regard—and perhaps at times a negative regard, though this is not likely in effective therapy. It is in this sense that unconditional positive regard exists as a matter of degree in any relationship.

tion we are endeavoring to describe. When the client's world is this clear to the therapist, and he moves about in it freely, then he can both communicate his understanding of what is clearly known to the client and can also voice meanings in the client's experience of which the client is scarcely aware. As one client described this second aspect: "Every now and again, with me in a tangle of thought and feeling, screwed up in a web of mutually divergent lines of movement, with impulses from different parts of me, and me feeling the feeling of its being all too much and such-like—then whomp, just like a sunbeam thrusting its way through cloudbanks and tangles of foliage to spread a circle of light on a tangle of forest paths, came some comment from you. [It was] clarity, even disentanglement, an additional twist to the picture, a putting in place. Then the consequence—the sense of moving on, the relaxation. These were sunbeams." That such penetrating empathy is important for therapy is indicated by Fiedler's (1950) research in which items such as the following placed high in the description of relationships created by experienced therapists:

> The therapist is well able to understand the patient's feelings.
> The therapist is never in any doubt about what the patient means.
> The therapist's remarks fit in just right with the patient's mood and content.
> The therapist's tone of voice conveys the complete ability to share the patient's feelings.

An operational definition of the therapist's empathy could be provided in different ways. Use might be made of the Q sort described under Condition 3. To the degree that items descriptive of accurate empathy were sorted as characteristic by both the therapist and the observers, this condition would be regarded as existing.

Another way of defining this condition would be for both client and therapist to sort a list of items descriptive of client feelings. Each would sort independently, the task being to represent the feelings which the client had experienced during a just completed interview. If the correlation between client and therapist sortings were high, accurate empathy would be said to exist, a low correlation indicating the opposite conclusion.

Still another way of measuring empathy would be for trained judges to rate the depth and accuracy of the therapist's empathy on the basis of listening to recorded interviews.

The Client's Perception of the Therapist

The final condition as stated is that the client perceives, to a minimal degree, the acceptance and empathy which the therapist experiences for him. Unless some communication of these attitudes has been achieved, then such attitudes do not exist in the relationship as far as the client is concerned, and the therapeutic process could not, by our hypothesis, be initiated.

Since attitudes cannot be directly perceived, it might be somewhat more accurate to state that therapist behaviors and words are perceived by the client as meaning that to some degree the therapist accepts and understands him.

An operational definition of this condition would not be difficult. The client might, after an interview, sort a Q-sort list of items referring to qualities representing the relationship between himself and the therapist. (The same list could be used as for Condition 3.) If several items descriptive of acceptance and empathy are sorted by the client as characteristic of the relationship, then this condition could be regarded as met. In the present state of our knowledge the meaning of "to a minimal degree" would have to be arbitrary.

Up to this point the effort has been made to present, briefly and factually, the conditions which I have come to regard as essential for psychotherapeutic change. I have not tried to give the theoretical context of these conditions nor to explain what seem to me to be the dynamics of their effectiveness. Such explanatory material will be available, to the reader who is interested, in the document already mentioned.

I have, however, given at least one means of defining, in operational terms, each of the conditions mentioned. I have done this in order to stress the fact that I am not speaking of vague qualities which ideally should be present if some other vague result is to occur. I am presenting conditions which are crudely measurable even in the present state of our technology, and have suggested specific operations in each instance even though I am sure that more adequate methods of measurement could be devised by a serious investigator.

My purpose has been to stress the notion that in my opinion we are dealing with an if-then phenomenon in which knowledge of the dynamics is not essential to testing the hypotheses. Thus, to illustrate from another field: if one substance, shown by a series of operations to be the substance known as hydrochloric acid, is mixed with another substance, shown by another series of operations to be sodium hydroxide, then salt and water will be products of this mixture. This is true whether one regards the results as due to magic, or whether one explains it in the most adequate terms of modern chemical theory. In the same way it is being postulated here that certain definable conditions precede certain definable changes and that this fact exists independently of our efforts to account for it.

THE RESULTING HYPOTHESES

The major value of stating any theory in unequivocal terms is that specific hypotheses may be drawn from it which are capable of proof or disproof. Thus, even if the conditions which have been postulated as necessary and sufficient conditions are more incorrect than correct (which I hope they are not), they could still advance science in this field by providing a base of operations from which fact could be winnowed out from error.

The hypotheses which would follow from the theory given would be of this order:

If these six conditions (as operationally defined) exist, then constructive personality change (as defined) will occur in the client.

If one or more of these conditions is not present, constructive personality change will not occur.

These hypotheses hold in any situation whether it is or is not labeled "psychotherapy."

Only Condition 1 is dichotomous (it either is present or is not), and the remaining five occur in varying degree, each on its continuum. Since this is true, another hypothesis follows, and it is likely that this would be the simplest to test:

If all six conditions are present, then the greater the degree to which Conditions 2 to 6 exist, the more marked will be the constructive personality change in the client.

At the present time the above hypotheses can only be stated in this general form—which implies that all of the conditions have equal weight. Empirical studies will no doubt make possible much more refinement of this hypothesis. It may be, for example, that if anxiety is high in the client, then the other conditions are less important. Or if unconditional positive regard is high (as in a mother's love for her child), then perhaps a modest degree of empathy is sufficient. But at the moment we can only speculate on such possibilities.

SOME IMPLICATIONS

Significant Omissions

If there is any startling feature in the formulation which has been given as to the necessary conditions for therapy, it probably lies in the elements which are omitted. In present-day clinical practice, therapists operate as though there were many other conditions in addition to those described, which are essential for psychotherapy. To point this up it may be well to mention a few of the conditions which, after thoughtful consideration of our research and our experience, are not included.

For example, it is _not_ stated that these conditions apply to one type of client, and that other conditions are necessary to bring about psychotherapeutic change with other types of client. Probably no idea is so prevalent in clinical work today as that one works with neurotics in one way, with psychotics in another; that certain therapeutic conditions must be provided for compulsives, others for homosexuals, etc. Because of this heavy weight of clinical opinion to the contrary, it is with some "fear and trembling" that I advance the concept that the essential conditions of psychotherapy exist in a single configuration, even though the client or patient may use them very differently. [3]

It is _not_ stated that these six conditions are the essential conditions for client-centered therapy, and that other conditions are essential for other types of psychotherapy. I certainly am heavily influenced by my own experience, and that experience has led me to a viewpoint which is termed "client centered." Nevertheless my aim in stating this theory is to state the conditions which apply to _any_ situation in which constructive personality change occurs, whether we are thinking of classical psychoanalysis, or any of its

---

[3] I cling to this statement of my hypothesis even though it is challenged by a just completed study by Kirtner (1955). Kirtner has found, in a group of 26 cases from the Counseling Center at the University of Chicago, that there are sharp differences in the client's mode of approach to the resolution of life difficulties, and that these differences are related to success in psychotherapy. Briefly, the client who sees his problem as involving his relationships, and who feels that he contributes to this problem and wants to change it, is likely to be successful. The client who externalizes his problem, feeling little self-responsibility, is much more likely to be a failure. Thus the implication is that some other conditions need to be provided for psychotherapy with this group. For the present, however, I will stand by my hypothesis as given, until Kirtner's study is confirmed, and until we know an alternative hypothesis to take its place.

modern offshoots, or Adlerian psychotherapy, or any other. It
will be obvious then that in my judgment much of what is considered to be essential would not be found, empirically, to be essential. Testing of some of the stated hypotheses would throw
light on this perplexing issue. We may of course find that various
therapies produce various types of personality change, and that
for each psychotherapy a separate set of conditions is necessary.
Until and unless this is demonstrated, I am hypothesizing that effective psychotherapy of any sort produces similar changes in personality and behavior, and that a single set of preconditions is
necessary.

It is not stated that psychotherapy is a special kind of relationship, different in kind from all others which occur in everyday
life. It will be evident instead that for brief moments, at least,
many good friendships fulfill the six conditions. Usually this is
only momentarily, however, and then empathy falters, the positive regard becomes conditional, or the congruence of the "therapist" friend becomes overlaid by some degree of facade or defensiveness. Thus the therapeutic relationship is seen as a heighten-
ing of the constructive qualities which often exist in part in other
relationships, and an extension through time of qualities which in
other relationships tend at best to be momentary.

It is not stated that special intellectual professional knowledge—psychological, psychiatric, medical, or religious—is required of the therapist. Conditions 3, 4, and 5, which apply
especially to the therapist, are qualities of experience, not intellectual information. If they are to be acquired, they must, in my
opinion, be acquired through an experiential training—which may
be, but usually is not, a part of professional training. It troubles
me to hold such a radical point of view, but I can draw no other
conclusion from my experience. Intellectual training and the acquiring of information has, I believe, many valuable results—but
becoming a therapist is not one of those results.

It is not stated that it is necessary for psychotherapy that the
therapist have an accurate psychological diagnosis of the client.
Here too it troubles me to hold a viewpoint so at variance with my
clinical colleagues. When one thinks of the vast proportion of
time spent in any psychological, psychiatric, or mental hygiene
center on the exhaustive psychological evaluation of the client or
patient, it seems as though this must serve a useful purpose insofar as psychotherapy is concerned. Yet the more I have observed
therapists, and the more closely I have studied research such as
that done by Fiedler (1953) and others, the more I am forced to

the conclusion that such diagnostic knowledge is not essential to psychotherapy.[5] It may even be that its defense as a necessary prelude to psychotherapy is simply a protective alternative to the admission that it is, for the most part, a colossal waste of time. There is only one useful purpose I have been able to observe which relates to psychotherapy. Some therapists cannot feel secure in the relationship with the client unless they possess such diagnostic knowledge. Without it they feel fearful of him, unable to be empathic, unable to experience unconditional regard, finding it necessary to put up a pretense in the relationship. If they know in advance of suicidal impulses they can somehow be more acceptant of them. Thus, for some therapists, the security they perceive in diagnostic information may be a basis for permitting themselves to be integrated in the relationship, and to experience empathy and full acceptance. In these instances a psychological diagnosis would certainly be justified as adding to the comfort and hence the effectiveness of the therapist. But even here it does not appear to be a basic precondition for psychotherapy.[5]

Perhaps I have given enough illustrations to indicate that the conditions I have hypothesized as necessary and sufficient for psychotherapy are striking and unusual primarily by virtue of what they omit. If we were to determine, by a survey of the behaviors of therapists, those hypotheses which they appear to regard as necessary to psychotherapy, the list would be a great deal longer and more complex.

Is This Theoretical Formulation Useful?

Aside from the personal satisfaction it gives as a venture in abstraction and generalization, what is the value of a theoretical statement such as has been offered in this paper? I should like to spell out more fully the usefulness which I believe it may have.

In the field of research it may give both direction and impetus to investigation. Since it sees the conditions of constructive per-

[4] There is no intent here to maintain that diagnostic evaluation is useless. We have ourselves made heavy use of such methods in our research studies of change in personality. It is its usefulness as a precondition to psychotherapy which is questioned.

[5] In a facetious moment I have suggested that such therapists might be made equally comfortable by being given the diagnosis of some other individual, not of this patient or client. The fact that the diagnosis proved inaccurate as psychotherapy continued would not be particularly disturbing, because one always expects to find inaccuracies in the diagnosis as one works with the individual.

sonality change as general, it greatly broadens the opportunities
for study. Psychotherapy is not the only situation aimed at constructive personality change. Programs of training for leadership
in industry and programs of training for military leadership often
aim at such change. Educational institutions or programs frequently aim at development of character and personality as well as
at intellectual skills. Community agencies aim at personality and
behavioral change in delinquents and criminals. Such programs
would provide an opportunity for the broad testing of the hypotheses
offered. If it is found that constructive personality change occurs
in such programs when the hypothesized conditions are not fulfilled, then the theory would have to be revised. If however the
hypotheses are upheld, then the results, both for the planning of
such programs and for our knowledge of human dynamics, would
be significant. In the field of psychotherapy itself, the application
of consistent hypotheses to the work of various schools of therapists may prove highly profitable. Again the disproof of the hypotheses offered would be as important as their confirmation,
either result adding significantly to our knowledge.

For the practice of psychotherapy the theory also offers significant problems for consideration. One of its implications is that
the techniques of the various therapies are relatively unimportant
except to the extent that they serve as channels for fulfilling one of
the conditions. In client-centered therapy, for example, the technique of "reflecting feelings" has been described and commented
on (Rogers, 1951, pp. 26-36). In terms of the theory here being
presented, this technique is by no means an essential condition of
therapy. To the extent, however, that it provides a channel by
which the therapist communicates a sensitive empathy and an unconditional positive regard, then it may serve as a technical channel by which the essential conditions of therapy are fulfilled. In
the same way, the theory I have presented would see no essential
value to therapy of such techniques as interpretation of personality
dynamics, free association, analysis of dreams, analysis of the
transference, hypnosis, interpretation of life style, suggestion,
and the like. Each of these techniques may, however, become a
channel for communicating the essential conditions which have
been formulated. An interpretation may be given in a way which
communicates the unconditional positive regard of the therapist.
A stream of free association may be listened to in a way which
communicates an empathy which the therapist is experiencing. In
the handling of the transference an effective therapist often communicates his own wholeness and congruence in the relationship.

Similarly for the other techniques. But just as these techniques may communicate the elements which are essential for therapy, so any one of them may communicate attitudes and experiences sharply contradictory to the hypothesized conditions of therapy. Feeling may be "reflected" in a way which communicates the therapist's lack of empathy. Interpretations may be rendered in a way which indicates the highly conditional regard of the therapist. Any of the techniques may communicate the fact that the therapist is expressing one attitude at a surface level, and another contradictory attitude which is denied to his own awareness. Thus one value of such a theoretical formulation as we have offered is that it may assist therapists to think more critically about those elements of their experience, attitudes, and behaviors which are essential to psychotherapy, and those which are nonessential or even deleterious to psychotherapy.

Finally, in those programs—educational, correctional, military, or industrial—which aim toward constructive changes in the personality structure and behavior of the individual, this formulation may serve as a very tentative criterion against which to measure the program. Until it is much further tested by research, it cannot be thought of as a valid criterion, but, as in the field of psychotherapy, it may help to stimulate critical analysis and the formulation of alternative conditions and alternative hypotheses.

SUMMARY

Drawing from a larger theoretical context, six conditions are postulated as necessary and sufficient conditions for the initiation of a process of constructive personality change. A brief explanation is given of each condition, and suggestions are made as to how each may be operationally defined for research purposes. The implications of this theory for research, for psychotherapy, and for educational and training programs aimed at constructive personality change, are indicated. It is pointed out that many of the conditions which are commonly regarded as necessary to psychotherapy are, in terms of this theory, nonessential.

REFERENCES

Bown, O. H. An investigation of therapeutic relationship in client-centered therapy. Unpublished doctor's dissertation, Univer. of Chicago, 1954.

Chodorkoff, B. Self-perception, perceptual defense, and adjustment. J. abnorm. soc. Psychol., 1954, 49:508-512.

Fiedler, F. E. A comparison of therapeutic relationships in psychoanalytic, non-directive and Adlerian therapy. J. consult.
Psychol., 1950, 14:436-445.

Fiedler, F. E. Quantitative studies on the role of therapists'
feelings toward their patients. In O. H. Mowrer (Ed.),
Psychotherapy: theory and research. New York: Ronald, 1953.

Kirtner, W. L. Success and failure in client-centered therapy as
a function of personality variables. Unpublished master's
thesis, Univer. of Chicago, 1955.

Rogers, C. R. Client-centered therapy. Boston: Houghton Mifflin,
1951.

Rogers, C. R., & Dymond, Rosalind F. (Eds.). Psychotherapy
and personality change. Chicago: Univer. of Chicago Press,
1954.

Standal, S. The need for positive regard: a contribution to client-
centered theory. Unpublished doctor's dissertation, Univer.
of Chicago, 1954.

X

REQUISITE CONDITIONS FOR BASIC PERSONALITY CHANGE

Albert Ellis

Are there any necessary and sufficient conditions which an emotionally disturbed individual <u>must</u> undergo if he is to overcome his disturbance and achieve a basic change in his personality? Yes and no–depending upon whether our definition of the word "conditions" is narrow or broad.

Carl Rogers (1957), in a notable paper on this subject, stuck his scientific neck out by listing six conditions that, he hypothesized, must exist and continue to exist over a period of time if personality change is to be effected. I shall now stick out my own scientific neck by contending that none of his postulated conditions are necessary (even though they may all be desirable) for personality change to occur.

For purposes of discussion, I shall accept Rogers' definition of "constructive personality change" as consisting of "change in the personality structure of the individual, at both surface and deeper levels, in a direction which clinicians would agree means greater integration, less internal conflict, more energy utilizable for effective living; change in behavior away from behaviors regarded as immature and toward behaviors regarded as mature." In my own terms, which I believe are a little more specific, I would say that constructive personality change occurs when an individual ⟨eliminates⟩ a significant proportion of his needless, unrealistically based self-defeating reactions (especially intense, prolonged, or repeated feelings of anxiety and hostility) which he

This chapter consists of an expanded version of a paper read at the workshop on psychotherapy of the American Academy of Psychotherapists, held in Madison, Wisconsin, August 9, 1958, and subsequently published in *J. Consult. Psychol.*, 1959, 23, 538-540. Reprinted by permission of the author and publisher from Albert Ellis. *Reason and Emotion in Psychotherapy*. New York: Lyle Stuart, 1962.

may consciously experience or whose subsurface existence may lead him to behave in an ineffective or inappropriate manner (Ellis, 1957a, 1958a).

According to Rogers, the six necessary and sufficient conditions for constructive personality change are as follows: 1. Two persons are in psychological contact. 2. The first (the client or patient) is in a state of incongruence, being vulnerable or anxious. 3. The second person, the therapist, is congruent or integrated in the relationship. 4. The therapist experiences unconditional positive regard for the patient. 5. The therapist experiences an empathic understanding of the patient's internal frame of reference and endeavors to communicate this experience to the patient. 6. The communication to the patient of the therapist's empathic understanding and unconditional positive regard is to a minimal degree achieved.

Let us now examine each of these six conditions to see if it is really necessary for basic personality change.

Two persons, says Rogers, must be in psychological contact. This proposition, I am afraid, stems from a kind of therapeutic presumptuousness, since it ignores thousands, perhaps millions, of significant personality changes that have occurred when a single individual (a) encountered external experiences and learned sufficiently by them to restructure his philosophy and behavior patterns of living, or (b) without being in any actual relationship with another, heard a lecture, read a book, or listened to a sermon that helped him make basic changes in his own personality.

I am reminded, in this connection, of many individuals I have read about, and a few to whom I have talked, who narrowly escaped death and who were significantly changed persons for the rest of their lives. I am also reminded of several people I have known who read books, ranging from Mary Baker Eddy's idiotic mishmash, Science and Health, with Key to the Scriptures, to my own How to Live with a Neurotic or my collaborative effort with Dr. Robert A. Harper, A Guide to Rational Living (1961), who immediately thereafter significantly changed their unconstructive behavior toward others and themselves.

I am not saying, now, that having dangerous life experiences or reading inspirational books is likely to be the most effective or frequent means of personality reconstruction. Obviously not—or psychotherapists would quickly go out of business! But to claim, as Rogers does, that these non-relationship methods of personality change never work is to belie considerable evidence to the contrary.

Rogers secondly contends that for personality change to occur the patient must be in a state of incongruence, being vulnerable or anxious. Incongruence he later defines as "a discrepancy between the actual experience of the organism and the self picture of the individual insofar as it represents that experience." Here again, although he may well be correct in assuming that most people who undergo basic personality changes are in a state of incongruence before they reconstruct their behavior patterns, he fails to consider the exceptions to this general rule.

I have met several individuals who were far above the average in being congruent and basically unanxious and yet who, as I said above, improved their personalities significantly by life experiences or reading. I have also seen a few psychologists, psychiatrists, and social workers who were distinctly congruent individuals and who came to therapy largely for training purposes or because they had some practical problem with which they wanted help. Most of these patients were able to benefit considerably by their therapy and to make significant constructive personality changes—that is, to become more congruent and less anxious. I often feel, in fact, that such relatively congruent individuals tend to make the most constructive personality changes when they come to therapy—largely because they are best able to benefit from the therapist's placing before them alternative philosophies of life and modes of adjustment which they had simply never seriously considered before.

It should be remembered, in this connection, that there are often two main reasons why an individual comes to and stays in therapy: (a) he wants to be healed, and (b) he wants to grow. Once he has been healed—that is, induced to surrender most of his intense and crippling anxiety or hostility—he still can significantly grow as a human being—that is, reëvaluate and minimize some of his less intense and less crippling negative emotions, and learn to take greater risks, feel more spontaneously, love more adequately, etc. Frequently I find that group therapy, in particular, is an excellent medium for individuals who have largely been healed in a prior (individual and/or group) therapeutic process, but who still would like to know more about themselves in relation to others, and to grow experientially and esthetically. And I find that relatively healed individuals, who are what Carl Rogers would call congruent persons, can still grow and make basic personality changes in themselves in some form of therapy.

The third requisite for constructive personality change, says Rogers, is "that the therapist should be, within the confines of this relationship, a congruent, genuine integrated person. It means that within the relationship he is freely and deeply himself, with his actual experience accurately represented by his awareness of himself. It is the opposite of presenting a facade, either knowingly or unknowingly." Here, once again, I feel that Rogers is stating a highly desirable but hardly a necessary condition.

Like most therapists, I (rightly or wrongly!) consider myself a congruent, genuine, integrated person who, within my relationships with my patients, am freely and deeply myself. I therefore cannot be expected to quote a case of my own where, in spite of my own lack of congruence, my patient got better. I can say, however, that I have seen patients of other therapists whom I personally knew to be among the most emotionally disturbed and least congruent individuals I have ever met. And some of these patients—not all or most, alas, but some—were considerably helped by their relationship with their disturbed and incongruent therapists.

In saying this, let me hasten to add that I am definitely not one of those who believes that a therapist is most helpful to his patient when he, the therapist, is or has been a victim of severe disturbance himself, since then he is supposedly best able to empathize with and understand his patients. On the contrary, I believe that the therapist who is least disturbed is most likely to serve as the best model for, and be able to accept without hostility, his severely disturbed patients; and I am consequently in favor of discouraging highly incongruent therapists from practicing. I distinctly agree, therefore, with Rogers' contention that congruence on the part of the therapist is very desirable. That such congruence is in all cases necessary, however, I would dispute.

Rogers next lists as a necessary condition for personality change the therapist's experiencing unconditional positive regard for the patient—by which he means "a caring for the client, but not in a possessive way or in such a way as simply to satisfy the therapist's own needs." Here, with almost nauseating repetition, I must insist that Rogers has again turned a desideratum of therapy into a necessity.

I have recently been in close contact with several ex-patients of a small, and I think highly unsavory, group of therapists who do not have any real positive regard for their patients, but who deliberately try to regulate the lives and philosophies of these patients for the satisfaction of the therapists' own desires. In all cases but one, I would say that the ex-patients of this group whom I have seen were not benefited appreciably by therapy and were sometimes harmed. But in one instance I have had to admit that the patient was distinctly benefited and underwent significant constructive personality change—though not as much as I would have liked to see him undergo—as a result of this ineffective and in some ways pernicious form of therapy. I have also seen many other ex-patients of other therapists who, I am quite certain, were emotionally exploited by their therapists; and some of them, surprisingly enough, were considerably helped by this kind of an exploitative relationship.

The fifth condition for constructive personality change, says Rogers, "is that the therapist is experiencing an accurate, empathic understanding of the client's awareness of his own experience. To sense the client's private world as if it were your own, but without ever losing the 'as if' quality—this is empathy, and this seems essential to therapy." This contention I again must dispute, although I think it is perhaps the most plausible of Rogers' conditions.

That the therapist should normally <u>understand</u> his patient's world and see the patient's behavior from this patient's own frame of reference is highly desirable. That the therapist should literally <u>feel</u> his patient's disturbances or believe in his irrationalities is, in my opinion, usually harmful rather than helpful to this patient. Indeed, it is precisely the therapist's ability to comprehend the patient's immature behavior <u>without</u> getting involved in or believing in it that enables him to induce the patient to stop believing in or feeling that this behavior is necessary.

Even, however, when we strictly limit the term "empathy" to its dictionary definition—"apprehension of the state of mind of another person without feeling (as in sympathy) what the other feels" (English and English, 1958), it is still doubtful that this state is always a necessary condition for effective therapy. I have had, for example, many patients whose problems I have been able to view from their own frame of reference and whom I have shown exactly how and why they have been defeating themselves and what alternate modes of thinking and behaving they could employ to help themselves. Some of these patients have then dogmatically and arbitrarily indoctrinated their friends or relatives with the new philosophies of living I have helped them acquire, without their ever truly understanding or empathizing with the private world of these associates. Yet, somewhat to my surprise, they have occasionally helped their friends and relatives to achieve significant personality changes with this non-empathic, dogmatic technique of indoctrination.

Similarly, some of the greatest bigots of all time, such as Savonarola, Rasputin, and Adolf Hitler, who because of their own

severe emotional disturbances had a minimum of empathy with
their fellow men, frequently induced profound personality changes
in their adherents, and at least in a few of these instances the
changes that occurred were constructive. This does not contradict
the proposition that to empathize with another's private world usually helps him become less defensive and more congruent; but it
throws much doubt on the hypothesis that empathically-motivated
therapy is the only kind that is ever effective.

Rogers' final condition for constructive personality change is
"that the client perceives, to a minimal degree, the acceptance
and empathy which the therapist experiences for him." This proposition I have disproved several times in my own therapeutic practice. On these occasions, I have seen paranoid patients who,
whether or not I was properly empathizing with their own frames
of reference, persistently insisted that I was not. Yet, as I kept
showing them how their attitudes and actions, including their anger
at me, were illogical and self-defeating, they finally began to accept my frame of reference and to make significant constructive
personality changes in themselves. Then, after they had surren-
dered some of their false perceptions, they were able to see, in
most instances, that I might not have been as unempathic as they
previously thought I was.

In one instance, one of my paranoid patients kept insisting, to
the end of therapy, that I did not understand her viewpoints and was
quite wrong about my perceptions of her. She did admit, however,
that my attitudes and value systems made a lot of sense and that
she could see that she'd better adopt some of them if she was going
to help herself. She did adopt some of these attitudes and became
more understanding of other people and considerably less paranoid.
To this day, even though she is making a much better adjustment
to life, she still feels that I do not really understand her.

In the light of the foregoing considerations, it may perhaps be
legitimately hypothesized that very few individuals significantly
restructure their personalities when Rogers' six conditions are all
unmet; but it is most dubious that none do. Similarly, it is equally
dubious that no patients make fundamental constructive improve-
ments unless, as Freud (1924-1950) contends, they undergo and
resolve a transference neurosis during therapy; or, as Rank (1945)
insists, unless they first have a highly permissive and then a
strictly limited relationship with the therapist; or as Reich (1949)
claims, unless they loosen their character armor by having it
forcefully attacked by the therapist's psychological and physical

uncoverings; or as Reik (1948) notes, unless they are effectively listened to by the therapist's "third ear"; or, unless as Sullivan (1953) opines, they undergo an intensive analysis of the security operations they employ with the therapist and with significant others in their environment. All these suggested therapeutic techniques may be highly desirable; but where is the evidence that any of them is necessary?

Are there, then, any other conditions that are absolutely necessary for constructive personality change to take place? At first blush, I am tempted to say yes; but on second thought, I am forced to restrain myself and say no, or at least probably no.

My personal inclination, after working for the last several years with rational-emotive psychotherapy, is to say that yes, there is one absolutely necessary condition for real or basic personality change to occur—and that is that somehow, through some professional or non-professional channel, and through some kind of experience with himself, with others, or with things and events, the afflicted individual must learn to recognize his irrational, inconsistent, and unrealistic perceptions and thoughts, and change these for more logical, more reasonable philosophies of life. Without this kind of fundamental change in his ideologies and philosophic assumptions, I am tempted to say, no deep-seated personality changes will occur.

On further contemplation, I nobly refrain from making this claim, which would so well fit in with my own therapeutic theories, for one major and two minor reasons. The minor reasons are these:

1. Some people seem to make significant changes in their personalities without concomitantly acquiring notably new philosophies of living. It could be said, of course, that they really, unconsciously, do acquire such new philosophies. But this would be difficult to prove objectively.

2. Some individuals appear to change for the better when environmental conditions are modified, even though they retain their old childish views. Thus, a person who irrationally hates himself because he is poor may hate himself considerably less if he inherits a fortune. It could be said that the security he receives from inheriting this money really does make him change his childish, irrational views, and that therefore he has had a philosophic as well as a behavioral change. But again: there would be difficulty in objectively validating this contention. It could also be alleged that this individual really hasn't made a constructive personality change if he can now be secure only when he is rich. But how, ex-

cept by a rather tautological definition, could this allegation be proven?

Which brings me to the major and I think decisive reason for my not contending that for constructive personality change to oc-cur, the individual must somehow basically change his thinking or his value system. Granted that this statement may be true–and I am sure that many therapists would agree that it is–it is largely tautological. For all I am really saying when I make such a state-ment is that poor personality integration consists of an individual's having unrealistic, self-defeating ideological assumptions and that to change his personality integration for the better he must some-how surrender or change these assumptions.

Although descriptively meaningful, this statement boils down to the sentence: in order to change his personality the individual must change his personality. Or: in order to get better he must get better. This proves very little about the "necessary" conditions for personality change.

Again: rational psychotherapy significantly differs from vir-tually all other theories and techniques in that, according to its precepts, it is desirable not merely for the therapist to uncover, understand, and accept the patient's illogical and unrealistic as-sumptions which cause him to remain immature and ineffective, but it is usually also required that he forthrightly and unequivocally attack and invalidate these assumptions. Is this desideratum of psychotherapy necessary?

Most probably not: since some patients and non-patients (al-though relatively few, I believe) seem to have significantly im-proved in spite of their not having the benefit of a competent ra-tional therapist to help them understand how they acquired, how they are currently sustaining, and how they can and should forth-rightly attack and annihilate their basic irrational attitudes and assumptions.

The conclusion seems inescapable, therefore, that although basic constructive personality change–as opposed to temporary symptom removal–seems to require fundamental modifications in the ideologies and value systems of the disturbed individual, there is probably no single condition which is absolutely necessary for the inducement of such changed attitudes and behavior patterns.

Many conditions, such as those listed by Freud, Rank, Reich, Reik, Rogers, Sullivan, and other outstanding theorists, or such as are listed in this book, are highly desirable; but all that seems to be necessary is that the individual somehow come up against significant life experiences, or learn about others' experiences, or sit down and think for himself, or enter a relationship with a therapist who is preferably congruent, accepting, empathic, rational, forceful, etc. Either/or, rather than this-and-that, seems to be the only realistic description of necessary conditions for basic personality change that can be made at the present time.

The basic contention of this book [Reason and Emotion in Psychotherapy], then, is not that RT is the only effective method of therapy. It is, rather, that of all the scores of methods that are variously advocated and employed, RT is probably one of the most effective techniques that has yet been invented. Certainly, in my twenty years as a counselor and psychotherapist, it is far and away the best method that I have found; and an increasing number of my professional colleagues are finding it unusually efficient in their own practices. Even when it is only partially employed, along with other basic therapeutic methods, it often produces fine results. And when it is consistently and thoroughly used, the results seem to be still better.

REFERENCES

Ellis, A. How to live with a neurotic. New York: Crown, 1957.

Ellis, A. Neurotic interaction between marital partners. J. counsel. Psychol., 1958, 5:24-28.

Ellis, A., & Harper, R. A. A guide to rational living. Englewood Cliffs, N. J.: Prentice-Hall, 1961.

English, H. B., & English, Ava C. A comprehensive dictionary of psychological and psychoanalytical terms. New York: David McKay, 1958.

Freud, S. Collected papers. London: Hogarth, 1924-1950.

Rank, O. Will therapy and truth and reality. New York: Knopf, 1945.

Reich, W. Character analysis. New York: Orgone Institute Press, 1949.

Reik, T. Listening with the third ear. New York: Rinehart, 1948.

Rogers, C. R. Client-centered therapy. Boston: Houghton Mifflin, 1951.

Sullivan, H. S. The interpersonal theory of psychiatry. New York: Norton, 1953.

XI

SOME BASIC PROPOSITIONS OF A GROWTH
AND SELF-ACTUALIZATION PSYCHOLOGY

Abraham H. Maslow

When the philosophy of man (his nature, his goals, his potentialities, his fulfillment) changes, then everything changes, not
only the philosophy of politics, of economics, of ethics and values,
of interpersonal relations and of history itself, but also the philosophy of education, the theory of how to help men become what they
can and deeply need to become.

We are now in the middle of such a change in the conception of
man's capacities, potentialities and goals. A new vision is emerging of the possibilities of man and of his destiny, and its implications are many, not only for our conceptions of education, but also
for science, politics, literature, economics, religion, and even
our conceptions of the non-human world.

I think it is now possible to begin to delineate this view of human nature as a total, single, comprehensive system of psychology
even though much of it has arisen as a reaction against the limitations (as philosophies of human nature) of the two most comprehensive psychologies now available—behaviorism (or associationism)
and classical, Freudian psychoanalysis. Finding a single label for
it is still a difficult task, perhaps a premature one. In the past I
have called it the "holistic-dynamic" psychology to express my
conviction about its major roots. Some have called it "organismic"
following Goldstein. Sutich and others are calling it the Self-psy-
chology or Humanistic psychology. We shall see. My own guess

Reprinted by permission of the author and publisher from Abraham H. Maslow.
Toward a Psychology of Being. Princeton, N.J.: Van Nostrand, 1962.

is that, in a few decades, if it remains suitably eclectic and comprehensive, it will be called simply "psychology."

I think I can be of most service by speaking primarily for myself and out of my own work rather than as an "official" delegate of this large group of thinkers, even though I am sure that the areas of agreement among them are very large. A selection of works of this "third force" is listed in the bibliography. Because of the limited space I have, I will present here only some of the major propositions of this point of view, especially those of importance to the educator. I should warn you that at many points I am way out ahead of the data. Some of these propositions are more based on private conviction than on publicly demonstrated facts. However they are all in principle confirmable or disconfirmable.

1. We have, each one of us, an essential inner nature which is instinctoid, intrinsic, given, "natural," i.e., with an appreciable hereditary determinant, and which tends strongly to persist (Maslow, 1954, Chapter 7).

It makes sense to speak here of the hereditary, constitutional and very early acquired roots of the individual self, even though this biological determination of self is only partial, and far too complex to describe simply. In any case, this is "raw material" rather than finished product, to be reacted to by the person, by his significant others, by his environment, etc.

I include in this essential inner nature instinctoid basic needs, capacities, talents, anatomical equipment, physiological or temperamental balances, prenatal and natal injuries, and traumata to the neonate. This inner core shows itself as natural inclinations, propensities or inner bent. Whether defense and coping mechanisms, "style of life," and other characterological traits, all shaped in the first few years of life, should be included is still a matter for discussion. This raw material very quickly starts growing into a self as it meets the world outside and begins to have transaction with it.

2. These are potentialities, not final actualizations. Therefore they have a life history and must be seen developmentally. They are actualized, shaped or stifled mostly (but not altogether) by extra-psychic determinants (culture, family, environment, learning, etc.). Very early in life these goalless urges and tendencies become attached to objects ("sentiments") by canalization (Murphy, 1947) but also by arbitrarily learned associations.

3. This inner core, even though it is biologically based and "instinctoid," is weak in certain senses rather than strong. It is easily overcome, suppressed or repressed. It may even be killed

off permanently. Humans no longer have instincts in the animal sense, powerful, unmistakable inner voices which tell them un-equivocally what to do, when, where, how and with whom. All that we have left are instinct-remnants. And furthermore, these are weak, subtle and delicate, very easily drowned out by learning, by cultural expectations, by fear, by disapproval, etc. They are hard to know, rather than easy. Authentic selfhood can be defined in part as being able to hear these impulse-voices within oneself, i.e., to know what one really wants or doesn't want, what one is fit for and what one is not fit for, etc. It appears that there are wide individual differences in the strength of these impulse-voices.

4. Each person's inner nature has some characteristics which all other selves have (species-wide) and some which are unique to the person (idiosyncratic). The need for love characterizes every human being that is born (although it can disappear later under certain circumstances). Musical genius however is given to very few, and these differ markedly from each other in style, e.g., Mozart and Debussy.

5. It is possible to study this inner nature scientifically and objectively (that is, with the right kind of "science") and to discover what it is like (discover—not invent or construct). It is also possi-ble to do this subjectively, by inner search and by psychotherapy, and the two enterprises supplement and support each other.

6. Many aspects of this inner, deeper nature are either (a) actively repressed, as Freud has described, because they are feared or disapproved of or are ego-alien, or (b) "forgotten" (neg-lected, unused, overlooked, unverbalized or suppressed), as Schachtel has described. Much of the inner, deeper nature is therefore unconscious. This can be true not only for impulses (drives, instincts, needs) as Freud has stressed, but also for ca-pacities, emotions, judgments, attitudes, definitions, perceptions, etc. Active repression takes effort and uses up energy. There are many specific techniques of maintaining active unconsciousness, such as denial, projection, reaction-formation, etc. However, re-pression does not kill what is repressed. The repressed remains as one active determinant of thought and behavior.

Both active and passive repressions seem to begin early in life, mostly as a response to parental and cultural disapprovals.

However, there is some clinical evidence that repression may arise also from intra-psychic, extra-cultural sources in the young child, or at puberty, i.e., out of fear of being overwhelmed by its own impulses, of becoming disintegrated, of "falling apart," ex-ploding, etc. It is theoretically possible that the child may spontaneously form attitudes of fear and disapproval toward its own impulses and may then defend himself against them in various ways. Society need not be the only repressing force, if this is true. There may also be intra-psychic repressing and controlling forces. These we may call "intrinsic counter-cathexes."

It is best to distinguish unconscious drives and needs from unconscious ways of cognizing because the latter are often easier to bring to consciousness and therefore to modify. Primary process cognition (Freud) or archaic thinking (Jung) is more recoverable by, e.g., creative art education, dance education, and other nonverbal educational techniques.

7. Even though "weak," this inner nature rarely disappears or dies, in the usual person, in the U.S. (such disappearance or dying is possible early in the life history, however). It persists underground, unconsciously, even though denied and repressed. Like the voice of the intellect (which is part of it), it speaks softly but it will be heard, even if in a distorted form. That is, it has a dynamic force of its own, pressing always for open, uninhibited expression. Effort must be used in its suppression or repression from which fatigue can result. This force is one main aspect of the "will to health," the urge to grow, the pressure to self-actualization, the quest for one's identity. It is this that makes psychotherapy, education and self-improvement possible in principle.

8. However, this inner core, or self, grows into adulthood only partly by (objective or subjective) discovery, uncovering and acceptance of what is "there" beforehand. Partly it is also a creation of the person himself. Life is a continual series of choices for the individual in which a main determinant of choice is the person as he already is (including his goals for himself, his courage or fear, his feeling of responsibility, his ego-strength or "will power," etc.). We can no longer think of the person as "fully determined" where this phrase implies "determined only by forces external to the person." The person, insofar as he is a real person, is his own main determinant. Every person is, in part, "his own project" and makes himself.

9. If this essential core (inner nature) of the person is frustrated, denied or suppressed, sickness results, sometimes in obvious forms, sometimes in subtle and devious forms, sometimes immediately, sometimes later. These psychological illnesses include many more than those listed by the American Psychiatric Association. For instance, the character disorders and disturbances are now seen as far more important for the fate of the world than the classical neuroses or even the psychoses. From this new

point of view, new kinds of illness are most dangerous, e.g., "the diminished or stunted person," i.e., the loss of any of the defining characteristics of humanness, or personhood, the failure to grow to one's potential, valuelessness, etc.

That is, general-illness of the personality is seen as any falling short of growth, or of self-actualization, or of full-humanness. And the main source of illness (although not the only one) is seen as frustrations (of the basic needs, of the B-values, [1] of idiosyncratic potentials, of expression of the self, and of the tendency of the person to grow in his own style and at his own pace) especially in the early years of life. That is, frustration of the basic needs is not the only source of illness or of human diminution.

10. This inner nature, as much as we know of it so far, is definitely not "evil," but is either what we adults in our culture call "good," or else it is neutral. The most accurate way to express this is to say that it is "prior to good and evil." There is little question about this if we speak of the inner nature of the infant and child. The statement is much more complex if we speak of the "infant" as he still exists in the adult. And it gets still more complex if the individual is seen from the point of view of B-psychology rather than D-psychology.

This conclusion is supported by all the truth-revealing and uncovering techniques that have anything to do with human nature: psychotherapy, objective science, subjective science, education and art. For instance, in the long run, uncovering therapy lessens hostility, fear, greed, etc., and increases love, courage, creativeness, kindness, altruism, etc., leading us to the conclusion that the latter are "deeper," more natural, and more basic than the former, i.e., that what we call "bad" behavior is lessened or removed by uncovering, while what we call "good" behavior is strengthened and fostered by uncovering.

11. We must differentiate the Freudian type of superego from intrinsic conscience and intrinsic guilt. The former is in principle a taking into the self of the disapprovals and approvals of persons other than the person himself, fathers, mothers, teachers, etc. Guilt then is recognition of disapproval by others.

Intrinsic guilt is the consequence of betrayal of one's own inner nature or self, a turning off the path to self-actualization, and is essentially justified self-disapproval. It is therefore not as culturally relative as is Freudian guilt. It is "true" or "deserved" or

[1]Editor's note: "B—values" = *Being* values, as contrasted with "D—values" = *Deficiency* values. The contrasts between Being and Deficiency are discussed more fully later in this article.

"right and just" or "correct" because it is a discrepancy from
something profoundly real within the person rather than from acci-
dental, arbitrary or purely relative localisms. Seen in this way it
is good, even <u>necessary</u>, for a person's development to have intrinsic guilt when he deserves to. It is not just a symptom to be avoided
at any cost but is rather an inner guide for growth toward actualization of the real self, and of its potentialities.

12. "Evil" behavior has mostly referred to unwarranted hostility, cruelty, destructiveness, "mean" aggressiveness. This we
do not know enough about. To the degree that this quality of hostility is instinctoid, mankind has one kind of future. To the degree
that it is reactive (a response to bad treatment), mankind has a very
different kind of future. My opinion is that the weight of the evidence so far indicates that indiscriminately destructive hostility is
reactive, because uncovering therapy reduces it, and changes its
quality into "healthy" self-affirmation, forcefulness, selective hostility, self-defense, righteous indignation, etc. In any case, the
<u>ability</u> to be aggressive and angry is found in all self-actualizing
people, who are able to let it flow forth freely when the external
situation "calls for" it.

The situation in children is far more complex. At the very
least, we know that the healthy child is also able to be justifiably
angry, self-protecting and self-affirming, i.e., reactive aggression. Presumably, then, a child should learn not only how to control his anger, but also how and when to express it.

Behavior that our culture calls evil can also come from ignorance and from childish misinterpretations and beliefs (whether in
the child or in the repressed or "forgotten" child-in-the-adult). For
instance, sibling rivalry is traceable to the child's wish for the exclusive love of his parents. Only as he matures is he in principle
capable of learning that his mother's love for a sibling is compatible
with her continued love for him. Thus out of a childish version of
love, not in itself reprehensible, can come unloving behavior.

The commonly seen hatred or resentment of or jealousy of
goodness, truth, beauty, health or intelligence, ("counter-values")
is largely (though not altogether) determined by threat of loss of
self-esteem, as the liar is threatened by the honest man, the
homely girl by the beautiful girl, or the coward by the hero. Every
superior person confronts us with our own shortcomings.

Still deeper than this, however, is the ultimate existential
question of the fairness and justice of fate. The person with a disease may be jealous of the healthy man who is no more deserving
than he.

Evil behaviors seem to most psychologists to be reactive as in these examples, rather than instinctive. This implies that though "bad" behavior is very deeply rooted in human nature and can never be abolished altogether, it may yet be expected to lessen as the personality matures and as the society improves.

13. Many people still think of "the unconscious," of regression, and of primary process cognition as necessarily unhealthy, or dangerous or bad. Psychotherapeutic experience is slowly teaching us otherwise. Our depths can also be good, or beautiful or desirable. This is also becoming clear from the general findings from investigations of the sources of love, creativeness, play, humor, art, etc. Their roots are deep in the inner, deeper self, i.e., in the unconscious. To recover them and to be able to enjoy and use them we must be able to "regress."

14. No psychological health is possible unless this essential core of the person is fundamentally accepted, loved and respected by others and by himself (the converse is not necessarily true, i.e., that if the core is respected, etc., then psychological health must result, since other prerequisite conditions must also be satisfied).

The psychological health of the chronologically immature is called healthy growth. The psychological health of the adult is called variously, self-fulfillment, emotional maturity, individuation, productiveness, self-actualization, authenticity, full-humanness, etc.

Healthy growth is conceptually subordinate, for it is usually defined now as "growth toward self-actualization," etc. Some psychologists speak simply in terms of one overarching goal or end, or tendency of human development, considering all immature growth phenomena to be only steps along the path to self-actualization (Goldstein, Rogers).

Self-actualization is defined in various ways but a solid core of agreement is perceptible. All definitions accept or imply, (a) acceptance and expression of the inner core or self, i.e., actualization of these latent capacities, and potentialities, "full functioning," availability of the human and personal essence. (b) They all imply minimal presence of ill health, neurosis, psychosis, of loss or diminution of the basic human and personal capacities.

15. For all these reasons, it is at this time best to bring out and encourage, or at the very least, to recognize this inner nature, rather than to suppress or repress it. Pure spontaneity consists of free, uninhibited, uncontrolled, trusting, unpremeditated expression of the self, i.e., of the psychic forces, with minimal interference by consciousness. Control, will, caution, self-criticism,

measure, deliberateness are the brakes upon this expression made intrinsically necessary by the laws of the social and natural worlds outside the psychic world, and secondarily, made necessary by fear of the psyche itself (intrinsic counter-cathexis). Speaking in a very broad way, controls upon the psyche which come from fear of the psyche are largely neurotic or psychotic, or not intrinsically or theoretically necessary. (The healthy psyche is not terrible or horrible and therefore doesn't have to be feared, as it has been for thousands of years. Of course, the unhealthy psyche is another story.) This kind of control is usually lessened by psychological health, by deep psychotherapy, or by any deeper self-knowledge and self-acceptance. There are also, however, controls upon the psyche which do not come out of fear, but out of the necessities for keeping it integrated, organized and unified (intrinsic counter-cathexes). And there are also "controls," probably in another sense, which are necessary as capacities are actualized, and as higher forms of expression are sought for, e.g., acquisition of skills through hard work by the artist, the intellectual, the athlete. But these controls are eventually transcended and become aspects of spontaneity, as they become self.

The balance between spontaneity and control varies, then, as the health of the psyche and the health of the world vary. Pure spontaneity is not long possible because we live in a world which runs by its own, non-psychic laws. It is possible in dreams, fantasies, love, imagination, sex, the first stages of creativity, artistic work, intellectual play, free association, etc. Pure control is not permanently possible, for then the psyche dies. Education must be directed then both toward cultivation of controls and cultivation of spontaneity and expression. In our culture and at this point in history, it is necessary to redress the balance in favor of spontaneity, the ability to be expressive, passive, unwilled, trusting in processes other than will and control, unpremeditated, creative, etc. But it must be recognized that there have been and will be other cultures and other areas in which the balance was or will be in the other direction.

16. In the normal development of the normal child, it is now known that, most of the time, if he is given a really free choice, he will choose what is good for his growth. This he does because it tastes good, feels good, gives pleasure or delight. This implies that he "knows" better than anyone else what is good for him. A permissive regime means not that adults gratify his needs directly but make it possible for him to gratify his needs, and make his own choices, i.e., let him be. It is necessary in order for children to

grow well that adults have enough trust in them and in the natural processes of growth, i.e., not interfere too much, not make them grow, or force them into predetermined designs, but rather let them grow and help them grow in a Taoistic rather than an authoritarian way.

17. Coordinate with this "acceptance" of the self, of fate, of one's call, is the conclusion that the main path to health and self-fulfillment for the masses is via basic need gratification rather than via frustration. This contrasts with the suppressive regime, the mistrust, the control, the policing that is necessarily implied by the belief in basic, instinctive evil in the human depths. Intrauterine life is completely gratifying and non-frustrating and it is now generally accepted that the first year or so of life had better also be primarily gratifying and non-frustrating. Asceticism, self-denial, deliberate rejection of the demands of the organism, at least in the West, tend to produce a diminished, stunted or crippled organism, and even in the East, bring self-actualization to only a very few, exceptionally strong individuals.

18. But we know also that the complete absence of frustration is dangerous. To be strong, a person must acquire frustration-tolerance, the ability to perceive physical reality as essentially indifferent to human wishes, the ability to love others and to enjoy their need-gratification as well as one's own (not to use other people only as means). The child with a good basis of safety, love and respect-need-gratification, is able to profit from nicely graded frustrations and become stronger thereby. If they are more than he can bear, if they overwhelm him, we call them traumatic, and consider them dangerous rather than profitable.

It is via the frustrating unyieldingness of physical reality and of animals and of other people that we learn about their nature, and thereby learn to differentiate wishes from facts (which things wishing makes come true, and which things proceed in complete disregard of our wishes), and are thereby enabled to live in the world and adapt to it as necessary.

We learn also about our own strengths and limits and extend them by overcoming difficulties, by straining ourselves to the utmost, by meeting challenge and hardship, even by failing. There can be great enjoyment in a great struggle and this can displace fear.

Overprotection implies that the child's needs are gratified for him by his parents, without effort of his own. This tends to infantilize him, to prevent development of his own strength, will and self-assertion. In one of its forms it may teach him to use other people rather than to respect them. In another form it implies a lack of trust and respect for the child's own powers and choices, i.e., it is essentially condescending and insulting, and can help to make a child feel worthless.

19. To make growth and self-actualization possible, it is necessary to understand that capacities, organs and organ systems press to function and express themselves and to be used and exercised, and that such use is satisfying, and disuse irritating. The muscular person likes to use his muscles, indeed, has to use them in order to "feel good" and to achieve the subjective feeling of harmonious, successful, uninhibited functioning (spontaneity) which is so important an aspect of good growth and psychological health. So also for intelligence, for the uterus, the eyes, the capacity to love. Capacities clamor to be used, and cease their clamor only when they are well used. That is, capacities are also needs. Not only is it fun to use our capacities, but it is also necessary for growth. The unused skill or capacity or organ can become a disease center or else atrophy or disappear, thus diminishing the person.

20. The psychologist proceeds on the assumption that for his purposes there are two kinds of worlds, two kinds of reality, the natural world and the psychic world, the world of unyielding facts and the world of wishes, hopes, fears, emotions, the world which runs by non-psychic rules and the world which runs by psychic laws. This differentiation is not very clear except at its extremes, where there is no doubt that delusions, dreams and free associations are lawful and yet utterly different from the lawfulness of logic and from the lawfulness of the world which would remain if the human species died out. This assumption does not deny that these worlds are related and may even fuse.

I may say that this assumption is acted upon by many or most psychologists, even though they are perfectly willing to admit that it is an insoluble philosophical problem. Any therapist must assume it or give up his functioning. This is typical of the way in which psychologists bypass philosophical difficulties and act "as if" certain assumptions were true even though unprovable, e.g., the universal assumption of "responsibility," "will power," etc. One aspect of health is the ability to live in both of these worlds.

21. Immaturity can be contrasted with maturity from the motivational point of view, as the process of gratifying the deficiency-needs in their proper order. Maturity, or self-actualization, from this point of view, means to transcend the deficiency-needs. This state can be described then as metamotivated, or unmotivated (if deficiencies are seen as the only motivations). It can also be de-

scribed as self-actualizing, Being, expressing, rather than coping. This state of Being, rather than of striving, is suspected to be synonymous with selfhood, with being "authentic," with being a person, with being fully human. The process of growth is the process of becoming a person. Being a person is different.

22. Immaturity can also be differentiated from maturity in terms of the cognitive capacities (and also in terms of the emotional capacities). Immature and mature cognition have been best described by Werner and Piaget. We can now add another differentiation, that between D-cognition and B-cognition (D = Deficiency, B = Being). D-cognition can be defined as the cognitions which are organized from the point of view of basic needs or deficiency-needs and their gratification and frustration. That is, D-cognition could be called selfish cognition, in which the world is organized into gratifiers and frustrators of our own needs, with other characteristics being ignored or slurred. The cognition of the object, in its own right and its own Being, without reference to its need-gratifying or need-frustrating qualities, that is, without primary reference to its value for the observer or its effects upon him, can be called B-cognition (or self-transcending, or unselfish, or objective cognition). The parallel with maturity is by no means perfect (children can also cognize in a selfless way), but in general, it is mostly true that with increasing selfhood or firmness of personal identity (or acceptance of one's own inner nature) B-cognition becomes easier and more frequent. (This is true even though D-cognition remains for all human beings, including the mature ones, the main tool for living-in-the-world.)

To the extent that perception is desire-less and fearless, to that extent is it more veridical, in the sense of perceiving the true, or essential or intrinsic whole nature of the object (without splitting it up by abstraction). Thus the goal of objective and true description of any reality is fostered by psychological health. Neurosis, psychosis, stunting of growth—all are, from this point of view, cognitive diseases as well, contaminating perception, learning, remembering, attending and thinking.

23. A by-product of this aspect of cognition is a better understanding of the higher and lower levels of love. D-love can be differentiated from B-love on approximately the same basis as D-cognition and B-cognition, or D-motivation and B-motivation. No ideally good relation to another human being, especially a child, is possible without B-love. Especially is it necessary for teaching, along with the Taoistic, trusting attitude that it implies. This is also true for our relations with the natural world, i.e., we can

treat it in its own right, or we can treat it as if it were there only for our purposes.

24. Though, in principle, self-actualization is easy, in practice it rarely happens (by my criteria, certainly in less than 1% of the adult population). For this, there are many, many reasons at various levels of discourse, including all the determinants of psychopathology that we now know. We have already mentioned one main cultural reason, i.e., the conviction that man's intrinsic nature is evil or dangerous, and one biological determinant for the difficulty of achieving a mature self, namely that humans no longer have strong instincts which tell them unequivocally what to do, when, where and how.

There is a subtle but extremely important difference between regarding psychopathology as blocking or evasion or fear of growth toward self-actualization, and thinking of it in a medical fashion, as akin to invasion from without by tumors, poisons or bacteria, which have no relationship to the personality being invaded. Human diminution (the loss of human potentialities and capacities) is a more useful concept than "illness" for our theoretical purposes.

25. Growth has not only rewards and pleasures but also many intrinsic pains and always will have. Each step forward is a step into the unfamiliar and is possibly dangerous. It also means giving up something familiar and good and satisfying. It frequently means a parting and a separation, even a kind of death prior to rebirth, with consequent nostalgia, fear, loneliness and mourning. It also often means giving up a simpler and easier and less effortful life, in exchange for a more demanding, more responsible, more difficult life. Growth forward is in spite of these losses and therefore requires courage, will, choice, and strength in the individual, as well as protection, permission and encouragement from the environment, especially for the child.

26. It is therefore useful to think of growth or lack of it as the resultant of a dialectic between growth-fostering forces and growth-discouraging forces (regression, fear, pains of growth, ignorance, etc.). Growth has both advantages and disadvantages. Non-growing has not only disadvantages, but also advantages. The future pulls, but so also does the past. There is not only courage but also fear. The total ideal way of growing healthily is, in principle, to enhance all the advantages of forward growth and all the disadvantages of not-growing, and to diminish all the disadvantages of growth forward and all the advantages of not-growing.

Homeostatic tendencies, "need-reduction" tendencies, and Freudian defense mechanisms are not growth-tendencies but are

often defensive, pain-reducing postures of the organism. But they
are quite necessary and not always pathological. They are generally prepotent over growth-tendencies.

27. All this implies a naturalistic system of values, a by-
product of the empirical description of the deepest tendencies of
the human species and of specific individuals. The study of the
human being by science or by self-search can discover where he is
heading, what is his purpose in life, what is good for him and what
is bad for him, what will make him feel virtuous and what will make
him feel guilty, why choosing the good is often difficult for him,
what the attractions of evil are. (Observe that the word "ought"
need not be used. Also such knowledge of man is relative to man
only and does not purport to be "absolute.")

28. A neurosis is not part of the inner core but rather a defense against or an evasion of it, as well as a distorted expression
of it (under the aegis of fear). It is ordinarily a compromise between the effort to seek basic need gratifications in a covert or disguised or self-defeating way, and the fear of these needs, gratifications and motivated behaviors. To express neurotic needs, emotions, attitudes, definitions, actions, etc., means not to express
the inner core or real self fully. If the sadist or exploiter or per-
vert says, "Why shouldn't I express myself?" (e.g., by killing),
or, "Why shouldn't I actualize myself?" the answer to them is that
such expression is a denial of, and not an expression of, instinctoid
tendencies (or inner core).

Each neuroticized need, or emotion or action is a loss of capacity to the person, something that he cannot do or dare not do except in a sneaky and unsatisfying way. In addition, he has usually
lost his subjective well-being, his will, and his feeling of self-control, his capacity for pleasure, his self-esteem, etc. He is diminished as a human being.

29. The state of being without a system of values is psycho-
pathogenic, we are learning. The human being needs a framework
of values, a philosophy of life, a religion or religion-surrogate to
live by and understand by, in about the same sense that he needs
sunlight, calcium or love. This I have called the "cognitive need
to understand." The value-illnesses which result from valuelessness are called variously anhedonia, anomie, apathy, amorality,
hopelessness, cynicism, etc., and can become somatic illness as
well. Historically, we are in a value interregnum in which all externally given value systems have proven to be failures (political,
economic, religious, etc.) e.g., nothing is worth dying for. What
man needs but doesn't have, he seeks for unceasingly, and he be-

comes dangerously ready to jump at any hope, good or bad. The cure for this disease is obvious. We need a validated, usable system of human values that we can believe in and devote ourselves to (be willing to die for), because they are true rather than because we are exhorted to "believe and have faith." Such an empirically based Weltanschauung seems now to be a real possibility, at least in theoretical outline.

Much disturbance in children and adolescents can be understood as a consequence of the uncertainty of adults about their values. As a consequence, many youngsters in the United States live not by adult values but by adolescent values, which of course are immature, ignorant and heavily determined by confused adolescent needs. An excellent projection of these adolescent values is the cowboy, "Western" movie, or the delinquent gang.

30. At the level of self-actualizing, many dichotomies become resolved, opposites are seen to be unities and the whole dichotomous way of thinking is recognized to be immature. For self-actualizing people, there is a strong tendency for selfishness and unselfishness to fuse into a higher, superordinate unity. Work tends to be the same as play; vocation and avocation become the same thing. When duty is pleasant and pleasure is fulfillment of duty, then they lose their separateness and oppositeness. The highest maturity is discovered to include a childlike quality, and we discover healthy children to have some of the qualities of mature self-actualization. The inner-outer split, between self and all else, gets fuzzy and much less sharp, and they are seen to be permeable to each other at the highest levels of personality development. Dichotomizing seems now to be characteristic of a lower level of personality development and of psychological functioning; it is both a cause and an effect of psychopathology.

31. One especially important finding in self-actualizing people is that they tend to integrate the Freudian dichotomies and trichotomies, i.e., the conscious, preconscious and the unconscious, (as well as id, ego, superego). The Freudian "instincts" and the defenses are less sharply set off against each other. The impulses are more expressed and less controlled; the controls are less rigid, inflexible, anxiety-determined. The superego is less harsh and punishing and less set off against the ego. The primary and secondary cognitive processes are more equally available and more equally valued (instead of the primary processes being stigmitized as pathological). Indeed, in the "peak-experience" the walls between them tend to fall together.

This is in sharp contrast with the early Freudian position in which these various forces were sharply dichotomized as (a) mutually exclusive, (b) with antagonistic interests, i.e., as antagonistic forces rather than as complementary or collaborating ones, and (c) one "better" than the other.

Again we imply here (sometimes) a healthy unconscious, and desirable regression. Furthermore, we imply also an integration of rationality and irrationality with the consequence that irrationality may, in its place, also be considered healthy, desirable or even necessary.

32. Healthy people are more integrated in another way. In them the conative, the cognitive, the affective and the motor are less separated from each other, and are more synergic, i.e, working collaboratively without conflict to the same ends. The conclusions of rational, careful thinking are apt to come to the same conclusions as those of the blind appetites. What such a person wants and enjoys is apt to be just what is good for him. His spontaneous reactions are as capable, efficient and right as if they had been thought out in advance. His sensory and motor reactions are more closely correlated. His sensory modalities are more connected with each other (physiognomical perception). Furthermore, we have learned the difficulties and dangers of those age-old rationalistic systems in which the capacities were thought to be arranged dichotomously-hierarchically, with rationality at the top, rather than in an integration.

33. This development toward the concept of a healthy unconscious, and of a healthy irrationality, sharpens our awareness of the limitations of purely abstract thinking, of verbal thinking and of analytic thinking. If our hope is to describe the world fully, a place is necessary for preverbal, ineffable, metaphorical, primary process, concrete-experience, intuitive and esthetic types of cognition, for there are certain aspects of reality which can be cognized in no other way. Even in science this is true, now that we know (1) that creativity has its roots in the nonrational, (2) that language is and must always be inadequate to describe total reality, (3) that any abstract concept leaves out much of reality, and (4) that what we call "knowledge" (which is usually highly abstract and verbal and sharply defined) often serves to blind us to those portions of reality not covered by the abstraction. That is, it makes us more able to see some things, but less able to see other things. Abstract knowledge has its dangers as well as its uses.

Science and education, being too exclusively abstract, verbal and bookish, don't have enough place for raw, concrete, esthetic experience, especially of the subjective happenings inside oneself.

For instance, organismic psychologists would certainly agree on the desirability of more creative education in perceiving and creating art, in dancing, in (Greek style) athletics and in phenomenological observation.

The ultimate of abstract, analytical thinking, is the greatest simplification possible, i.e., the formula, the diagram, the map, the blueprint, the schema, the cartoon, and certain types of abstract paintings. Our mastery of the world is enhanced thereby, but its richness may be lost as a forfeit, <u>unless</u> we learn to value B-cognitions, perception-with-love-and-care, free-floating attention, all of which enrich the experience instead of impoverishing it. There is no reason why "science" should not be expanded to include both kinds of knowing.

34. This ability of healthier people to dip into the unconscious and preconscious, to use and value their primary processes instead of fearing them, to accept their impulses instead of always controlling them, to be able to regress voluntarily without fear, turns out to be one of the main conditions of creativity. We can then understand why psychological health is so closely tied up with certain universal forms of creativeness (aside from special-talent), as to lead some writers to make them almost synonymous.

This same tie between health and integration of rational and irrational forces (conscious and unconscious, primary and secondary processes) also permits us to understand why psychologically healthy people are more able to enjoy, to love, to laugh, to have fun, to be humorous, to be silly, to be whimsical and fantastic, to be pleasantly "crazy," and in general to permit and value and enjoy emotional experiences in general and peak experiences in particular and to have them more often. And it leads us to the strong suspicion that learning <u>ad hoc</u> to be able to do all these things may help the child move toward health.

35. Esthetic perceiving and creating and esthetic peak-experiences are seen to be a central aspect of human life and of psychology and education rather than a peripheral one. This is true for several reasons. (1) All the peak-experiences are (among other characteristics) integrative of the splits within the person, between persons, within the world, and between the person and the world. Since one aspect of health is integration, the peak-experiences are moves toward health and are themselves, momentary healths. (2) These experiences are life-validating, i.e., they make life worth while. These are certainly an important part of the answer to the question, "Why don't we all commit suicide?" (3) They are worth while in themselves, etc.

36. Self-actualization does not mean a transcendence of all human problems. Conflict, anxiety, frustration, sadness, hurt and guilt can all be found in healthy human beings. In general, the movement, with increasing maturity, is from neurotic pseudo-problems to the real, unavoidable, existential problems, inherent in the nature of man (even at his best) living in a particular kind of world. Even though he is not neurotic he may be troubled by real, desirable and necessary guilt rather than neurotic guilt (which isn't desirable or necessary), by an intrinsic conscience (rather than the Freudian superego). Even though he has transcended the problems of Becoming, there remain the problems of Being. To be untroubled when one should be troubled can be a sign of sickness. Sometimes, smug people have to be scared "into their wits."

37. Self-actualization is not altogether general. It takes place via femaleness or maleness, which are prepotent to general-humanness. That is, one must first be a healthy, femaleness-fulfilled woman or maleness-fulfilled man before general-human self-actualization becomes possible.

There is also a little evidence that different constitutional types actualize themselves in somewhat different ways (because they have different inner selves to actualize).

38. Another crucial aspect of healthy growth of selfhood and full-humanness is dropping away the techniques used by the child, in his weakness and smallness for adapting himself to the strong, large, all-powerful, omniscient, godlike adults. He must replace these with the techniques of being strong and independent and of being a parent himself. This involves especially giving up the child's desperate wish for the exclusive, total love of his parents while learning to love others. He must learn to gratify his own needs and wishes, rather than the needs of his parents, and he must learn to gratify them himself, rather than depending upon the parents to do this for him. He must give up being good out of fear and in order to keep their love, and must be good because he wishes to be. He must discover his own conscience and give up his internalized parents as a sole ethical guide. All these techniques by which weakness adapts itself to strength are necessary for the child but immature and stunting in the adult (Maslow, Rand and Newman, 1960). He must replace fear with courage.

39. From this point of view, a society or a culture can be either growth-fostering or growth-inhibiting. The sources of growth and of humanness are essentially within the human person and are not created or invented by society, which can only help or hinder the development of humanness, just as a gardener can help

or hinder the growth of a rosebush, but cannot determine that it shall be an oak tree. This is true even though we know that a culture is a sine qua non for the actualization of humanness itself, e.g., language, abstract thought, ability to love; but these exist as potentialities in human germ plasm prior to culture.

This makes theoretically possible a comparative sociology, transcending and including cultural relativity. The "better" culture gratifies all basic human needs and permits self-actualization. The "poorer" cultures do not. The same is true for education. To the extent that it fosters growth toward self-actualization, it is "good" education.

As soon as we speak of "good" or "bad" cultures, and take them as means rather than as ends, the concept of "adjustment" comes into question. We must ask, "What kind of culture or subculture is the 'well adjusted' person well adjusted to?" Adjustment is, very definitely, not necessarily synonymous with psychological health.

40. The achievement of self-actualization (in the sense of autonomy) paradoxically makes more possible the transcendence of self, and of self-consciousness and of selfishness. It makes it easier for the person to be homonomous, i.e., to merge himself as a part in a larger whole than himself (Angyal, 1941). The condition of the fullest homonomy is full autonomy, and to some extent, vice versa, one can attain to autonomy only via successful homonomous experiences (child dependence, B-love, care for others, etc.). It is necessary to speak of levels of homonomy (more and more mature), and to differentiate a "low homonomy" (of fear, weakness, and regression) from a "high homonomy" (of courage and full, self-confident autonomy), a "low Nirvana" from a "high Nirvana," union downward from union upward (Weisskopf, 1958).

41. An important existential problem is posed by the fact that self-actualizing persons (and all people in their peak-experiences) occasionally live out-of-time and out-of-the-world (atemporal and aspatial) even though mostly they must live in the outer world. Living in the inner psychic world (which is ruled by psychic laws and not by the laws of outer-reality), i.e., the world of experience, of emotion, of wishes and fears and hopes, of love, of poetry, art, and fantasy, is different from living in and adapting to the non-psychic reality which runs by laws he never made and which are not essential to his nature even though he has to live by them. (He could, after all, live in other kinds of worlds, as any science fiction fan knows.) The person who is not afraid of this inner, psychic world, can enjoy it to such an extent that it may be called

Heaven by contrast with the more effortful, fatiguing, externally responsible world of "reality," of striving and coping, of right and wrong, of truth and falsehood. This is true even though the healthier person can also adapt more easily and enjoyably to the "real" world, and has better "reality testing," i.e., doesn't confuse it with his inner psychic world.

It seems clear now that confusing these inner and outer realities, or having either closed off from experience, is highly pathological. The healthy person is able to integrate them both into his life and therefore has to give up neither, being able to go back and forth voluntarily. The difference is the same as the one between the person who can visit the slums and the one who is forced to live there always. (Either world is a slum if one can't leave it.) Then, paradoxically, that which was sick and pathological and the "lowest" becomes part of the healthiest and "highest" aspect of human nature. Slipping into "craziness" is frightening only for those who are not fully confident of their sanity. Education must help the person to live in both worlds.

42. The foregoing propositions generate a different understanding of the role of action in psychology. Goal-directed, motivated, coping, striving, purposeful action is an aspect or by-product of the necessary transactions between a psyche and a non-psychic world.

(a) The D-need gratifications come from the world outside the person, not from within. Therefore adaptation to this world is made necessary, e.g., reality-testing, knowing the nature of this world, learning to differentiate this world from the inner world, learning the nature of people and of society, learning to delay gratification, learning to conceal what would be dangerous, learning which portions of the world are gratifying and which dangerous, or useless for need-gratification, learning the approved and permitted cultural paths to gratification and techniques of gratification.

(b) The world is in itself interesting, beautiful and fascinating. Exploring it, manipulating it, playing with it, contemplating it, enjoying it are all motivated kinds of action (cognitive, motor, and esthetic needs).

But there is also action which has little or nothing to do with the world, at any rate at first. Sheer expression of the nature or state or powers (Funktionslust) of the organism is an expression of Being rather than of striving (Buhler, 1924). And the contemplation and enjoyment of the inner life not only is a kind of "action" in itself but is also antithetical to action in the world, i.e., it produces stillness and cessation of muscular activity. The ability to wait is a special case of being able to suspend action.

43. From Freud we learned that the past exists now in the person. Now we must learn, from growth theory and self-actualization theory that the future also now exists in the person in the form of ideals, hopes, duties, tasks, plans, goals, unrealized potentials, mission, fate, destiny, etc. One for whom no future exists is reduced to the concrete, to hopelessness, to emptiness. For him, time must be endlessly "filled." Striving, the usual organizer of most activity, when lost, leaves the person unorganized and unintegrated.

Of course, being in a state of Being needs no future, because it is already there. Then Becoming ceases for the moment and its promissory notes are cashed in the form of the ultimate rewards, i.e., the peak-experiences, in which time disappears and hopes are fulfilled.

REFERENCES

Angyal, A. Foundations for a science of personality. New York: Commonwealth Fund, 1941.

Buhler, K. Die geistige Entwicklung des Kindes. 4th ed. Jena: M Fischer, 1924.

Maslow, A. H. Motivation and personality. New York: Harper, 1954.

Maslow, A. H., Rand, H., & Newman, S. Some parallels between the dominance and sexual behavior of monkeys and the fantasies of psychoanalytic patients. J. nerv. ment. Dis., 1960, 131: 202-212.

Murphy, G. Personality. New York: Harper, 1947.

Weisskopf, W. Existence and values. In A. H. Maslow (Ed.) New knowledge of human values. New York: Harper, 1959.

Specific Issues in Counseling and Psycotherapy

XII

THE ETHICS OF COUNSELING

C. Gilbert Wrenn

In November, 1950, Dr. L. E. Drake and I worked as a team in the first oral examinations administered by the American Board of Examiners in Professional Psychology. We were responsible for examining the candidates in the areas of research and of ethics and it became embarrassingly apparent at that time that there was no generally understood code of ethics upon which to examine the candidates. Drake and I agreed upon certain principles and raised what we considered crucial questions but we worked in something of a fog. It was at that time that I determined to discuss this topic with the Division of Counseling and Guidance at the 1951 meetings.

For some years counselors have been concerned with confidential information that is transmitted within the counseling relationship. There has been some discussion of just what is confidential and what is not and thought has been given as to just how to record information considered confidential. More recently has arisen the question of the legal position of the counselor who possesses information given to him in counseling. If this information suggests that the client is a law breaker, a violator of mores, or contemplates harm to others is the counselor legally obligated to reveal this information? Beyond this, under what conditions can he be legally required to disclose information given to him by a client while the two were in a counseling relationship to each other?

Presidential address before the Division of Counseling and Guidance of the American Psychological Association, Chicago, Ill., September 30, 1951. Reprinted by permission of the author and *Educational and Psychological Measurement*, 1952, 12:161–77.

During the year 1951, section 3 of the very important formulations of the APA Hobbs' Committee on Ethical Standards for Psychology was made available in the February and May issues of The American Psychologist. (The revised version of these standards is given in the Appendix, page 293.) The present paper is built upon this published statement of ethics in clinical and consulting relationships, soon to become the official code of the APA. I can claim little originality therefore, although my self-confidence was strengthened by comparing my notes of last November for this paper with the codified statement of the official committee. Perhaps I should not have been surprised at the degree of agreement because the code was built upon the problems supplied by hundreds of operating psychologists throughout the country. It is an operational code, not one spun out of gossamer abstractions. It is a statement of principles that grew out of the experiences of many practicing psychologists. Since I am one such psychologist, it might be expected that the ethical problems that seem significant to me also seem important to others.

This discussion is, therefore, concerned with the implications for counselors of the proposed code. I have selected some of the more significant principles for comparison and application and have occasionally added one that I thought should be considered by counselors. There is one important conflict in counseling ethics that will be carefully explored but before engaging that issue allow me to state briefly two or three other considerations.

WHY A CONCERN FOR ETHICS

First of all, why this greatly increased interest in the ethics of counseling? There are, perhaps, two major reasons. Counseling is becoming a profession and as such is at once concerned with its dual obligation to society and to the client. For generations the concept of a profession has been linked with that of service to society. Roscoe Pound defines a profession very simply in these terms —"(it is) an organized calling in which men pursue a learned art and are united in the pursuit of public service" (Pound, 1936). If people generally are to regard counseling with respect because counselors consider themselves to be professional men, then the members of this profession must have a clear understanding of its social purpose and obligation. So long as the counseling function is merely an arm or a projection of some institution there is little problem, for under these conditions it tacitly adopts the principles and procedures of its parent organization. If, however, counseling is to operate independently or is to have professional independence within an institution then its status as an independent profession demands a clear understanding of its ethical obligations. One of the generally accepted criteria of a profession—or so Darley and I stated in 1947 (Wrenn and Darley, 1947, pp. 283-284)—is the development and adoption of a code of ethics by the members of that occupational group. Counseling—and psychology in general—is all too tardy in this respect. [1]

A further consequence of arriving at professional status is the closer relationship between professional skill and professional ethics. As a body of professional knowledges and skills develops, it becomes an ethical concern if a counselor attempts to operate without these skills. The statement "I didn't know" is no longer an excuse if there exists a body of knowledge that he should know. Still another outgrowth of professional status is the need for defining our relationships with the members of other professions. We must know clearly the conditions under which a counselor discloses client information to a member of another profession. We must also know what is ethically sound in receiving and using client information from others. There are questions of both skill and ethics in referring a client to a colleague either within or without the counseling profession.

A second reason for our growing interest in ethics—and perhaps a more compelling one—is the changing emphasis in counseling itself. The shift is in the direction of more self-information being disclosed in counseling, more of the client's attitudes, emotions, and self concepts being shared with the counselor. There is still, and will continue to be, concern about information that should be given to the client, and concern about the quality of the counselor's judgment in introducing interpretations or in discussing outcomes of projected action. These are interview elements that are outside the client, relating to his environment or to the attitudes of the counselor. It is still true that both counselor and client may be guilty of serious misinterpretations of personality unless they give full recognition to the cultural influences that shape their concepts of themselves and of others (Ichheiser, 1943).

Regardless of these considerations the trend of our knowledge of personality dynamics leads the counselor to emphasize that which happens within the client, leads him to encourage the client

[1]Note the published codes of ethics for 133 professions and businesses in Heermance, 1924; see also the very complete code for the medical profession, "Principles of Medical Ethics," 1945.

to explore his own attitudes and feelings. In doing this the client discloses much that is very vitally a part of him—he gives to the counselor a part of himself and in that disclosure places a heavy burden of responsibility upon the counselor. This burden of knowledge is one which the counselor sometimes wishes he did not have, but it is one which he cannot avoid. The ethics of dealing with the intimate self-stuff of a counseling interview takes both personal discernment and professional standards of behavior. Without a code of carefully conceived ethical principles a counselor may unwittingly injure himself in the eyes of both his client and his professional colleagues.

LEGAL POSITION OF COUNSELOR

The counselor's concern for his legal position was earlier mentioned and perhaps an expansion of this point belongs also in our prologue. Upon several occasions I have had law professors in this field of law speak to seminars in personnel work. The counselor has more legal leeway than he may recognize. For example, he does not have to release any personnel or counseling records merely upon the request of an officer of a court, a state, or the Federal government. In fact he probably should _not_, for the client can sue the counselor for failing to protect his interests. A warrant for the release of the records is necessary. Furthermore, the counselor may keep confidential notes on his clients in the form of personal memoranda and since these do not become part of the official records of the institution or of his office they do not have to be released when the personnel records of an individual are taken into custody.

In states where a psychologist has no "privileged communication" status by law he is not under obligation to reveal that which he considers confidential _unless_ he is under oath before a grand jury or a court of law. The mere request for specific or general information about a client, even though made by a person in uniform or with an imposing title, does not obligate a counselor to reveal information that he considers confidential unless he is under oath. If he refuses to answer when under oath he _may_ be cited for contempt of court. What would actually happen if such a situation arose we do not know for no precedent exists. I have been told that there is no assurance at all that a counselor would be cited for contempt of court if he refused to answer giving as his reason that to do so would be violating the confidential nature of his relationship with his client. Lawyers, physicians, and ministers are in

most states protected by "privileged communication." Counselors
and clinical psychologists should seek the same type of protection.
But a precedent would be set by a court <u>acknowledging</u> privileged
status if some counselor, with legal aid, pled for recognition of
his professional ethics and refused to disclose interview information.

This is a fascinating subject because so little exists in print
which acknowledges the professional nature of the client-counselor
relationship, but the counselor still has certain privileges in law.
(See Fowerbaugh, 1945.) It should be noted, for example, that information given to a counselor by a client is almost always "hearsay" evidence and therefore not admissible in court. For example,
the counselor did not see the client injure someone else, he merely
heard him tell about it. For the purpose of proving the fact of in-
jury this statement to the counselor is hearsay evidence and not admissible over objection in most instances. Certainly much that is
told in an interview is "hearsay" in every sense of the word. We
seldom have more evidence than what the client said.

Here is another point. The possession of information that a
client gave in an interview to the effect he <u>said</u> that he violated a
law or a social convention does not make the counselor legally li-
able to disclose this information to any official or officer of the
law. He has an ethical problem on his hands but no legal one until
he is under oath. Certainly lawyers, ministers and physicians are
frequently recipients of information indicating criminal behavior
upon the part of their client but they are not obligated to reveal this
information. As a matter of fact they are under ethical compulsion
<u>not</u> to do so. So is the counselor. He differs from the members of
these other professions only when he is under oath, for then he does
not know what is his legal right with regard to "privileged communication" as they do.

Nothing of what has been said here should be interpreted as
suggesting that counselors should not cooperate with an officer of
the law or of any other agent of society. We are citizens and obligated to uphold the duly constituted law of the state or nation. What
I have tried to suggest is that when questions of ethics arise, particularly those regarding the disclosure of information transmitted
in an interview, the counselor has some discretion even in states
where he is not legally recognized as a member of a profession.
He is not obligated to "tell all" merely because some one requests
him to do so and, as a matter of fact, he is professionally obligated
to his client <u>not</u> to tell. This dilemma of client versus society is
given further attention a little later.

LITERATURE ON ETHICS IN COUNSELING

It is a sad commentary on the maturity of our profession that the published literature on ethics in counseling can be discussed quite briefly. Reference has been made to one published report of the currently operating Committee on Ethical Standards of APA, that on Ethics in Clinical and Consulting Relationships, but not to the report of the Sub-Committee on the Distribution of Psychological Tests that was published in the November 1950 American Psychologist. Aside from the work of this Committee the literature on ethics in counseling is generalized and discursive.[2] The Committee on Ethical Practices of the National Vocational Guidance Association has, during the past five years, developed a published statement and working standards regarding the counseling done in vocational guidance agencies. The latest directory of approved guidance agencies[3] is a marked contribution to professional and ethical practices in counseling and in vocational guidance in general. Its two chairmen during the five-year period, Albert Harris and Nathan Kohn, and the chairman for the succeeding year, Robert Kamm, are members of this Division, as have been several members of the Committee—Daniel Harris, Donald Super, Henry McDaniel, and myself. The extent of my personal concern for ethics in vocational guidance is suggested in an address I gave before NVGA in 1947. At the conclusion of a review of trends in this field I stated a kind of personal creed for counselors which contained the following two paragraphs:

> I will respect the integrity of each individual with whom I deal. I will accord to him the same right to self-determination that I want for myself. I will respect as something sacred the personality rights of each person and will not attempt to manipulate him or meddle in his life.
> I will define my personal and ethical responsibility to my client as well as my legal and vocational responsibility to my organization and to society. I work for both the group to which I am responsible and for each individual that I serve as a client. This dual responsibility must be defined and understood by my employers and by myself (Wrenn, 1947).

[2] One must of course note that the literature contains reference to several smaller groups of psychologists, in the United States and elsewhere, who have adopted ethical codes. Illustrative is the recently adopted Code of Ethical Standards of the New York State Psychological Association which is based upon Section 3 of the APA code, and the Code of the Victorian Group of the Australian Branch of the British Psychological Society, cited in The American Psychologist, May, 1951, p. 176.

[3] 1951 Directory of Vocational Counseling Services. Ethical Practices Committee of the National Vocational Guidance Association, Box 64, Washington University, St. Louis, Missouri.

The Committee on Professional Ethics of the National Education Association is in the process of preparing a revision of the
N. E. A. code which has been in effect for 21 years. The revision,
which will be completed in 1952, is based upon 1,309 teachers' reports of what are considered to be ethical problems. It is cited
here because it will contain some reference to the nature of confidential relations between teachers and pupils and to the ethics of
professional relations among teachers themselves (School and Soc.,
1950).

Some of the recent textbooks dealing with counseling give pass-
ing attention to the question of ethics—two pages in Watson's Readings book, one in Robinson's text on counseling procedures, one or
two in my book on college personnel work. Thorne's book has one
chapter (Thorne, 1950) on "Problems of Professional Responsibility," dealing with the counselor's responsibility to society, family
or friends, the profession, and himself, as well as his administrative responsibilities. It is the best and most complete textbook
treatment of the ethics of counseling, although somewhat closely
tied in with medical ethics and with ethical problems that arise
with psychotics and severe neurotics. The professional relation of
the psychologist to the medical man is appropriately emphasized
since Thorne himself is both an M. D. and a psychologist.

The periodical literature is not very rewarding. There is
great need for a thoughtful paper on the place of the psychologist
in our society and the ethical implications of that societal responsibility. During the coming year someone should write such a paper. Someone should also write a paper on our legal position that
is the result of a study of state laws and court decisions. One re-
markable series of journal articles on ethics in psychotherapy and
in counseling deals with the basic issue raised in this paper—client
versus society. This series of four articles in four successive
volumes of the Journal of Abnormal and Social Psychology (Sutich,
1944; Sargent, 1945; Bixler and Seeman, 1946; Meehl and Mc-
Closky, 1947) is probably known to most readers. It was started
by Anthony Sutich in 1944 with an extensive statement of 51 duties
and rights of counselors who practice within a "democratic counseling relationship." The 51 statements of the code were grouped
under such headings as psychologists' duties and rights, third party
duties and rights, client's rights, and interprofessional responsibilities that are suggestive of the divisions of our present code.
The publication was a pioneer effort of considerable significance
but its reception was influenced by the fact that the code was postulated upon Sutich's particular modification of the non-directive

point of view. It was, in a sense, an exposition of a philosophy of counseling.

Helen Sargent in 1945 published a reply that expressed agreement in general with Sutich but took him to task at two points: (1) where he departs from simple non-directive theory with his "democratic counseling relationship," and (2) where his code becomes so detailed and didactic that it must be explained formally to the client. The succeeding year, 1946, saw a contribution by Ray Bixler and Julius Seeman in an urgent plea for a code under the three headings of (1) Responsibility to the individual, (2) Responsibility to related professions, and (3) Responsibility to society. There is an interesting distinction made between the confidentiality of diagnostic data and of treatment data of referred cases that is not too well reflected in the present code.

In 1947 Paul Meehl and Herbert McClosky took issue with Sutich's use of the concepts of "democracy" and "authoritarianism." These are stated to be political concepts and not applicable to the ethics of counseling. Furthermore this team of psychologist and political scientist object to Sutich's failure to distinguish between ethics and procedures. The latter must be accepted or not in terms of whether they are found to be effective and contributing to the client's needs, but not because they do or do not fit a system of ethics. One may question "advice" as a procedure because it often (not always) does not work but not because it is authoritarian and therefore unethical. "The most fundamental ethical commitment of a counselor is to help the client to achieve the client's end . . . ."

This series is not, unfortunately, a straightforward presentation of points of view regarding the therapist's responsibility to his client and to society. The articles, with the possible exception of that by Bixler and Seeman, are expositions of, or refutations of, the philosophy of non-directive counseling. The implications of a philosophy of human relationships are of deep significance but we were still without a code of ethics.

The 1949 conference on Graduate Education in Clinical Psychology—The Boulder Conference—gave consideration to ethical problems in both the training and practice of clinical psychology (Raimy, 1950). No code was suggested, of course, because the Hobb's Committee results were anticipated, but attention was given to (1) ethical problems in the psychologist's functioning in the dual role of scientist and practitioner, and (2) to the ethics of his interprofessional relations. Nothing definitive was proposed for the ethics of training, but there was a clear statement of the responsibility of the university for eliminating from graduate training students guilty of unethical practices. In general, this chapter of the report raises questions without answering them.

ISSUES OF THIS PAPER

This paper has arrived at a point where it can delay no longer in the statement of its major argument. In brief, this argument is that there is a conflict between a counselor's loyalties to his client and his corresponding loyalties to his society, his employing institution, his profession and himself. This conflict is outlined by a series of ethical principles that have been grouped under the headings of the basic loyalties named above. After some analysis of the principles, this paper will propose that the conflict in counseling ethics can be resolved only by recourse to a framework of values.

The statement of principles as taken directly from the Hobb's Committee Report, or as modified or added to by the writer, follows.

ETHICAL PRINCIPLES IN COUNSELING[4]

I. Responsibility to Client. *1. The counselor is primarily responsible to his client and ultimately to society; these basic loyalties guide all his professional endeavors. The counselor is at all times to respect the integrity and guard the welfare of the person with whom he is working as a client.*

2. The counselor must obtain his client's permission before communicating any information about the client that has been given in a counseling relationship to another person or agency such as a parent, family physician, a social agency, an employer. This principle must be observed even though the action may be perceived by the counselor as only in the interest of the client. An exception to this is contained in principle three.

3. The counselor should guard professional confidences as a trust and reveal such confidences without the client's permission only after most careful deliberation and when there is clear and imminent danger to an individual or to society; i.e., threatened suicide, homicide, or treason.

4. Psychological information, such as the results of tests or of a diagnostic appraisal, should be given to a client at such time and in such a manner when it is most likely to be accepted by him as part of his self-concept; *i.e., when it is most likely to be helpful to the client's efforts to solve his problems.*

---

[4] The wording of the principles is the same as that proposed by the A.P.A. Committee and reported in the February and May, 1951, issues of *The American Psychologist* except for material in roman type. This indicates changed wording or new material by the author.

5. *The counselor must refer his client to an appropriate specialist when there is evidence of a difficulty with which the counselor is not competent to deal. In such cases the counselor's responsibility for the welfare of the client continues until this responsibility is assumed by the professional person to whom the client is referred.* In schools or institutions referral should be made through channels, and, where children are involved, with parents' consent.

6. *Clinical materials should be used in teaching and writing only* when the permission of those involved is secured or *when their identity is obscured beyond likelihood of recognition.*

7. Interviews held within a counseling relationship are not to be mechanically recorded for training or other purposes without the knowledge and consent of the client. The exception may be the recording of interviews for valid research purposes under circumstances where only the research worker can identify the client in the typescript.

8. *When a counselor's position in an organization is such that some departure is required from the normal expectation that counseling relationships are confidential, it is essential that the counselor make clear to the client the nature of his role before counseling is begun.*

It is with this last stated principle that the counselor's conflict of loyalties becomes specific although it has been made clear in principles 1 and 3 that he has a dual responsibility to client and to society. The pinch really comes however, when the counselor has a known responsibility to a specific organization or to an employer that may affect his complete loyalty to his client. To say that a counselor should not have a double loyalty is to be unrealistic. He <u>has</u> them—the question is how can he resolve them? The principles to follow make clear the variety of relationships that cloud the clear waters of single-minded loyalty to his client.

It has been suggested that the confidential nature of the interview is less to be stressed when the client is a child and that permission to transmit is not necessary for children. I doubt this assumption. A child's trust in a counselor may be betrayed as well as an adult's. A child is very much a person and the integrity of his personality must be protected while at the same time admitting that parents' consent must be obtained for treatment or referral.

II. <u>Responsibility to Society.</u> *(Principle 1), (Principle 3).* 9. *It is unethical for a counselor,* and a betrayal of his responsibility to society, *to offer services outside his area of training and experience or beyond his level of competence,* or to accept assignments of this nature that are made by his employer.

10. Where a counselor is not granted the rights of "privileged communication" in his state, he must decide for himself whether his professional ethics regarding the confidential nature of his relationship to his client are subordinate to the demands of the state as these may be made by an agent of the state or in a court of law. It follows that the counselor must be informed regarding his legal rights and limitations.

III. Responsibility to Employing Institution and to Colleagues. *11. Counselors are obligated to define for themselves the nature and direction of
their loyalties and responsibilities in any particular undertaking, to inform
all involved of these commitments, and to carry them out conscientiously.*

*12. In counseling situations where a possible division of loyalties ex-
ists, as between the client and the employer of the counselor, an agreement concerning the handling of confidential material must be worked out
and the nature of the agreement made known to all concerned.*

*13. Information obtained in counseling relationships should be dis-
cussed only in professional settings and with professional persons who
are clearly concerned with the case.*

*14. Case records prepared for the counselor or for professional com-
munication should not be shown to a client.*

*15. A counselor should not accept a private fee or other form of re-
muneration for professional work with a person who is entitled to his services through an institution or agency.*

IV. Responsibility to Self and to the Profession. *16. It is desirable in
counseling, where sound inter-personal relationships are essential to effective endeavor, that a counselor be aware of the inadequacies in his own
personality which may bias his appraisals of others or distort his relationships with them. He should refrain from undertaking any activity where his
personal limitations and preconceptions are likely to result in inferior professional services, or harm a client.*

*17. The counselor must distinguish between his own values and those
held by his client or his client's associates in order to guard against a
subtle imposition of his own values and moral code upon his client.*

*18. In situations where referral is indicated and the client refuses re-
ferral, the counselor must carefully weigh the possible harm to the client,
to himself and his profession, that might ensue from continuing the relationship. If the client is in clear and imminent danger, the counselor
should insist on referral or refuse to continue the relationship.*

*19. Counseling activities, such as administering diagnostic tests, en-
couraging self-revelations, or engaging in psychotherapy, should be undertaken only with serious intent and not in casual relationships.*

Lest I be misunderstood may the first principle—first for the
Committee and first in my list—be repeated: "The counselor is
primarily responsible to his client and ultimately to society . . . .
The counselor is at all times to respect the integrity and guard the
welfare of the person with whom he is working as a client" (italics
mine).

It is clear the client comes first but there is all too often a
second and a third to be considered. It is difficult to point out
where the shoe pinches most. I believe that for many school, college, or institutionally employed counselors there is greatest danger of unethical conduct in communicating officially to one's superior what is confidential and in discussing case information too
freely and casually with colleagues. In some situations the unau-

thorized mechanical recording of case data that is played back to others is an equally grave violation of ethics.

Where pressure is placed upon a counselor for the transmittal of interview information what is his recourse? Sometimes recommendations for constructive or protective action can be made without divulging the reason for such action and thus violating confidences. Sometimes the client's permission for transmittal of information can be secured. But at other times the issue cannot be avoided—and it is as sharp an issue ethically when a colleague asks us for information that should not be shared as it would be if we were under oath and in a witness chair. There is a clear ethical question in both cases with a difference only in the first situation possessing a more subtle temptation to violate confidences.

It is clear that there is frequently a real question as to whom the counselor's loyalty is due. Is it due the client and not the employer, the client and not the colleague, the client and not the professional training need, the client and not the state? The answer lies in the judgment of the counselor. He and he alone can decide. The profession has said "Here is the code of ethics—you apply it. Upon you rests the responsibility of deciding who must be protected in these matters of confidential information and interprofessional relationships—the client, the employer, or the state." Sometimes it is simpler than that but much harder—who gets hurt, someone else or you?

ETHICS WITHIN A VALUE SYSTEM

In the ethical judgments that must be made by the counselor some system of values must be employed. One doesn't decide in terms of logic—the logic may lead in opposing directions—one decides in terms of this value or that. The relation of values to psychotherapy in general is crucial. A discussion by Arnold Green of the University of New Hampshire of social values inherent in the practice of psychotherapy starts out with this statement: "The history of modern psychotherapy can be viewed as an unsuccessful struggle to evaluate the role of social values" (Green, 1946). Green is speaking here of social values in the life of both the client and the counselor, for later he states that one of the shortcomings of modern psychotherapy is the failure to distinguish between three value areas—that of the therapist, that of the client, and that of the persons and groups with whom the client is interacting. The therapist must be aware of the values held by the client's associates but he must also, in matters of ethics, be aware of the values held by his own associates. All of us "maintain a series of relations with others whose values comprise effective limits to the implementation of our own."

Incidentally, Green contends that modern psychotherapy is sociologically naive—that it does not realize what social values are being recognized in the process of therapy. He criticizes the nondirective counselor for believing that he is doing something that he is not doing but at the same time proposes that the non-directive approach is best equipped of all therapies for dealing with a modern social trend toward separateness rather than wholism. To point up Green's provocative analysis this proposition might be made—there may be debate as to whether or not a science considers values but there is no doubt that the practice of a therapy does.

Values enter deeply into the field of ethics, for ethical principles in any field are based upon the value system of that field of endeavor. In psychology, and in the application of psychology in counseling, we now have a code of ethics. Such a code is a crystallization of the value system of our profession. This paper has tried to suggest that the adoption of this code, excellent as it is, will not solve the ethical problems of the counselor. For the code clearly shows the several obligations and loyalties that the counselor must attempt to reconcile. In general these loyalties are grouped into two categories and the perplexing question can be stated as follows—"Which is to be elevated, the integrity of the individual or the welfare of the state?" It is no weakness of our code that this problem remains to be resolved. Not at all, for counselors clearly have loyalties to others than the client, even though these loyalties are secondary. Responsibilities to society, employer, and colleague are clearly a part of our code and these may conflict with the counselor's responsibility to the client. When this happens what values determine the counselor's decision?

For some, there is little conflict, for the will of the state or of society is paramount. The individual is never as important as the group. The state or the institution exists for the protection and welfare of the individual and must at all costs be preserved. The fact that the state or the group punishes when its values are rejected doubtless influences all of us, but some individuals cleave to conformity as a matter of principle rather than because of fear. They will also be loyal to their employer and will rationalize any harm that comes to their client because of information about the client that has been transmitted to the employer.

To other counselors the reverse always seems true—the individual is always more important than a social institution and must

be protected at all costs. Institutional or group welfare is sacri-
ficed in favor of the individual as a matter of deep principle. For
most counselors however, no consistency is possible and each situation presenting a conflict of loyalties must be analyzed anew.
Sometimes the group or employer is favored, and at other times
the client is protected, even at cost to the counselor. Both types
of decisions may be individually defensible but one observation
should be made. It takes more courage and strength of conviction
to take a stand to protect the client than it does to make a decision
to protect the employer. Courage is variable too, however, a variable in any man's life. Because this is true it ill fits any of us to
be critical of a colleague when he was not as courageous as we
thought he should have been. We have lacked in courage too at
times—"He that is without sin among you, let him first cast a
stone."

What system of values does the counselor have recourse to
when an ethical conflict arises? To whose, indeed, but his own.
Each man has his own pattern of values, with limits indeed, that
are set by his state, his society, his immediate associates, but
for all that, a man's beliefs are his own. Back of these personal
values, which sometimes must be pitted against those of his society, is another set of values. These are part of our great human
heritage, great principles of truth and mercy and justice that are
as yet, and perhaps will always be, only dimly understood. Certainly the life of man is more than he can see and hear or even understand. Each of us is his own way is trying to apprehend truths
that are part of the ultimate. So it is with some of the values that
transcend that which is legalized or accepted by a man's associates

A counselor to be ethical has to do more than observe a code
of ethics. He must be great within himself because he relates himself to God and the greatness of the Infinite. He must consider how
important or unimportant he is as compared with principles for
which men have in centuries past suffered and died. Some men
have formerly believed in the great truths of life but their experiences have soured them. They could not live up to greatness.
Some men have gotten too big for their intellectual britches and
have discarded all but that which they can understand. For these
we can be truly sorry but for the young in age or spirit there is
still greatness possible—greatness of faith in the unseen, of belief
in the intangible, of expectation of the impossible.

Henry Luce spoke recently in Texas to a group of eminent ju-
rists on Justice Oliver Wendell Holmes. He proposed that Holmes
had a cynical philosophy of life and that the influence of this cyni-

cism had done harm to the legal profession. He closed with these words:

> And now, gentlemen, if I have spoken extravagantly, I ask your indulgence and plead that if your profession is in want of anything, it is not in want of sobriety, caution, discretion, prudence; if it is in want of anything, it is in want of extravagance, enthusiasm, heroism, and these qualities I would willingly incite (Luce, 1951).

I close with a paraphrase of this—spoken gently and with affection for all of you who are my colleagues. I propose that our profession is not in want of a respect for evidence and scientific truth, nor in want for a drive to serve individuals and to advance human welfare. We are aware of our technical and knowledge limitations and have a great discontent with the imperfectness of much that we do. If this profession is in want of anything it is in a neglect of the proposition that man is spiritual as well as intellectual in nature— it is in a failure to recognize that man has a relationship to the Infinite as well as to other men. The profession has established a code of ethics but its application calls for decisions that will require great personal courage and depth of conviction. It is at this point that the counselor may have to have recourse to the great values and principles of the human race in order to resolve the ethical conflict. The counselor may truly have to think more of others than of himself. Counselors need to strengthen their moral courage as well as their understandings and skills, for it is the constellation of all these qualities that provides true professional competence.

REFERENCES

Bixler, R., & Seeman, J. Suggestions for a code of ethics for consulting psychologists. J. abnorm. soc. Psychol., 1946, 41:486-490.

Fowerbaugh, C.C. Legal status of psychologists in Ohio. J. consult. Psychol., 1945, 9:196-200.

Green, A. W. Social values and psychotherapy. J. Pers., 1946, 14:199-228.

Heermance, E. L. Codes of ethics, a handbook. Burlington, Vt.: Free Press, 1924.

Ichheiser, G. Misinterpretations of personality in everyday life and the psychologist's frame of reference. Charact. & Pers., 1943, 12:145-160.

Luce, H. R. Holmes was wrong. _Fortune_, June 1951.

Meehl, P. E., & McClosky, H. Ethical and political aspects of applied psychology. _J_. _abnorm_. _soc_. _Psychol_., 1947, 43:91-98.

Pound, R. What is a profession? _Rev_. _of_ _Reviews_, 1936, 94:84-85.

Principles of medical ethics. _J_. _clin_. _Psychol_., 1945, 1:336-342.

Raimy, V. C. (Ed.) _Training_ _in_ _clinical_ _psychology_. New York: Prentice-Hall, 1950.

Sargent, Helen. Professional ethics and problems of therapy. _J_. _abnorm_. _soc_. _Psychol_., 1945, 40:47-60.

School _&_ _Soc_., 1950, 72:396.

Sutich, A. Toward a professional code for psychological consultants. _J_. _abnorm_. _soc_. _Psychol_., 1944, 39:329-350.

Thorne, F. C. _Principles_ _of_ _personality_ _counseling_. Brandon, Vt.: Journal of Clinical Psychology, 1950.

Wrenn, C. G. Trends and predictions in vocational guidance. _Occupations_, May 1947, 503-515.

Wrenn, C. G., & Darley, J. G. Student personnel work as a profession; I and II. In E. G. Williamson (Ed.) _Trends_ _in_ _Student_ _Personnel_ _Work_. Minneapolis: Univer. of Minnesota Press, 1950.

XIII

ON THE PHILOSOPHICAL NEUTRALITY OF COUNSELORS

Robert L. Browning and Herman J. Peters

There appears to be an urgent demand among guidance counselors for a clarification of the relationship between the counselor's
basic philosophy and his counseling procedures. Can a counselor
remain philosophically neutral, on the one hand, and should the
counselor do so, on the other hand. Is Vordenberg's dictum true
that "Regardless of the kind of personal philosophy evolved by the
counselor, it must surely affect the techniques he uses and the
evaluation of the effectiveness of his work" (Vordenberg, 1953)?

DEMANDS FOR THE CONSIDERATION
OF THE INFLUENCE OF PHILOSOPHY OF COUNSELING

After giving a survey of the inadequacies of the current attempts to develop a philosophical foundation and direction for guidance, Donald Walker and Herbert Peiffer issue a call to action.
They say, ". . . we would urge close and careful attention to the
problems of the goals of counseling, both at the general theoretical
level and as they affect the progress of the individual counseling
case. . . . We are handicapped by the fact that in psychotherapy we
are, to some extent, the victims of our disease orientation, our
bias against value judgments and our contradictory cultural goals"
(Walker and Peiffer, 1957, p. 209). Mathewson says that the old
myth of economic man is inadequate. He says, "A new myth may
be forming; we cannot tell what it may be and perhaps we cannot
hasten its formation, or even consciously affect its form. But un-

Reprinted by permission of the authors and *Educational Theory*, 1960,
10:142-47.

less we wish to take a completely passive position in the determination of our national destiny, it seems necessary to think about and to choose between alternative sets of social and moral values, especially in the education and guidance of our youth" (Mathewson, 1955, p. 26).

Arbuckle (1953) compares the counselor and the surgeon, saying that the philosophy of the surgeon may have very little effect on the recovery or death of a patient. "The attitude and the philosophy of the counselor, however, are all important and in any research it is difficult to keep such an inconsistent factor consistent." In Arbuckle's thinking the personnel point of view must include a consideration of every aspect in the development of the student— ". . . his intellect, his emotions, his physical being, his moral values, his skills and aptitudes, his means of recreation, his esthetic and religious values, his social adjustment, and his environmental situation" (Arbuckle, 1953, p. 3). This is a big order! The fulfillment of such a goal in guidance is greatly complicated by the fact that the counselor, in dealing with the counselee's development along such broad lines, is confused about whether or not his own loyalties, his own philosophy of life, should be shared, or whether, in fact, he can keep himself from sharing it!

> Counseling involves the interaction of two personalities through the medium of speech and other symbolic behavior. It is reasonable to suppose, therefore, that the structure of each of these personalities will have a marked influence on the interaction. It may be hypothesized further that the ways in which the personality structure of each of the counseling participants is symbolized in the speech of the interview will also have a marked effect upon the interaction.
>
> If it is true that the counselor's personality influences the direction, course, and outcome of the counseling interaction, it might be profitable to speculate about the kinds of counselor personality traits which are likely to facilitate counseling and those which are not (Arbuckle, 1953).

Strang states,

> The counselor should be himself but not impose himself. He should be genuine and sincere. He is likely to fail if he tries to play a role that is not natural for him. If a person cannot risk being himself in the counseling relationship, he should not try to be a counselor. Moreover, he is consciously or unconsciously influenced by his theory of counseling; his attitude toward school policies, his outlook on life, his attitude toward people. In short, his counseling is an expression of his personality, not merely a technic applied at will (Strang, 1953).

Pepinsky and Pepinsky, writing in 1954, state,

> There is no denying that the counselor's behavior, also, is subject to change as a function of his experience in working with clients (p. 173).

A little later under this same topic, "The Primary Function of Interaction," they go on to say,

> Indeed, the more closely we examine the counselor's motives, the more they become suspect! It appears to be, at best, nonsense and, at worst, a delusion to try to maintain that the counselor does or ought to leave his own needs parked outside the door while he interviews a client. We can state only that the explicit function of the counseling relationship—to help the client to change—should not be interfered with or destroyed (Pepinsky & Pepinsky, 1954, p. 74).

Perhaps the greatest single influence on counselors to be philosophically neutral has come from the work of Carl Rogers. His non-directive theory of psychotherapy was built on the belief that man could be trusted to work his way through to insights and new orientation if he could have a genuinely permissive relationship with the counselor in which he could open his inner life to himself and the helping person. Early research by Rogers led him to state that, "One can read through a complete recorded case or listen to it, without finding more than a half dozen instances in which the therapist's views on any point are evident. . . . One could not determine his diagnostic views, his standards of behavior, his social class" (Rogers, 1947, p. 358). Rogers did not, at that time, comment on the effect of the half dozen times and the absolute inevitability of such sharing of values. More recently, but only after a number of years of general confusion about the issue, has he addressed himself more directly to this pressing concern. In 1957, he said, in answer to certain articles challenging his position, that, "One cannot engage in psychotherapy without giving operational evidence of an underlying value orientation and view of human nature. It is definitely preferable, in my opinion, that such underlying views be open and explicit, rather than covert and implicit" (Rogers, 1957), p. 199). Rogers' insistence upon as much neutrality as possible has been a helpful research technique and allowed him and his associates to see deeply into the inner dynamics of the self. From his research there is ample evidence that the self, when free from threat or attack, is able to consider "hitherto rejected perceptions, to make new differentiations and to reintegrate the self in such a way as to include them" (Rogers, 1947, p. 365). Rogers' method seems honestly to help the person change. ". . . as changes occur in the perception of self and in the perception of reality, changes occur in the behavior" (Rogers, 1947, p. 363). The fact that persons often integrate their lives on levels that are not ultimately satisfactory but which only give the illusion of well-being must now be faced by Rogers and others.

ATTEMPTS TO CLARIFY THE RELATIONSHIP
OF BASIC PHILOSOPHY TO COUNSELING

One of the most powerful attempts to do away with philosophical relativism has been made by the humanistic psychotherapist and author, Erich Fromm, in his several writings, especially in The Sane Society. Fromm seeks to establish a solid foundation for the development of mental health for all men in whatever society. He observes that man has not only physiological and anatomical commonalities but that he is governed universally by certain basic psychic factors as well. His system of right and wrong is therefore built squarely upon whether or not man as man, in his essential being, is having his basic human needs fulfilled.

Fromm's inclusion in his list of basic needs of the necessity for a "frame of orientation and devotion" has led him to be most sympathetic toward the insights of the great religions and philosophies of the past and present. He is sensitive also to the moral standards propagated in our varying societies, because he believes that whole cultures can become full of defects which can and do tend to make men mentally ill. Societal arrangements, therefore, often must be changed before man's needs can be met. This observation forces counselors to be concerned with social, political, and religious philosophies which have created and are sustaining, often, such unhealthy social structures.

Fromm's theory is an attempt to build on what man's needs are objectively and not on what man feels his needs to be. This concept challenges in many ways the goal of non-directive counseling which tends to center on the process of man's expression of his inner feelings of need without reference to the fact that such needs are often a result of cultural defects which will not and cannot bring ultimate health to the client. This is true because of the very nature of his human condition, and the breadth of his needs which are in the area of ultimate loyalties and basic, undergirding frames of orientation, about which most counselors feel insecure and from which discussions they tend to steer clear!

A similar trend to that of Fromm's can be seen in the writings of Kurt Lewin. He stated as far back as 1935 that, "The individual psychical experiences, the actions and emotions, purposes, wishes and hopes, are rather embedded in quite definite psychical structures, spheres of the personality, and whole process" (Lewin, 1935, p. 54).

Also to be found in Fromm and Lewin thought is an emphasis on man's freedom and the necessity to broaden the range of that freedom in psychotherapy as well as in intelligent political action. Lewin observed that often the individual area of freedom is very small due to the vectors and forces in his field of psychic experience, built on past identifications, inhibitions and loyalties. Yet, this freedom existed. Man as man had qualities beyond the realm of the animal. Therapy should help man use his freedom to find the paths to growth, and to overcome the psychic barriers.

One of the most dramatic and controversial attempts to deal with the question of philosophy in psychotherapy has been made by Dr. Viktor E. Frankl, the Director of the Neurological Polyclinic in Vienna and a Professor of Psychiatry at the University of Vienna. Frankl's point of view grows out of the emphasis in existentialist philosophy on man's actual conditions of existence. Man in his essence is endowed with certain capacities for freedom, for decision making, for determining his destiny. Man is a responsible being with the power to transcend his own situation and to prophesy the results of his decisions. His intellectual powers and his psychic powers are qualitatively different from other animals. Frankl joins Fromm, at this point, in that he is seeking to analyze man's basic need for a value system on which he can base his decisions, as a result of which he will increase his freedom and his meaning.

He recognizes the significance of both individual psychology, stemming from Adler, and psychoanalysis, stemming from Freud. He maintains, however, that psychotherapy will be incomplete until man has a "psychotherapy of the mind" which deals with philosophical issues. Differing with Freud and others, he says, "The individual's philosophical attitude is part and parcel of his psychological one and emerges in every case" (Frankl, 1955, p. 34). He also believes, against the stream of thought in psychotherapy, that, "In no case should the intellectual problems of a person be written off as a 'symptom'" (p. 33).

Frankl honestly discusses the many profound problems related to his point of view, and pushes ahead, along with Fromm, to establish certain fundamental values inherent in man's situation. And yet, he maintains that existential analysis must not interfere with the ranking of values. ". . . what values he elects is and remains the patient's own affair. Existential analysis must not be concerned with what the patient decides for, what goals he sets himself, but only that he decides at all. . . . The physician should never be allowed to take over the patient's responsibility; he must never permit that responsibility to be shifted to himself; he must never anticipate decisions or impose them upon the patient. His job is to make it possible for the patient to reach decisions; he must endow the patient with the capacity for deciding" (Frankl, 1955, p. 270).

Such a view has been given great impetus by the philosophical writings of Martin Buber. Buber's philosophy urges man to relationships of trust with other men—very much like that between the counselor and the client in a permissive setting; and yet, he believes that real trust must allow and encourage honest dialogue between both parties. When there is a real meeting of persons (Buber describes this meeting in terms of an I—Thou relationship—very similar to Schweitzer's "reverence for life" concept) each person is bringing his full self to the dialogue. He must "be willing. . . to say what is really in his mind about the subject of conversation. And that means further that on each occasion he makes the contribution of his spirit without reduction and without shifting ground" (Buber, 1957, p. 112).

Dialogue on a philosophical level, on the level of the quest for ultimate meaning, is a basic need for every human being. The counselor must be sensitive, nevertheless, to the existential situation in which the client finds himself at any given time.

Gordon Allport emphasizes the profundity of this renewed interest in studying the basic conditions of man's existence. He says, "Existentialism calls for a doctrine of an active intellect, for more emphasis upon propriate functions, including self-objectification and oriented becoming. In particular it calls for a wider and fresher view of anxiety, of courage, and of freedom (Allport, 1955, p. 80). Allport stresses the fact that Freud and his followers have dealt mostly with the anxiety in man aroused by feelings of guilt and fear of punishment and not at all the anxiety which comes from a fear of nonbeing (death—either actual or psychological, in the Buber sense of being not in relation; not affirmed and confirmed by others).

Allport believes that the consideration of philosophical matters has been greatly de-emphasized in counseling, to the detriment of our whole concept of personality structure. Philosophic and religious decisions have to do with what he terms Intentional Characteristics which become a part of the personality. He believes that, "Intentional characteristics represent above all else the individual's primary modes of addressing himself to the future. As such they select stimuli, guide inhibitions and choices, and have much to do with the process of adult becoming. Relatively few theories of personality recognize the pre-emptive importance of intentional characteristics" (Allport, 1955, p. 89).

So, we are seeing a powerful movement within the guidance field, psychotherapy, philosophy, theology, and psychology for a deeper view of man's problems of existence, his wide and deep needs, his essential freedom of being, and his finite situation which forces him to go beyond knowledge to an ultimate devotion —built on faith (not an irrational faith, but faith, nonetheless).

Buber, in his William Alanson White Lectures given at the Washington School of Psychiatry, says that the counselor or educator "cannot wish to impose himself, for he believes in the effect of the actualizing forces. . . . The propagandist who imposes himself, does not really believe even in his own cause, for he does not trust it to attain the effect of its own power, without his special methods" (Buber, 1957, p. 111). While Buber believes so strongly in the power of honest meeting between persons in an I—Thou relationship of mutual trust and confirmation, even with differences of loyalties, he is very cautious about the right of the psychotherapist to embark upon a "treatment of the essential in man." He agrees with the late Viktor von Weizsaecker who said that it is not the privilege of the therapist or counselor to deal with the final destiny of man.

Returning to the area of guidance and student personnel services, it is becoming equally well established that basic educational philosophy does inevitably influence the procedures of the guidance counselor. If he is thoroughly pragmatic in his orientation he will probably be inclined to play down or ignore the importance of religious or metaphysical beliefs that the student brings to the counseling situation. He may feel that value judgments must be left out of the considerations. Of course, with this Pragmatic Philosophy which seems on the surface to be a neutral position, goes a basic commitment just as much so as the student may have, with his religious commitment. It seems to us that considerations of ultimate values cannot be avoided by the counselor as a person, and that he must operate from some philosophical point of view— some form of Idealism, Realism (Christian or otherwise), Pragmatism, Naturalism, or Existentialism (again religious or otherwise).

It seems imperative that guidance counselors and educators must join other leaders in education, psychology, psychotherapy, philosophy and religion in doing basic research in this field.

In this spirit of scientific inquiry (even with its obvious limitations in the area of ultimate values) and also in the spirit of dialogue (with free discussion of important questions related to man's basic needs and his basic conditions of existence) we should proceed to clarify and come to decisions about the foundation and goals of counseling.

194

Recently, Williamson has stated that, "I have further argued
for making explicit our own value orientations as individual counselors, not in order that we may adopt a counselor's orthodox
creed, but rather that we may responsibly give societal and moral
direction to our individual work in terms of the explicitly desired
goals chosen by our student clients" (Williamson, 1958, p. 528).

When guidance counselors, psychotherapists, or religious
counselors admit that they are not philosophically neutral, then
we will be able to study more systematically the effect of our
philosophical loyalties upon our counseling.

REFERENCES

Allport, G. W. Becoming: Basic considerations for a psychology
    of personality. New Haven: Yale Univer. Press, 1955.
Arbuckle, D. S. Student personnel services in higher education.
    New York: McGraw-Hill, 1953.
Arbuckle, D. S. Teacher counseling. Cambridge, Mass.: Addison-
    Wesley, 1950.
Buber, M. William Alanson White memorial lectures. Psychiatry,
    1957, 20 (2): 95-114.
Buber, M. The teacher and teaching. Unpublished manuscript. In
    collection compiled by Dr. Ross Snyder, Univer. of Chicago.
Frankl, V. E. The doctor and the soul. New York: Alfred Knopf,
    1955.
Fromm, Erich. The sane society. New York: Rinehart, 1955.
Lewin, K. A dynamic theory of personality. New York: McGraw-
    Hill, 1935.
Mathewson, R. H. Guidance policy and practice. New York: Harpe
    1955.
Oates, W. E. The religious dimensions of personality. New York:
    Association Press, 1957.
Pepinsky, H. B., & Pepinsky, Pauline N. Counseling: Theory and
    practice. New York: Ronald, 1954.
Rogers, C. R. Some observations on the organization of person-
    ality. Amer. Psychologist, 1947, 2: 358-368.
Rogers, C. R. A note on the nature of man. J. counsel. Psychol.,
    1957, 4: 199-203.
Strang, Ruth. The role of the teacher in personnel work. (4th ed.)
    New York: Teachers College (Columbia University), 1953.

Tillich, P. Systematic theology. Vol. 1. Chicago: Univer. of Chicago Press, 1952.

Vordenberg, W. The impact of personal philosophies on counseling. Personnel Guid. J., 1953, 31:439-440.

Walker, D., & Peiffer, H. The goals of counseling. J. counsel. Psychol., 1957, 4:204-209.

Weitz, H. Counseling as a function of the counselor's personality. Personnel Guid. J., 1957, 35:276-280.

Williamson, E. G. Value orientation in counseling. Personnel Guid. J., 1958, 36:520-528.

XIV

CHANGE IN VALUES: A GOAL IN COUNSELING

Joseph Samler

It seems a safe statement in an otherwise hazardous paper that psychologists are no longer defensive about being concerned with values. Hobbs' summary is only the most recent in a series of essays on ethics, values, science, and psychology (1959). In her presentation of concepts of positive mental health, Marie Jahoda devotes a brief section to the value dilemma (1958). In the last three years, Williamson has written a number of articles on values and counseling. Patterson's chapter on Values and Psychotherapy in his current <u>Counseling and Psychotherapy</u> (1959) cites 52 references to pertinent literature. Wrenn's contributions and Meehl's great clarity on this problem are well known. The current puzzling courtship of religion by psychotherapy (or the other way around) is a related phenomenon.

ON THE DERIVATION OF VALUES

We are at the core, here, of man's search for meaning in life, of his attempt to provide structure where in fact none may exist. Out of this overwhelming need, answers inevitably arose. For millennia they came from the wisdom and intuition of the noblest (a most value-laden term) among us.

The second Isaiah and the other Hebrew prophets, Jesus, the deeply perceptive poets, novelists, playwrights and our modern-day moral leaders, supplied the need out of their own deep feeling and identification with humankind. The nature of the values thus adduced is well known. They are absolute and final and not readily subject to question. They are an integral part of given institutions

Reprinted by permission of the author and the *Journal of Counseling Psychology*, 1960, 7:32-39.

and to question them is to attack the institutions. Since this not in-
frequently brings personal guilt and anxiety into play, it is done at
some hazard.

As against values thus derived, and in spite of the unnerving
cold shower Hobbs' clarity provides, is the method of science. Its
disadvantages in the field of values are clearly evident. Out of the
scientific-instrumental approach flow values which are relative by
definition, take context into account, represent stages in progress,
and are, therefore, open-ended. They are necessarily partial,
tentative and qualified. Wheelis' (1958) informed exposition of the
etiology of these different value systems warrants the attention of
all who are concerned with this problem.

Hobbs' (1959) conclusion (which sounds somehow regretful)
seems to be that psychology, as a science, has no major contribution to make to value organization. But psychology is _not_ any other
science; it is the science of man, the science of human behavior.
Also courage can be taken from his statement that he is as yet
highly tentative about some of his formulations and that he is not
yet able to let the problem alone. "For a science of man," Ashley
Montagu cites Julian Huxley as saying, "the problem is not whether
or not to have anything to do with values, but how to devise methods
of studying them and discovering how they work."

There is another aspect of this general problem that does not
relate to choice between traditional and scientifically derived value
systems. Maslow probably has been most articulate about it, although he is joined by others. This point is that the prime disease
of our time is valuelessness. It is a state variously described as
amorality, rootlessness, emptiness, alienation, hopelessness, the
lack, in short, of something to believe in and be devoted to. We
are confronted with a vacuum in values which must be filled. The
point of view is that traditional values have failed and in Maslow's
terms, we "need a validated, usable system of human values that
we can believe in and devote ourselves to because they are true
rather than because we are exhorted to believe and have faith"
(1959).

THREE BASIC PROPOSITIONS

Yet with all of the disadvantages of the scientific method in
the derivation of values granted, a number of points remain stubbornly in mind: That for the first time in the history of man there
is a systematic means of exploring his needs and their fulfillment;
that its appeal is widespread and has captured the interest and de-

votion of highly intelligent and creative workers; that its methodology is increasing in its sophistication; and that there is already a body of substantive information about the nature and condition of man.

Therefore, the first in a series of propositions:

1. Man's increasing scientific knowledge about himself should supply the basic data for derivation of his values.

Obviously we lack the tightly designed researches with findings validated at high levels of confidence, but we are not without theoretical contributions out of which we can identify necessary lines of research and testable hypotheses. The contributions by psychological workers are too well known to cite extensively, but they should be called to attention even if only to remind ourselves that we are least of all without such ideas.

The characteristics of Erich Fromm's productive personality are very much in point here as in his formulation of human needs in society. Sullivan's mature personality belongs here. Probably there would be a certain amount of difficulty in living in a world of Goldstein's and Maslow's self-actualizing people, but their validity and force are indubitable. Sorokin and Ashley Montagu and Shoben have contributed in this area. Of very great interest is Maslow's well known hierarchy of needs with its strong instinctoid overtones. Needs, it may be granted, are without undue difficulty translatable into values, also capable of hierarchial ordering.

With these contributions in mind, it is possible to offer, however tentatively, a second proposition:

2. The theoretical models of the psychologically healthy person, his orientation to himself and others, the choices he makes, and his criteria for making these choices, offer us meaningful material for value determinations.

A third proposition reaches for even if it does not quite grasp the horn of another dilemma:

3. Values should be subject to explicit examination as criteria for choice, as determinants of behavior.

Here I have learned from John E. Smith's discerning essay on Jacob's study (1958), and it is congruent with our current professions relative to mental health, specifically with the importance of bringing unconscious motivation into awareness. Smith's emphasis is on the critical response which requires a standard or criterion in accordance with which the actual judgment or evaluation is made.

We have a choice of a kind here. If we do not examine our value predispositions, or indeed our valuelessness, our beliefs and behavior must flow from our present value orientation which exists at various levels of awareness and clarity and understanding. All of this affects our ability to move toward or away from them.

Thus far this paper (a) urged the need for values derived from man's increasing knowledge about himself, at least as a goal if not as an immediate program, (b) called attention to theoretical models of the well-functioning individual and (c) made Smith's point that in final analysis, values must stand as the referent points, as the criteria for choice. All of these have pertinence in considering the particular enterprise, the learning task we call counseling.

VALUES AND THE COUNSELING TASK

It is hardly news that we have yet to define clearly and cleanly the job of counseling, its distinguishing characteristics relative to psychotherapy, or the appropriate range of effort in such specific goals as vocational counseling or marriage counseling. But it can be agreed that in some measure personality appraisal, evaluation of misperception, examination of self-acceptance, resulting change of behavior, acceptance of responsibility, and assumption of independence are common to all counseling tasks. Differential goals are also, of course, to be noted, e.g., reduction in guilt, acceptance of appropriate feelings of dependence, and the experience of feeling.

Whatever the true nature of these tasks, it seems quite a circumspect statement that the counselor plays a central role in them. For some workers in therapy and counseling he is clarifier of feelings, for others teacher and mentor, for still others a vehicle for safe reliving of the past and its examination. He is other things still, depending on what one feels actually takes place in the consulting room, and of course, the nature and cause and effect of behavior change in counseling or therapy are still largely unknown. Probably it is these different and partial theoretical views of counseling interaction that compel us to assign differing behavior to the counselor. The fourth proposition is based upon the idea now gaining increasing acceptance that as Sullivan's participant observer, as himself his most useful tool, the counselor is in effect an instrument which itself must be calibrated.

4. The counselor's values must be held in awareness.

In his usual comprehensive fashion C. H. Patterson (1959) has pulled together the literature on this problem. As against a previously adopted fancied neutrality, he cites theory and research relative to the impossibility of keeping the therapist's values out of his work. The evidence indicates that the influence can be unintended and quite below awareness levels. Logic compels us to the same conclusion, for to say that the counselor manifests no values is to require that he have no feelings and whatever great drama this may be it is not counseling. The unreality of such a devastating neutrality requires no comment. The least we can learn from this is that the counselor's awareness of his values is of prime importance.

The impression is gained in moving among professional colleagues and in reading that this need for search of self is accepted readily enough. It seems to be, in fact, the preferred style but whether this is only the cut of cloth or really integrated personality style is an open question. To be sure, life is a great teacher and the practicum leader's comments on taped interviews may go some distance, but it is doubtful that much light is shed in the dark area of unconscious motivation by these means. Yet how many counselors have been subject to the systematic and painful and enriching (and expensive) experience of truly investigating their behavior and its motivation, that is to say their values? The point that short of analytic procedures, we have been remiss in investigating and putting into effect systematic self-exploration methods, is defended elsewhere (Samler, 1959).

The point comes home in its specifics. Williamson points out in a recent article (1959) that in vocational counseling the counselor takes for granted that choice of occupation should reflect the individual's optimum potential, that interests should be capitalized, that university training is the summum bonum, and that job stability is much to be preferred to job hopping, which at times in fact is seen as a clinical symptom. The point Dean Williamson makes is that these values which determine basic counselor attitudes and behavior probably are quite out of the counselor's awareness.

It seems useful to note that these are relatively "safe" value areas. That is, we do not deal here with the counselor's own deeply rooted value system relating to this regard for himself, the nature and extent of his guilt, his strong feelings of dependence and so on, although connections there may be. Yet these value assumptions also are in quite a mysterious and unlighted area.

Like the apocryphal story of the paranoid patient who was advised he could continue in his delusions if only he kept his mouth shut, it may be possible to have behavioral change without fundamental change in values, but this is hardly an acceptable counseling goal. It is only making the obvious explicit to say that behavior constitutes a reflection, sometimes twisted and distorted as in peculiar mirrors, of values. How is it possible, for instance, to divorce values from Tyler's description of counseling which reads in part "a process by which each person can be helped to develop and understand his own characteristic life pattern, his own identity," or from the core of Super's statement relative to vocational counseling—"helping a person develop and accept an integrated and adequate picture of himself and his role in the world of work."

The next proposition, therefore, is that,

5. Values are at the heart of the counseling relationship, are reflected in its content, and affect the process.

It is clear that the very availability of counseling has deeply imbedded in it a particular value orientation. All counseling by definition is for the benefit of the counselee (with society's needs in mind, to be sure) and, therefore, the behavior, attitudinal set and basic relationship of the counselor to his client is characterized at least by interest, probably by concern, and possibly by a form of love. The need for respecting the client is a counseling byword. As silent preceptor, advocate of a particular way of relating to others, and as a respecting and expert helper, the counselor at the very least affects client attitudes. The literature is abundant on this point.

The counseling process as such is aimed at providing insight, changing behavior, and the exercise of choice along lines leading to more adequate functioning and greater comfort in living in terms of specified values. In vocational counseling, Super's phrase in his definition "helping the individual develop and accept an adequate picture of himself," is value loaded, as are other personality oriented counseling definitions. If the counselor functions along these lines he is inevitably, one way or another, addressing himself to the client's values. This is perhaps best illustrated by the studied observation not of a psychologist, but by the economist, researcher, and general gad-fly Eli Ginsberg (1951). In assessing the situation of vocational counseling he and his colleagues point out that:

> The connection between occupational choice process and work satisfaction is not contained in the specific decision which the individual reaches, but in how he clarifies the goals and values which are associated with the satisfactions he seeks in work. This clarification is an essential part of his occupational decision making, for he cannot make a choice without determining, at least preliminarily, what he wants to get out of work. If he fails to clarify his goals and values and fails to crystallize his choice, it is more than likely that his work experience will prove frustrating. Not knowing what he wants from work, he will be unable to choose from among such alternatives as he may have. *True crystallization and specification cannot take place until a clarification of goals and values has been made.* (Italics supplied)

Equally significant is understanding of the differential value systems of occupations. Here our colleagues in related fields have contributed heavily to understanding of social, class, and occupational expectations, roles, and their related values. It is difficult to conceive of counseling related to psychological realities which does not take these data into account.

We need not deal with the problem only on presumptive grounds. In his 1958 APA paper in this area, Paul Meehl, without offering his own support, cites workers (e.g., Wolpe, Herzberg, Maeder, Phillips, Frankl, Ellis, Thorpe) who, in his words "not only permit but who encourage a detailed consideration of value problems. These practitioners prefer not to treat the patient's value-orientation as merely a symptom or derivative of something else . . . but rather conceive that a patient's value orientation may itself be one of the important determiners of his unhappiness."

Proposition 6. "Intervention" by the counselor in the client's values is an actuality and should be accepted as a necessary part of the process.

Almost the question answers itself. If the counseling task is in a context of values, and if counseling goals must explicate and integrate them, then the counselor's activity in this area should be taken for granted. But I doubt that many will be satisfied with this abstraction. Specifics may help:

Given a highly talented 17-year-old youngster in educational and vocational counseling from a lower socio-economic stratum, I submit that the counselor assumes a given attitude set. This has to do with the client's self-actualization to be sure, and will allow for unique solutions. But for the generality of cases, the desirability of college will be very much in his mind. He has set a goal, tentative to be sure, for the youngster—it is obviously value oriented. I submit that the counselor will work toward that goal for and with the youngster.

Given impulsive and acting-out behavior with another client of whatever age, the role of the worker and his goals for the client are quite clear—more rational behavior and repression of some impulses.

One can list a set of troubles, the therapies of choice and their underlying value orientation:

for the demanding and infantile—assumption of responsibility;

for the vocationally disoriented—assumption of a working role congruent with the picture the client will develop of himself;

for the guilt-ridden—tolerance for himself and life's reality;
for the unloved and unloving—self-acceptance and kindliness;
for the achievement and power-ridden—appreciation of the
    rich resources in human beings;
for the highly controlling—reduction of anxiety and a more
    trusting and optimistic outlook.

The point I am making is that these goals in terms of change in client behavior and the accompanying assumption of congruent values, are clearly in the minds of the workers, and that they will address their efforts toward these ends.

In an oft-quoted article Gardner Murphy (1955) also addressed himself to this central issue. To the dilemma of activity relative to client values, Murphy's answer is unequivocal and along three lines. He feels that the counselor "cannot help conveying directly or indirectly to every client what he himself sees and feels, and the perspective in which his own life is lived." Second, "it is not true that the wise man's sharing of a philosophy of life is an arrogant imposition upon a defenseless client." Third, in addressing himself to our work, he says "it is often said that all philosophies are subjective and arbitrary, and that one system of values is as good as another. But if you believed that, you would not have chosen personnel and guidance as a way of life. Your experience, moreover, has shown you that some values, such as those of sympathy, tenderness, generosity, and self-control resonate to the deeper chords of human nature, and that they are for that reason intensely practical and dependable.

In Meehl's paper referred to before (1958), the therapists he cites, he states, "are willing to step into a pedagogical role and engage in direct behavioral retraining. Some would pay only incidental attention to cognitive issues; others view cognitive clarification—including persuasion and intellectual argument—as fundamental to the therapeutic process." Those who heard this thoughtful paper will recall that he goes on to say

> In the course of ordinary secular psychotherapy there occur, from time to time, exchanges between patient and therapist which are not defensive intellectualizations but which (whatever may be called within the therapist's preferred theoretical scheme) are, in their actual verbal structure, rather like a segment out of one of the Platonic dialogues. I suspect that one reason why so many therapists are skittish about getting involved in this kind of thing is that they lack talent and training for the Socratic dialogue; and that this deficiency, together with their own personal ambiguity about the value-question, makes them feel unsafe if they treat any such material in its own right, rather than as a derivative calling for a psychodynamic interpretation at some other level.

It is of the greatest possible interest that the same point is made in very much the same way be Allen Wheelis (1958) in the rich context of his novelette-essay-autobiography.

Proposition 7. Promotion of given values and counseling technique are now seen as constituting an indissoluble unit. They should be regarded as separable.

It seems to me that the actuality of counselor intervention in client values is beyond dispute. While such intervention is now accomplished through a basic relationship technique, it does not follow that this must be our only means. Even if methods determine ends it is still for consideration whether these are immutably the only proper means at our disposal.

We know that in their behavior, defenses, and values, human beings change least of all by exhortation, but this does not mean that the person to whom high achievement or power is a prime value and a way of maintaining self-respect, should not change; it only means that exhortation will not work with him. We have found that it is possible for people to learn to be loving, to like people (a value), but only by living through the experience of themselves being loved, being allowed suspiciously to test the lover-therapist in a thousand different ways. We have changed a value, in awareness, with full intention of doing so, but we have done it in a very particular way.

To the client who for the best of reasons has put a tight lid on his feelings, and is defended by intellect and emptiness, the therapist may sometimes want to say "try feeling, only the learning is painful," but he will not, because it will not work. But the encouraged experience, as it were, of creeping up on feeling, can work. The value is identified and sought out, change is encouraged, but again, the way of achieving it is very particular.

Probably the examples can be multiplied many times. There is a cause and effect relationship between the experience of being accepted and feeling the concern of another and increase in self-esteem, but it should not follow that this is the only way of achieving the desired effect in change in values. One is a very special kind of learning, a particular rich experience, but it is still a technique, and it should be seen as such. I keep on wondering whether if we deny the goal (specified change in values) and emphasize the means (our present relationship techniques), we are not selling ourselves short on the possibility of finding other ways of helping.

This proposition is based in part on the discerning discussion by Meehl and McClosky (1947) of the relationship between ethics and technique in therapeutic work. It is tempting to cite any number of sharp and clear paragraphs in this discussion. It is required reading for all of us concerned with this problem.

If we can separate out technique of choice from the necessary goal of change in values, the inevitable question arises as to which values. It is this critical question that prompts the last proposal:

Proposition 8. Drawing upon the available models of the mature personality, it should be possible to develop testable hypotheses relative to the values to be supported in counselor-client interaction.

The hazards in this are tremendous: Jahoda (1958) points out for instance that

> While it is easy to speculate about the relation of each criterion to a vast number of high values, we do not know whether such relations actually obtain. Does self-actualization really benefit the development of the species, as Fromm would claim? Is interpersonal competence a prerequisite for the happiness of the individual? Is happiness or productivity the value underlying an active orientation to problem-solving?

Yet what recourse have we other than the dictum that the individual will develop his own? More than that: the omniscient answers that these questions appear to require are not really necessary. We do not need to solve them for the next few millennia, the job is difficult enough if we get answers that are better than any others and that will work for the next 25 years or for that part of such a period until better answers emerge. In any case, the models provide the best answers that theory making and clinical experience have yet made available to us.

I do not want to be mistaken. The notion, for example, of a congress of psychologists determining by vote whatever values should be, scares the daylight out of me as well. This is not the way. Our faith must be put on the scientific derivation of desirable behavior, orientation to life, and their underlying values.

Should we embark on such an enterprise, after coming to terms with the values implicit in it, it would follow that the professed neutrality of the counselor relative to his client's values would have to be abandoned in favor of an affirmation of given values. The attendant possibility might arise of opening up the important process of values as referent points.

Least of all am I concerned with the shibboleth of democracy and authoritarianism in the counseling relationship. These ghosts were laid by Meehl and McClosky in 1947, and what is required is a courageous editor nowhere available to reprint that sterling article. An affirmative stand in values is contrary also to Patterson's summation (1959, p. 74). He says in part about the counselor that:

> He would not feel that the counseling relationship is the place to teach moral or ethical standards, or a philosophy of life. He is confident, as apparently some are not, that the client in the therapeutic relationship will be aware of and influenced by social realities. He will leave to the family, the church and the school, as institutions representing the moral and ethical standards of society, the teaching of such standards.

These three sentences appear to represent the orthodox opinion in the field and yet I believe they must be subject to serious examination. They bypass the reality that values are in fact learned in the consulting room. But more important, they disregard the counseling situation as a learning experience of the greatest possible import, ethically bound as are very few others, constantly under the scrutiny of a highly self-conscious professional community. It is not an opportunity to be lightly dismissed. It is an opportunity for the learning of values to be affirmed, explored, and made the subject of our most serious concern.

The written word takes on a finality that goes beyond intention. Personal experience and consideration of these serious problems argues a greater tentativeness than these propositions offer. But the unequivocal certitude of a great deal of present thinking on values, counselor role, and client change, is too troublesome to leave alone. This much is certain: We must examine our present value commitments and carry them sharply in awareness. In the light of our growing knowledge of human behavior we must ourselves map the country and travel a road of our own choosing. We should be able to accept without quibbling the objective in counseling of modification of client behavior and therefore of attitudes and values. With the purpose unequivocally clear our task remains that of determining how it can best be accomplished whatever our present commitments.

REFERENCES

Ginsberg, E., et al. Occupational choice, an approach to a general theory. New York: Columbia Univer. Press, 1951.

Hobbs, N. Science and ethical behavior. Amer. Psychol., 1959, 14:217-225.

Jahoda, Marie. Current concepts of positive mental health. Monograph Series No. 1, Joint Commission on Mental Health. New York: Basic Books, 1958.

Maslow, A. H. (Ed.) New knowledge in human values. New York: Harper, 1959.

Meehl, P. E. Some technical and axiological problems in the therapeutic handling of religious and valuational material. Unpublished paper delivered at APA convention, 1958.

Meehl, P. E., & McClosky, H. Ethical and political aspects of applied psychology. J. abnorm. soc. Psychol., 1947, 42:91-98.

Montagu, M. F. The direction of human development: Biological and social bases. New York: Harper, 1955.

Murphy, G. The cultural context of guidance. Personnel Guid. J., 1955, 34: 4-9.

Patterson, C. H. Counseling and psychotherapy: Theory and practice. New York: Harper, 1959.

Samler, J. Basic approaches to mental health, an attempt at synthesis. Personnel Guid. J., 1959, 37:638-643.

Smith, J. E. Value convictions and higher education. New Haven: Edward W. Hazen Foundation, 1958.

Wheelis, A. The quest for identity. New York: Norton, 1958.

Williamson, E. G. The meaning of communication in counseling. Personnel Guid. J., 1959, 38:6-14.

XV

THE FUSION OF DISCIPLINE AND COUNSELING IN THE EDUCATIVE PROCESS

E. G. Williamson

Of the many opposite and contradictory concepts to be found in the literature of education, discipline and counseling are perhaps most sharply separated.

Discipline is characterized as	Counseling is described as
repressive	growth producing
regulatory	ego strengthening
forced conformity	self-regulating
law abiding	affect integration
orderliness	confidence development
imposed	self-initiated
forced control	self-centered

Discipline and counseling differ sharply in other respects: Discipline is imposed by external restraining authority of parents, teachers, fellow pupils, community mores, law authorities, or principals. It is not requested by pupils in elementary school and least of all by high school students whose idea of a pure democracy is a society of adolescents with no adults anywhere in the vicinity.

Counseling long has been a self-initiated relationship at the adolescent age and a seemingly wanted one at the child level. It is centered not on the community, school or group but upon the indi-

This paper originally appeared in *Discipline and the Guidance Program* (1953 Potsdam Guidance Conference). Reprinted by permission of the author and the *Personnel and Guidance Journal*, 1955, 34:74–79.

vidual and his own unique problems—as though he were more important than everyone else in the home, school, and community.
This centering of counseling upon the isolated individual pupil has
been characterized recently as an instance of individual relativism
as opposed to cultural relativism.

Discipline is a "public" matter in two respects: It is imposed
conformity to other persons, and there is nothing private or confidential about it. One either conforms voluntarily publicly to
group requirements or else one is compelled to do so by social
pressures, punishment, or some other means of regulation.

Counseling is highly personal and confidential. Except for
certain persons who are motivated to be abnormal publicly, most
persons desire to discuss their intimate adjustments with one
counselor at a time. This is the reason that the highly prized confidentiality of counseling is a necessity—the pupil desires it, prof-
its most through it, and suffers relapses when it is dissipated.
From the viewpoint of a counselor, the absence of privacy and confidentiality are among the four most devastating weaknesses in
most programs of discipline. The ineffective use of punishment
for rehabilitation is a third weakness, and the fourth is the inhuman, impersonal manner in which human beings often are handled
and processed, sometimes even in education.

Discipline, as I am now using the term, is a discordant note
in that type of education designed to stimulate the growth of individuality—social, moral, and intellectual. Indeed, forcing conformity in behavior is often an indication that other educational
methods have failed and that in desperation we have abandoned efforts to persuade and have turned to the use of superior authority.
It needs to be re-emphasized, however, that many times we face
situations in which too much damage to morale has been done to
permit persuasion to have any effect. In such cases, we must use
compulsion, but we must not deceive ourselves that we are using
an educational method. And we ought to return to persuasion as
soon as we can.

Let me continue my contrast of discipline and counseling. I
am leading up to a re-definition of discipline achieved by fusing
the two into a new type of relationship between teacher and admin-
istrator, on the one hand, and pupils and students, on the other.

In a distant university, a teacher of counseling is said to have
told his trainees: No counselor should have anything to do with reg-
istration of students in subjects or with discipline. Presumably, in
such a school, unruly and destructive behavior would be handled by
the principal or superintendent, and they, harassed by many other

pressures and crises, quickly would be forced to dispose of disciplinary cases by assigning penalties, once guilt had been established. As one result of such "drum head" justice, resentment would be added to conflict and the pupil would make a test case to determine who was boss. Such conflict psychology of relationship would often preclude rehabilitation.

Moreover, the counselor, in such a school, would be freed from such conflict so that he could deal with the "behaving" students about their personal problems. Thus the delinquents, who most desperately need clarification of their own chaotic emotions, would often turn to stronger misbehavior as a substitute of counseling.

And counseling, by avoiding such disciplinary responsibilities, would become limited in its usefulness since it takes place only with "good" citizens in the school or home, requires voluntary seeking of counseling, and is of no help in dealing with the pupils who rebel against conformity. These consequences might not be a serious matter if we were content to dismiss delinquency and disciplinary cases by asserting that they are caused by pure cussedness, moral depravity, and other uncontrollable factors and that "nice" persons don't behave that way.

But we now know that misbehavior occurs in some pupils who are otherwise fine persons and quite capable of good citizenship. It is to discover the correctible causes of misbehavior that I believe discipline must be infused with counseling. Discipline as punishment is no corrective of misbehavior unless it is a part or a consequence of a counseling relationship. Alone, punishment is repressive and growth arresting. With counseling, it can become educative, corrective, and growth producing.

This is my thesis, and I now turn to a defense of it.

Many counselors are willing to be used as consultants in exploring the deeper motivations underlying misbehavior, but they understandably do not wish to play any role whatsoever when it comes to imposing restrictions and "punishment" upon the offending student. They wish to be completely without authority and to be perceived by the client as having no possible authority which could be a threat to him. Rather do they wish to serve as his advocate and friend even to the extent of pleading his case with the school authority.

In terms of its effectiveness in maintaining counseling relationships, such a course of action is necessary. But the principal is thus segregated and symbolized with all the trapping of "harsh" authority and is often perceived by the counselor and misbehaving student alike as being a repressive and threatening authority symbol. In my opinion, the counselor does not play his full and proper counseling role in an educational institution when he thus completely segregates and separates himself from such an authority symbol.

It seems to me that, in addition to the consultant role, there are three other functions that counselors properly have in disciplinary situations: first, counseling as active rehabilitation of misbehaving offenders; second, the prevention of misbehavior through counseling to achieve normal development in inner-control of self; and, finally, counseling as a way of aiding students to perceive and to accept that external authority which influences inner development and modifies unbridled individualism.

Counseling as Rehabilitation. My point is best illustrated by quoting from the field of child psychology. In her delightful book, New Ways in Discipline, Baruch (1949) has illuminated the major revolution that has taken place in the home with respect to the parental-child relationship, now reconstructed so that counseling techniques, emphasis, and points of view are built into the changed normal relationship of parent and child. Baruch's book is replete with insightful transposing reorientation guidelines, such as: "If a child misbehaves, we'll recognize that he must have unsatisfied emotional needs . . . we'll try to satisfy it all we can." And again, "When unwanted negative feelings have been emptied out sufficiently then—warm and good positive feelings flow in." And again, "All children need release and acceptance of 'mean' feelings. All children have 'mean' feelings that need to be released." The logic of therapy as rehabilitation in disciplinary cases is thus made clear. Misbehavior stems from the repression of "mean" feelings, and if the "mean" feelings are aired, brought up to the level of conscious communication, then the basic drive for misbehavior is lessened, if not eliminated. Rehabilitation consists, therefore, of straightforward therapy in which the individual finds substitute channels for his repressed feelings of aggression and disappointment.

So far so good. But it is one thing for the parent-child to restructure the relationship within the imposition of the home in which the child is scarcely willing or able to reject the parent, except symbolically; it is quite another thing for an adolescent, with some degree of possible freedom to reject a non-parental relationship, to be given that kind of release therapy which he does not want because he does not see the necessity of correcting his misbehavior or of being rehabilitated through counseling relationships. Here we run squarely into the complex problem of imposed counseling relationships. Counseling as rehabilitation in a disciplinary situation seems to work well when it is accepted by the counselee, but when it is not thus accepted, such voluntary counseling obviously will not be operative—according to the assumption of current therapists. Our experiences lead us to question the generalization that in all instances and in all respects, imposed counseling relationships are ineffective as well as "bad." I shall return to this point below.

There is a second way in which counseling can serve as the rehabilitation of offending students, and that way is through the transposition of points of view, techniques, and emphases from the customary one-to-one relationship of the counseling interview to the entire school situation. In much the same way as parent-child relationships in the home are now being restructured according to counseling generalizations and experiences, likewise the entire school atmosphere and the relationships between teachers and students, principals and students, and teachers and parents may be restructured with the counseling interview serving as a model. In many schools, such a revolution is well under way, but there are many counselors who do not accept this opportunity to extend the influence of counseling far beyond the one-to-one counseling interview.

Prevention of Misbehavior through Counseling. I come to my second point, the use of counseling techniques and emphases to facilitate the achievement of normal development of self-control and self-discipline. Every counselor understands some phases of the process by means of which warm and positive feelings become a normal part of the child's development through the maintenance of satisfying affective relationships with others and with adults. Optimum development of the individual is indeed achievable, as far as affect is concerned, through the emotional climate of the school and home in which the child is encouraged, assisted, and permitted to grow up with a minimum of repression and negative attitudes and feelings.

Baruch (1949) summarizes this generalization with respect to misbehavior and behavior when she says, "The more we accept a child's FEELINGS, the more will he accept our RULES." It is quite true that if the relationships of the home and school are satisfying, affectively, to the child, then there seems to be little motivation for misbehaving; that is, the child thus achieves satisfaction through conforming to the requirements of his social environment, and there is no desire or motivation to do otherwise. He is, in this sense, a normally developing individual, and he does not experience the necessity of conflicting or warring with his environment because his environment thwarts him. Thus developing effective school situations provides another opportunity for counselors to prevent misbehavior.

Counseling as an Aid to Perception and Acceptance of External Authority. I turn to my third point, counseling as a process of reorientation to the reality of external authority. As a facilitator of normal development, the school counselor enters the disciplinary situation, or at least can enter it, in a new and in many ways more important role, as an educator-counselor who seeks to help the misbehaving student perceive and accept the role of authority as it impinges upon his own "autonomous" inner life and behavior. Within the friendly home, the consequences of misbehavior are soon forgotten, and there is frequently no external legal authority acting for society to impose consequences, restrictions, and limitations upon the autonomy of the individual in the light of or as a result of his misbehavior. In most home-centered misbehavior, all is soon forgiven, and certainly the term "punishment" has no long-term connotation. But as a child grows into adolescence and begins to misbehave away from his home, all is not so readily forgiven and forgotten. Consequences flow from misbehavior and are sometimes legally imposed in the form of punishment as retribution following upon the heels of misbehavior. It is at this point that the counselor can play a very significant role in helping the individual to learn to live in a universe in which his autonomy is hedged about and "infringed" upon by external authority and to understand how the role of the forgiving parent, who generates positive feelings and warmth, is often set aside in many instances by a harsh, repressive, and sometimes vengeful authority symbol-role.

I am not advocating that a counselor enter into partnership with such a vengeful authority. But I feel certain that a counselor can play a significant role in helping the individual to perceive, and to accept emotionally, the inevitability of authority in some form or another acting as a restrictive agency upon the individual's free play of self-directed freedom. This learning is a profound one and most necessary in a democratic society of cooperative and interrelated individual persons. To be sure, it is not easy to teach such a generalization to an individual who has come into conflict with that society, or even in conflict with other individuals in a small, restricted club or school. Such an individual has already alienated himself from other individuals and from authority by his misbehavior. How then can he be aided to accept that which he has flaunted? As Kurt Lewin (1948) so cogently states:

We can now formulate the dilemma which re-education has to face in this way: How can free acceptance of a new system of values be brought about if the person who is to be educated is, in the nature of things, likely to be hostile to the new values and loyal to the old?

Re-education influences conduct only when the new system of values and beliefs dominates the individual's perception. The acceptance of the new system is linked with the acceptance of a specific group, a particular role, a definite source of authority as new points of reference. It is basic for re-education that this linkage between acceptance of new facts or values and acceptance of certain groups or roles is very intimate and that the second frequently is a prerequisite for the first (Lewin 1948).

At this point counselors can and should, I believe, pioneer in testing Lewin's hypothesis by searching for counseling techniques that will aid a misbehaving individual to learn and to like the "imposed" role and the new values required of him as a member of a group, his home, and his school.

I have now stated what I mean by the fusion of discipline and counseling in an educative process—discipline becomes not "forced" conformity or punishment, but a type of re-education designed to aid the individual to so understand his emotions and feelings and to so redirect them into new behavior channels that he no longer wants to or is forced to misbehave as an unsuccessful attempt to rid himself of external authority. Parenthetically, it escapes the attention of some counselors that the state of individualistic autonomy that some students seek is, in its extreme form, self destructive or at least not a full measure of self fulfillment in the case of human beings.

There are, I repeat, two arguments for attempting such a fusion of discipline and counseling: Counseling is our present chief prospect for changing discipline from punishment to rehabilitation; and counseling as a form of growth-producing and morale building human relationship will aid the individual to achieve that degree of self-control and self-restraint so necessary in all members of an inter-dependent democratic society. And I borrow the words of a cultural anthropologist who describes the way in which one individual can achieve his individuality through, and not in spite of, the imposed discipline of membership in a society:

... to belong to a society is to sacrifice some measure of individual liberty, no matter how slight the restraints which the society consciously imposes. The so-called free societies are not really free. They are merely those societies which encourage their members to express their individuality along a few minor and socially acceptable lines. At the same time they condition their members to abide by innumerable rules and regulations, doing this so subtly and completely that these members are largely unconscious that the rules exist. If a society has done its work of shaping the individual properly, he is no more conscious of most of the restrictions it has imposed than he is of the restraints which his habitual clothing imposes on his movements (Linton, 1945).

Let me quote my summary of a recent conference on discipline and counseling:

To achieve full personal development, each pupil must learn to live mutually helpfully with others in group life.

This means that each individual must learn self control or at least develop in the direction of that ideal of our democracy.

It follows that the individual cannot grow toward self control in a social vacuum of rampant and selfish individualism.

And that aspect involves the school (and counselor) in helping (and insisting) that the individual "conform" to the requirements of group living involving the needs of other pupils. Such a concept bothers those who feel guilty about "imposing" any restrictions from the outside upon the inner growth processes of the individual. Nevertheless, it is clear that both types of discipline (self and group) must be fused in the personality of the individual if he is to avoid disintegration and self conflict.

The crux of the matter is the methods the school and the counselor use to achieve this self control adjusted to group conformity. And rigid regimentation involving sharp punishment for deviation from official pathways of behavior is an ineffective way. Conversely, the maintenance of a friendly school atmosphere and the offering of a rich variety of growth-producing experiences in learning self control are effective ways of teaching self discipline.

If we redefine "discipline" as a constructive life-style of living as a human being involving the maintaining of human relationships with others, we then see new ways in which counseling can play a significant role in discipline.

But, and this is a troublesome spot, many individuals deviate in their learning and some deviate destructively to self and to others. It is at this point that the legal authorities step in, both in the school and community, and force conformity as well as "punish" deviation.

Up to this point, counselors participate in discipline through their normal activities of helping the individual to achieve optimum growth and also by insisting upon accommodation to standards required by membership in society. In this sense, the counselor does not permit unbridled self-growth of any kind that is destructive of self or other selves.

In the conflict state of disciplinary situations, the counselor becomes a teamwork consultant to the "authorities," participating within school and community in rehabilitating the "offender." It follows that he must make clear to the student that he, the counselor, is on the side of morality and "law and order." He is not neutral in such a situation. He also makes it clear that part of a student's behavior which is destructive of the "right" kind of self control is balanced in counseling between the needs and rights of the disciplined student and the needs and rights of other individuals within the group (Williamson, 1954).[1]

[1] The above nine paragraphs are taken from my article, "Discipline and Counseling," *Education*, 1954, 74:513–16.

I can sum up my point of view about the fusion of discipline and counseling by quoting a wise psychiatrist who played a major role in the conference referred to above. Dr. Carson of Potsdam, New York, capsuled the point in these words: "Discipline must be given a matrix of love." All human beings, and especially children and adolescents, have great "affect hunger" and misbehaving children and adolescents have greater need. If their misbehavior erupts out of affect hunger and resentment from rejection in home or community, then the school and especially the counselors must substitute affection for that hunger. Punishment will not completely fill such a deep void, but the humanized relationship of counseling will be effective. Therefore, in the area of behavior (as contrasted with "inert" knowledge of the classroom), human relationships in the school will often prove to be effective in helping pupils to achieve maturity, social, moral, intellectual, and other kinds. It is not unreasonable to restructure schools so that human beings are related to each other in a way characterized as humane.

In this way, self-control discipline is cultivated by the very personal relationships of the persons in the school, and this is one of the most important goals of counseling. Discipline then becomes restructured through the adoption of counseling methods and points of view as substitutes for discipline by inhumane punishment.

REFERENCES

Baruch, Dorothy W. New ways in discipline. New York: McGraw-Hill, 1949.

Lewin, K. Resolving social conflicts. New York: Harper, 1948.

Linton, R. The cultural background of personality. New York: Appleton-Century-Crofts, 1945.

Williamson, E. G. A conference summary: Counseling in a disciplinary situation. 1953 Potsdam Guidance Conference, State Univer. Teachers College, Potsdam, New York.

Williamson, E. G. Discipline and counseling. Education, 1954, 74:513-16.

XVI

SOME CONSTRUCTIVE FEATURES
OF THE CONCEPT OF SIN

O. Hobart Mowrer

As long as one adheres to the theory that psychoneurosis implies no moral responsibility, no error, no misdeed on the part of the afflicted person, one's vocabulary can, of course, remain beautifully objective and "scientific." But as soon as there is so much as a hint of personal accountability in the situation, such language is, at the very least, wide of the mark and, conceivably, quite misleading. Therefore, if "moral judgment" does enter the picture, one might as well beard the lion and use the strongest term of all, sin. This is the strategy involved in the present and following chapter.

But there is also a deeper objective here. "Sickness," as we shall see increasingly in later chapters [of The Crisis in Psychiatry and Religion], is a concept which generates pervasive pessimism and confusion in the domain of psychopathology; whereas sin, for all its harshness, carries an implication of promise and hope, a vision of new potentialities. Just so long as we deny the reality of sin, we cut ourselves off, it seems, from the possibility of radical redemption ("recovery").

In some ways it is perhaps not surprising that we are assembled here today to explore the question of whether real guilt, or sin, is relevant to the problem of psychopathology and psychotherapy. For half a century now we psychologists, as a profession, have very largely followed the Freudian doctrine that human beings

One of four papers comprising a symposium on "The Role of the Concept of Sin in Psychotherapy" held at the 1959 meeting of the American Psychological Association, in Cincinnati, Ohio (American Psychologist, 1959, 14:356) and later published in the Journal of Counseling Psychology, 1960, 7:185–188. This paper has also appeared, without authorization, in Catholic Mind, 1960, 58:151–155.)

become emotionally disturbed, not because of their having done anything palpably wrong, but because they instead lack insight. Therefore, as would-be therapists we have set out to oppose the forces of repression and to work for understanding. And what is this understanding, or insight, which we so highly prize? It is the discovery that the patient or client has been, in effect, too good; that he has within him impulses, especially those of lust and hostility, which he has been quite unnecessarily inhibiting. And health, we tell him, lies in the direction of recognizing and expressing these impulses.

But there are now widespread and, indeed, ominous signs that this logic and the practical strategies it seems to demand are ill-founded. The situation is, in fact, so grave that, as our presence here today suggests, we are even willing to consider the possibility that misconduct may, after all, have something to do with the matter and that the doctrine of repression and insight are more misleading than helpful.

However, as soon as we psychologists get into a discussion of this problem, we find that our confusion is even more fundamental than might at first appear. We find that not only have we disavowed the connection between manifest misconduct and psychopathology; we have, also, very largely abandoned belief in right and wrong, virtue and sin, in general.

On other occasions when I have seen this issue under debate and anyone has proposed that social deviousness is causal in psychopathology, there is always a chorus of voices who clamor that sin cannot be defined, that it is culturally relative, that it is an unscientific concept, that it is a superstition—and therefore not to be taken seriously, either in psychopathology or in ordinary, everyday experience. And whenever an attempt is made to answer these objections, there are always further objections—often in the form of reductions to absurdity—which involve naivity or sophistry that would ill-become a schoolboy. Historically, in both literate and non-literate societies, human beings are supposed to have reached the age of discretion by early adolescence; yet here we have the spectacle of grown men and women soberly insisting that, in effect, they cannot tell right from wrong—and that no one else can.

Now I realize how futile it is to try to deal with this kind of attitude in a purely rational or logical way. The subversive doctrine that we can have the benefits of orderly social life without paying for it, through certain restraints and sacrifices, is too alluring to be counteracted by mere reason. The real answer, I believe, lies along different lines. The unassailable, brute fact is that personality disorder is the most pervasive and baffling problem of our time; and if it should turn out that persons so afflicted regularly display (or rather hide) a life of too little, rather than too much, moral restraint and self-discipline, the problem would take on an empirical urgency that would require no fine-spun argument.

Sin used to be—and, in some quarters, still is—defined as whatever one does that puts him in danger of going to Hell. Here was an assumed cause-and-effect relationship that was completely metaphysical and empirically unverifiable; and it is small wonder that it has fallen into disrepute as the scientific outlook and method have steadily gained in acceptance and manifest power. But there is a very tangible and very present Hell-on-this-earth which science has not yet helped us understand very well; and so I invite your attention to the neglected but very real possibility that it is this Hell—the Hell of neurosis and psychosis—to which sin and unexpiated guilt lead us and that it is this Hell that gives us one of the most, perhaps the most realistic and basic criteria for defining sin and guilt. If it proves empirically true that certain forms of conduct characteristically lead human beings into emotional instability, what better or firmer basis would one wish for labeling such conduct as destructive, self-defeating, evil, sinful?[1]

If the Freudian theory of personality disorder were valid, one would expect neurotic and psychotic individuals to have lead exemplary, yea saintly lives—to have been just too good for this world. The fact is, of course, that such individuals typically exhibit lives that have been disorderly and dishonest in extreme degree. In fact, this is so regularly the case [see Chapters 8 and 13] that one cannot but wonder how so contrary a doctrine as that of Freud ever gained credence. Freud spurned The Wish and exalted Reality. What he regarded as Reality may yet prove to have been the biggest piece of wishfulness of all.

Or, it may be asked, how is it if sin and psychic suffering are correlated that not all who sin fall into neurosis or psychosis? Here the findings of the Kinsey studies are likely to be cited, show-

---

[1]There is, admittedly, an element of circularity in the above argument. If it is maintained that mental illness is caused by unacknowledged and unexpiated sin, or real guilt, then it adds nothing to our knowledge to *define* sin as that which causes mental illness. In fact, there is a sense in which such a definition is not only circular but misleading (see Chapter 13 [*The Crisis in Psychiatry and Religion*]). Obviously, what is needed is an *independent criterion for identifying* sin or guilt—cf. Chapters 10-11 and Mowrer, 1961.

ing that, for example, many persons have a history of sexual perversity who are later quite normal. In other words, the argument is that since sin and persistent suffering do not always go hand-in-hand, there is perhaps no relationship at all. The answer to this question is surely obvious. Some individuals, alas, simply do not have enough character, or conscience, to be bothered by their sins. These are, of course, the world's psychopaths. Or an individual may have been caught in his sin and punished for it. Or it may have weighed so heavily on his conscience that he himself has confessed it and made appropriate expiation. Or, quite conceivably, in some instances the individual, without either detection or confession, may have set upon a program of service and good works which has also brought him peace and redemption. In other words, there is, surely, no disposition on the part of anyone to hold that sin, as such, necessarily dooms a person to interminable suffering in the form of neurosis or psychosis. The presumption is rather that sin has this effect only where it is acutely felt but not acknowledged and corrected.

Also, it is sometimes contended that individuals who eventually come to the attention of psychotherapists have, to be sure, been guilty of major errors of conduct; but, it is held, the illness was present first and the misconduct was really just an expression or symptom thereof. If this were true, where then would we draw the line? Is there no such thing as moral responsibility and social accountability at all? Is every mean or vicious thing that you or I, as ordinary individuals, do not sin but rather an expression of "illness"? Who would seriously hold that a society could long endure which consistently subscribed to this flaccid doctrine?

Then there is, of course, the view that, in the final analysis, all psychopathology—or at least its profounder forms—have a constitutional or metabolic basis. One must, I believe, remain open-minded with respect to this possibility—indeed, perhaps even somewhat hopeful with respect to it; for how marvelous it would be if all the world's madness, stupidity, and meanness could be eliminated through biochemistry. But over the years we have seen one approach after another of this kind come into prominence, with much heralding as the long-awaited break-through on the problem of mental disease, only to fade out as manifestly not quite the panacea we had imagined it to be. Some of us may, at this point, even suspect that today the main incentive for keeping the biochemical hypothesis alive is not so much the supporting empirical evidence, which is meager enough, but instead the fact that it at least obliquely justifies the premise that the whole field of mental disorder is the proper and exclusive domain of medicine. Also, and again somewhat obliquely, it excuses the clergy from facing squarely the responsibilities that would devolve among them if neurosis and psychosis should indeed turn out to be essentially moral disorders.

The conception of personality disturbance which attaches major etiological significance to moral and interpersonal considerations thus faces formidable resistance, from many sources; but programs of treatment and prevention which have been predicated on these other views have gotten us nowhere, and there is no clear reason to think they ever will. Therefore, in light of the total situation, I see no alternative but to turn again to the old, painful, but also promising possibility that man is preeminently a social creature and that he lives or dies, psychologically and personally, as a function of the openness, community, relatedness, and integrity which by good action he attains and by evil action destroys.

As long as we could believe that the psychoneurotic's basic problem was not evil but a kind of ignorance, it did not seem too formidable a task to give him the requisite enlightenment or insight. But mental hospitals are now full of people who have had this kind of therapy, in one guise or another, and found it wanting; and if we are thus forced to reconsider the other alternative, the therapeutic or redemptive enterprise, however clear it may be in principle, is by no means simple in practice. If the problem is genuinely one of morality, rather than pseudo-morality, most of us in the secular healing professions, of psychology, psychiatry, or social work, find ourselves reduced to the status of laymen, with no special training or competence for dealing with or even approaching the problem in these terms. We know something, of course, about procedures for getting disturbed persons to talk about themselves, free-associate, "confess"; but the whole aim of this strategy has been insight, not redemption and personal reformation. And clergymen themselves have so often been told, both by their own leaders and by members of the secular healing professions, that they must recognize their own "limitations" and know when to "refer" that they, too, lack the necessary confidence and resources for dealing with these problems adequately cf. Chapters 11, 12].

Many present-day psychoanalysts will offer no serious objection to the way in which classical Freudian theory and practice have been evaluated in this paper; but they will insist that many "advances" have been made since Freud's time and that these put the whole problem in a very different light. If we ask, "Precisely what are these advances?" we are told that they have to do with the new emphasis upon "ego psychology" rather than upon "the unconscious." But what did Emalian Gutheil (1958) tell us at our convention last year in Washington about ego psychology? He said that although analysts now recognize the ego as much more important than formerly, they know next to nothing about the conditions for modifying or strengthening it; and the same position has been voiced earlier by Lawrence Kubie (1956) and in one of his very last papers (1937) even by Freud himself [see also Chapter 13].

Therefore, I do not see how we can avoid the conclusion that at this juncture we are in a real crisis with respect to the whole psychotherapeutic enterprise. But I do not think we are going to remain in this crisis, confused and impotent, indefinitely. There is, I believe, growing realism with regard to the situation on the part of both psychologists and psychiatrists, on the one hand, and ministers, rabbis, and priests, on the other; and I am hopeful and even confident that new and better ways of dealing with the situation are in the making.

What, precisely, these ways will be I do not know; but I venture the impression that Alcoholics Anonymous provides our best present intimation of things to come and that the therapeutic programs of the future, whether under religious or secular auspices, will, like AA, take guilt, confession, and expiation seriously and will involve programs of _action_ rather than mere groping for "insight."

REFERENCES

Freud, S. Analysis terminable and interminable. In Collected Papers. Vol. 5. London: Hogarth, 1950.

Kubie, L. S. Some unsolved problems of psychoanalytic psychotherapy. In Fromm-Reichmann & Moreno (Eds.), Progress in psychotherapy. New York: Grune & Stratton, 1956.

Gutheil, E. Pseudoneurotic symptoms in psychosis. Amer. Psychol., 1958, 13: 350.

XVII

SIN AND PSYCHOTHERAPY

Albert Ellis

One of the most challenging and lucid of recent thinkers on the subject of psychotherapy has been the eminent psychologist, O. Hobart Mowrer. Vigorously condemning the Freudian attitudes regarding the id, ego, and superego, Professor Mowrer has for the last decade upheld the thesis that if the psychotherapist in any way gives his patients the notion that they are not responsible for their sins, he will only encourage them to keep sinning; and that they cannot become emotionally undisturbed, since at bottom disturbance is a moral problem, unless they assume full responsibility for their misdeeds—and, what is more, stop their sinning.

In a recent symposium in which I participated with Dr. Mowrer, he made some excellent points with which I heartily agree (Mowrer, 1960a): namely, that psychotherapy must largely be concerned with the patient's sense of morality or wrongdoing; that classical Freudianism is mistaken in its implication that giving an individual insight into or understanding of his immoral or antisocial behavior will usually suffice to enable him to change that behavior; that if any Hell exists for human beings it is the Hell of neurosis and psychosis; that man is pre-eminently a social creature who psychologically maims himself to the degree that he needlessly harms others; that the only basic solution to the problem

This chapter is an expanded version of two previously published articles: "There is No Place for the Concept of Sin in Psychotherapy" (*J. Consult. Psychol.*, 1960, 7: 188-192) and "Mowrer on 'Sin'" (*Amer. Psychologist*, 1960, 15: 713). Reprinted by permission of the author and publisher from Albert Ellis. *Reason and Emotion in Psychotherapy*. New York: Lyle Stuart, 1962.

of emotional disturbance is the correction or cessation of the disturbed person's immoral actions; and that the effective psychotherapist must not only give his patient insight into the origins of his mistaken and self-defeating behavior but must also provide him with a highly active program of working at the eradication of this behavior.

On the surface, then, it would appear that I am in close agreement with Mowrer's concepts of sin and psychotherapy. This, however, is not true: since one of the central theses of rational-emotive psychotherapy is that there is no place whatever for the concept of sin in psychotherapy and that to introduce this concept in any manner, shape, or form is highly pernicious and antitherapeutic. The rational therapist holds, on the contrary, that no human being should ever be blamed for anything he does; and it is the therapist's main and most important function to help rid his patients of every possible vestige of their blaming themselves, blaming others, or blaming fate and the universe.

My pronounced differences with all those who would advocate making patients more guilty than they are, in order presumably to get them to change their antisocial and self-defeating conduct, can perhaps best be demonstrated by my insistence on a more precise and reasonably operational definition of the terms "sin" and "guilt" than is usually given by those who uphold this concept.

In their recent Comprehensive Dictionary of Psychological and Psychoanalytical Terms, English and English (1958) give a psychological definition of "sin" as follows: "Conduct that violates what the offender believes to be a supernaturally ordained moral code." They define a "sense of guilt" in this wise: "Realization that one has violated ethical or moral or religious principles, together with a regretful feeling of lessened personal worth on that account." English and English do not give any definition of "blame" but Webster's New World Dictionary defines it as: 1. "a blaming; accusation; condemnation; censure. 2. responsibility for a fault or wrong."

The beauty of these definitions, if one pays close attention to them, is that they include the two prime requisites for the individual's feeling a sense of sin, or guilt, or self-blame: (a) I have done the wrong thing and am responsible for doing it; and (b) I am a blackguard, a sinner, a no-goodnik, a valueless person, a louse, for having done this wrong deed. This, as I have shown my patients for the last several years, and as I and my co-author, Dr. Robert A. Harper, have noted in several recent publications on rational-emotive psychotherapy (Ellis, 1957; Ellis and Harper,

1961a, 1961b), is the double-headed essence of the feeling of sin, guilt, and blame: not merely the fact that the individual has made a mistake, an error, or a wrong move (which we may objectively call "wrongdoing") but the highly insidious, and I am convinced quite erroneous, belief or assumption that he is worthless, no good, valueless as a person for having done wrong.

I fully accept Hobart Mowrer's implication that there is such a thing as human wrongdoing or immoral behavior. I do not, as a psychologist, believe that we can have any absolute, final, or God-given standards of morals or ethics.

However, I do believe that, as citizens of a social community, we must have some standards of right and wrong. My own feeling is that these standards are best based on what I call long-range or socialized hedonism—that is, the philosophy that one should primarily strive for one's own satisfactions while, at the same time, keeping in mind that one will achieve one's own best-good, in most instances, by giving up immediate gratifications for future gains and by being courteous to and considerate of others, so that they will not sabotage one's own ends. I am also, however, ready to accept almost any other rationally planned, majority-approved standard of morality that is not arbitrarily imposed by an authoritarian clique of actual men or assumed gods.

With Mowrer and almost all ethicists and religionists, then, I accept it as fact that some standard of morality is necessary as long as humans live in social groups. But I still completely reject the notion that such a standard is only or best sustained by inculcating in individuals a sense of sin or guilt. I hold, on the contrary, that the more sinful and guilty a person tends to feel, the less chance there is that he will be a happy, healthy, or law-abiding citizen.

The problem of all human morality, it must never be forgotten, is not the problem of appeasing some hypothetical deity or punishing the individual for his supposed sins. It is the very simple problem, which a concept of sin and atonement invariably obfuscates, of teaching a person (a) not to commit an antisocial act in the first place, and (b) if he does happen to commit it, not to repeat it in the second, third, and ultimate place. This problem, I contend, can consistently and fully be solved only if the potential or actual wrongdoer has the philosophy of life epitomized by the internalized sentences: (a) "If I do this act it will be wrong," and (b) "Therefore, how do I not do this act?" Or: (a) "This deed I have committed is wrong, erroneous, and mistaken." (b) "Now, how do I not commit it again?"

If, most objectively, and without any sense of self-blame, self-censure, or self-guilt, any human being would thoroughly believe in and continually internalize these sentences, I think it would be almost impossible for him to commit or keep committing immoral acts. If, however, he does not have this objective philosophy of wrongdoing, I do not see how it is possible for him to prevent himself from being immoral, on the one hand, or for him to be moral and emotionally healthy, on the other. For the main alternatives to the objective philosophy of nonblaming morality which I have just outlined are the following:

1. The individual can say to himself: (a) "If I do this act it will be wrong," and (b) "If I do this wrong act, I will be a sinner, a blackguard." If this is what the individual says to himself, and firmly believes, he will then perhaps be moral in his behavior, but only at the expense of having severe feelings of worthlessness —of deeply feeling that he is a sinner. But such feelings of worthlessness, I submit, are the essence of human disturbance: since disturbance basically consists of intense anxiety (that is, the feelings following from the internalized sentence, "I am worthless and therefore I cannot live confortably and safely in a world filled with much more worthwhile persons") or sustained hostility (that is, the feeling often following from the sentence, "He is more worthwhile than I, and I cannot live comfortably and compete with him, and therefore I hate him").

So, at best, if a human being remains moral mainly because he would feel guilty and worthless if he did not so remain, he will most probably never be able to rid himself of his underlying feelings of worthlessness and his fear of these feelings showing through if he did, by some chance, prove to be fallible and did behave immorally. We have, then, a moral individual who keeps himself so only by plaguing himself with feelings of sin or worthlessness. And since none of us are angels, and all must at some time make mistakes and commit immoral acts, we actually have a moral individual who actively (as well as potentially) hates himself. Or we would have, as Mowrer might well put it if he were more precise about what a sense of sin actually is and what it does to human beings, an individual who perpetually keeps himself on the verge of or actually in the Hell of neurosis or psychosis.

2. The self-blaming or guilty individual can say to himself, as I contend that most of the time he does in actual practice: (a) "If I do this act it will be wrong," and (b) "If I am wrong I will be a sinner." And then, quite logically taking off from this wholly irrational and groundless conclusion, he will obsessively-compul-

sively keep saying to himself, as I have seen patient after patient say, "Oh, what a terrible sinner I will be (or already am). Oh, what a terrible person! How I deserve to be punished!" And so on, and so forth.

In saying this nonsense, and thereby equating his potential or actual act of wrongdoing with a concomitant feeling of utter worthlessness, this individual will never be able to focus on the simple question, "How do I not do this wrong act?" or "How do I not repeat it now that I have done it?" He will, instead, keep focusing senselessly on "What a horrible sinner, what a blackguard I am!" Which means, in most instances, that he will—ironically enough—actually be diverted into doing the wrong act or repeating it if he has already done it. His sense of sin will tend literally to drive him away from not doing wrong and toward "sinning." Or, in other words, he will become a compulsive wrongdoer.

To make matters still worse, the individual who blames himself for acting badly (or, sometimes, for even thinking about acting badly) will usually feel (as blamers normally do) that he should be punished for his poor behavior. His internalized sentences therefore will tend to go somewhat as follows: "I committed a horrible crime. I am therefore a terrible sinner and must atone for my sins, must punish myself for this crime. But if I keep doing badly, keep committing these kinds of crimes, I will certainly be caught or will have to keep being anxious about the danger of being caught. My being caught and punished or my being anxious about being caught will itself be a hard, punishing thing. Therefore, maybe it would be better if I kept committing crimes like this, in order to punish myself, and thereby atone for my sins."

In other words, the individual who construes his misdeeds as sins will often compulsively drive himself to more misdeeds in order, sooner or later, to bring punishment for these sins on his own head.

3. The self-blaming person (or, synonymously, the person with a pronounced sense of sin) may say to himself the usual sequence: (a) "If I do this act it will be wrong," and (b) "If I am wrong, I am a worthless sinner." Then, being no angel and being impelled, at times, to commit wrong deeds, and being prepared to condemn himself mercilessly (because of his sense of sin) for his deeds, he will either refuse to admit that he has done the wrong thing or admit that he has done it but insist that it is not wrong. That is to say, the wrongdoer who has an acute sense of sin will either repress thoughts about his wrongdoing or psychopathically insist that he is right and the world is wrong.

Any way one looks at the problem of morality, therefore, the individual who sanely starts out by saying (a) "It is wrong to do this act" and then who insanely continues (b) "I am a sinner or a black-guard for doing (or even for thinking about doing) it" can only be expected to achieve one or more of four most unfortunate results: (1) a deepseated feeling of personal worthlessness; (2) an obsessive-compulsive occupation with a consequent potential re-performance of the wrong act for which he is blaming himself; (3) denial or repression of the fact that his immoral act was actually committed by him; and (4) psychopathic insistence that the act was committed but was not really wrong.

To make matters infinitely worse, the individual who has a sense of sin, guilt, or self-blame inevitably cannot help blaming others for their potential or actual wrongdoings—and he therefore becomes angry or hostile to these others. And he cannot help blaming fate, circumstances, or the universe for wrongly or unjustly frustrating him in the attainment of many of his desires—and he consequently becomes self-pitying and angry at the world.

In the final analysis, then, blaming, in all its insidious ramifications, is the essence of virtually all emotional disturbances; and, as I tell my patients on many occasions, if I can induce them never, under any circumstances, to blame or punish anyone, including and especially themselves, it will be virtually impossible for them ever to become seriously upset. This does not mean that no child or adult should ever be objectively or dispassionately penalized for his errors or wrongdoings (as, for example, psychologists often penalize laboratory rats by shocking them when they enter the wrong passage of a maze); but merely that no one should ever be blamefully punished for his mistakes or crimes.

There are several other reasons why, almost invariably, giving an individual a sense of sin or of self-worthlessness in connection with his wrongdoing will not make for less immorality or greater happiness or mental health. Let me briefly mention some of these reasons.

For one thing, guilt and self-blame induce the individual to bow nauseatingly low to some arbitrary external authority, which in the last analysis is always some hypothetical deity; and such worship renders him proportionately less self-sufficient and self-confident. Secondly, the concept of guilt inevitably leads to the unsupportable sister concept of self-sacrifice for and dependency upon others—which is the antithesis of true mental health. Thirdly, guilty individuals tend to focus incessantly on past delinquencies and crimes rather than on present and future constructive behavior. Fourthly, it is psychophysically impossible for a person to concentrate adequately on changing his moral actions for the better when he is obsessively focused upon blaming himself for his past and present misdeeds. Fifthly, the states of anxiety created in an individual by his self-blaming tendencies induce concomitant breakdown states in which he cannot think clearly of anything, least of all constructive changes in himself.

The full measure of the harmfulness of self-blaming is perhaps best seen in regard to its interference with the reestablishment of mental health once it has set the wheels of emotional disturbance in working order. The vicious circle usually goes somewhat as follows. Jim Jones, who is a fairly normal, fallible human being, first demands that he be perfect and infallible, because he very falsely equates making mistakes with being incompetent and equates being incompetent with being worthless (that is, blameworthy). Naturally, he does not achieve perfection or infallibility; and, in fact, just because he is so overconcerned about being error-less, and focuses on how rather than on what he is doing, he tends to make many more mistakes than he otherwise would make if he did not blame himself and consider himself worthless for being error-prone.

So Jim Jones excoriates himself severely for his mistakes and develops some kind of neurotic symptom—such as severe anxiety or hostility against those he thinks are less incompetent than he. Once he develops this symptom, Jim soon begins to notice that he is afflicted with it, and then he blames himself severely for having the symptom—for being neurotic. This second-level self-blaming of course causes him to be still more neurotic.

Thus, where he was originally anxious about his potential incompetence, and then became more anxious because his original anxiety drove him to become actually incompetent, he now goes one step further, and becomes anxious about being anxious. In the process—naturally!—he tends to become still more incompetent, since he is even less than ever focused on problem-solving and more than ever concentrated on what a terrible person he is for being such a poor problem-solver.

Finally, after he has become anxious (that is, self-blaming) about (a) the possibility of being incompetent, (b) actual incompetence, stemming from (a), and (c) his anxiety or acute panic state resulting from both (a) and (b), Jim sees that he is terribly disturbed and goes for psychotherapeutic aid. But here again he is smitten down by his self-blaming tendencies and tends to sabotage his therapeutic efforts in several significant ways:

1. The more the therapist helps him see what he is doing to himself—that is, the more insight he is helped to acquire into how he is blaming himself—the more he tends to blame himself for being so stupid or incompetent or sick. Otherwise stated, the more he sees how he is blaming himself, the more he may, especially at the beginning of therapy, blame himself for blaming himself. He thereby may actually become considerably worse before he starts to get better.

2. As soon as he sees that therapy requires that he do something in order to get better—which it always does, since it is no magic formula for self-improvement without effort on the part of the patient—he frequently starts worrying about whether he is going to be able (meaning, competent enough) to do what he has to do to help himself. His internalized sentences may therefore run something along these lines: "My therapist is showing me that I have to see what I am doing to create my disturbances, and to challenge and contradict my own negative thinking in this connection. From what I can see, he is perfectly right. But wouldn't it be awful if I tried to do this kind of challenging of my own nonsense and failed! Wouldn't it be terrible if I proved to him and myself that I couldn't do what I have to do! Perhaps, since it would be so awful to try and to fail, I'd better not even try, and in that way at least save face."

In telling himself these kinds of sentences, the patient often gives himself an excuse to give up trying to cure himself early in the game; and he either continues therapy in a half-hearted and ineffective manner, or he gives it up entirely by convincing himself that "Well, maybe it works with other people, but obviously not with me. I guess I'm just hopeless."

3. If the patient continues in therapy for a while, and if he begins surely but fairly slowly to improve (as is usually the case, since he has become so habituated for so many years to mistaken patterns of thinking and acting), he then often starts to tell himself: "How disgusting! Here I've been going for therapy for quite a while now and I'm still not better. Why, considering how I blew up the other day, I'm probably just as bad as I was when I started! How stupid! Obviously, I'm not really trying at all—in which case I'm idiotically wasting my time and money in therapy—or I'm trying and I just haven't got what it takes to get better. Other people I know have made much greater strides in equal or lesser periods of time. I guess I really am no good!"

4. Sometimes the patient is sorely disappointed with his own progress in therapy but, realizing that if he frankly admits that

he has not been working too hard or consistently to help himself, he will mercilessly blame himself, he fails to face his own avoidance of the problem and bitterly starts resenting his therapist for not helping him enough. Knowing little but a basic philosophy of blame, he cannot conceive that neither he nor his therapist could be reprehensible (though either or both of them might be responsible) for his lack of progress; so he is faced with the choice of hating one of the two—and in this instance picks the therapist, and either quits therapy completely (telling himself that all therapists are no damn good) or keeps shopping around for another, and perhaps another, and perhaps still another therapist. In any event, he refuses to admit that probably he is responsible—though not blameworthy—for his lack of progress, and that he'd therefore better get back to the task of therapy with more effort and much less blaming.

The vicious circle, in instances like these, is now complete. First the individual upsets himself by his self-excoriating philosophy; then he blames himself (or others) for his becoming so upset; then, if he goes for therapeutic help, he again blames himself (or others) for his not immediately becoming completely cured. Under such triply self-blaming blows, it is virtually certain that he will not only become, but often forever remain, exceptionally disturbed.

It should be quite patent, then, that giving an individual a sense of sin, guilt or self-blame for his misdeeds is enormously disadvantageous. This is not to say that blame never helps human beings to correct their mistaken or criminal behavior. It certainly seems to work with many children and with some adults. But often it is highly ineffective—as shown by the fact that after thousands of years of censuring, ridiculing, jailing, killing, and otherwise severely blaming and punishing human beings for their immoralities, we still have not greatly reduced the quantity or quality of wrongdoing that goes on in this world.

Even, moreover, when blame is effective, and people do commit significantly fewer misdeeds because of harsh social sanctions which are leveled against them in their formative and later years, it is most dubious whether the game is worth the candle. For the toll, in terms of the immense amounts and intense degrees of anxiety and hostility that ensue, is so great as to call into question almost any amount of morality which is thereby achieved.

The concept of sin (as distinguished from the objective appraisal of wrongdoing) is so humanly inhuman that it would be difficult even to conceive a more pernicious technique for keeping mankind moral. And because any deity-positing religion almost by necessity involves endowing those members who violate the laws of its gods with a distinct concept of blameworthiness or sinfulness, I am inclined to reverse Voltaire's famous dictum and to say that, from a mental health standpoint, if there were a God it would be necessary to uninvent Him.

It is sometimes objected, when rational therapists talk of the distinction between "sin" and "wrongdoing," that they are merely quibbling and that the two are essentially the same. Thus, Mowrer (1960b), in a recent issue of the American Psychologist, argues that because "sin" is a stronger word than "wrongdoing" or "irresponsibility" it is better for the neurotic individual to admit his "sins" than to accept his "wrongdoings." Says Mowrer:

> The only way to resolve the paradox of self-hatred and self-punishment is to assume, not that it represents merely an "introjection" of the attitudes of others, but that the self-hatred is realistically justified and will persist until the individual, by radically altered attitude *and action*, honestly and realistically comes to feel that he now deserves something better. As long as one remains, in old-fashioned religious phraseology, hard-of-heart and unrepentant, just so long will one's conscience hold him in the vise-like grip of "neurotic" rigidity and suffering. But if, at length, an individual confesses his past stupidities and errors and makes what poor attempts he can at restitution, then the superego (like the parents of an earlier day—and society in general) forgives and relaxes its stern hold; and the individual once again is free, "well."

In upholding the concept of individual (if not original) "sin," Mowrer is contending that the neurotic individual must, if he is to get well, accept the following syllogism: (a) Sinning is unjustified; (b) I have sinned; (c) therefore, I must justify my existence by acknowledging my sins, changing my ways, and becoming a non-sinner.

At first blush, this seems like a perfectly valid syllogism. But, as Mowrer himself suggests, it rarely works because "there is some evidence that human beings do not change radically unless they first acknowledge their sins; but we also know how hard it is for one to make such an acknowledgment unless he has already changed. In other words, the full realization of deep worthlessness is a severe ego 'insult'; and one must have some new source of strength, it seems, to endure it. This is a mystery (or is it only a mistaken observation?) which traditional theology has tried to resolve in various ways—without complete success. Can we psychologists do better?"

I am sure that psychologists can do better—if they avoid the trap which Mowrer, by insisting on replacing the naturalistic words, "wrongdoing" and "responsibility," with the moralistic word, "sin," has got himself into.

Let us first see what is wrong with Mowrer's syllogism and why, because of the manner in which it is stated, it virtually forces the individual to think that he is "worthless" and consequently to be unable to change his immoral behavior. Mowrer's premise is that sinning is unjustified or that the sinner's "self-hatred is realistically justified." By this statement he appears to mean two important things, only the first of which can be objectively validated: (a) the sinner's act is mistaken or wrong (because it is, in some early or final analysis, self- or society-defeating); and (b) therefore, the sinner is personally blameworthy or integrally worthless for performing this mistaken or wrong act.

Although (a) may be a true observation, (b) is an arbitrary value judgment, or moralistic definition, that can never possibly be objectively validated and that, as Epictetus, Hartman (1959), Lewis (1949), Mead (1936), and other writers have shown, is philosophically untenable. No matter how responsible, in a causative sense, an individual may be for his mistaken or wrong behavior, he becomes a villain or a worthless lout only if members of his social group view or define him as such and if, more importantly, he accepts their moralistic views. Where Mowrer, for example, obviously thinks that the average murderer should hate himself, I (for one) believe that he should fully acknowledge and deplore his murderous act, but that he should in no way despise himself for committing this act.

The paradox, therefore, that Mowrer posits—that the neurotic sinner will not get better until he acknowledges and actively repents his sins and that he will not acknowledge his sins until he gets better—is a direct and "logical" result of explicitly or implicitly including the concept of personal worthlessness in the definition of "sin." Naturally, (as noted previously in this chapter) if someone believes that his acts are sinful—meaning (a) that he is wrong (self- or socially-defeating) for perpetrating them, and (b) that he is blameworthy or worthless for being wrong—he will not dare acknowledge that he has sinned; or he will make invalid excuses for so doing; or he will feel so worthless after his acknowledgement that he will hardly have the energy or efficiency to change his wrong or mistaken behavior.

How can the non-moralistic and rational psychologist help his neurotic patients resolve this paradox? Very simply: by taking the objective and "weaker" (that is, unmoralistic) words, such as "wrongdoing" and "irresponsibility," that Mowrer abandons in place of "sin," and putting them into his original syllogism. The syllogism then becomes: (a) Wrongdoing is self- or society-defeating;

(b) I have made a mistake or committed a wrong act; (c) therefore, I'd better stop being self-defeating by acknowledging my wrongdoing and take considerable time and effort to work at not repeating it, so that eventually I'll become a less frequent wrongdoer.

If the neurotic wrongdoer states his syllogism in this form, he will never think that he is quite worthless, will never experience any ego "insult," and will easily be able to acknowledge his wrongdoings before he has changed and stopped committing them. The artificial problem that was created by his feeling he was a sinner and therefore blaming himself immediately for any wrongdoing that he may have perpetrated is no longer created when a misdeed is viewed as a serious mistake rather than as a heinous crime.

Although I still agree heartily with Hobart Mowrer that the healthy and happy human being should have a clear-cut sense of wrongdoing, and that he should not only try to understand the origin of his antisocial behavior but to do something effective to become more morally oriented, I contend that giving anyone a sense of sin, guilt, or self-blame is the worst possible way to help him be an emotionally sound and adequately socialized individual.

A rational psychotherapist certainly helps show his patients that they have often behaved wrongly, badly, and self-defeatingly by performing antisocial actions, and that if they continue to act in this kind of self-defeating manner they will inevitably continue to defeat their own ends. But he also shows them that this is no reason why they should feel sinful or guilty or self-blaming about the actions for which they may well have been responsible. He helps his patients to temporarily accept themselves as wrongdoers, acknowledge fully their responsibility for their acts, and then focus intently, in their internalized sentences and their overt activities, on the only real problem at hand—which is: How do I not repeat this wrong deed next time?

If, in this thoroughly objective, non-guilty manner, we can teach patients (as well as the billions of people in the world who, for better or worse, will never become patients) that even though human beings can be held quite accountable or responsible for their misdeeds, no one is ever to blame for anything he does, human morality, I am sure, will be significantly improved and, for the first time in human history, civilized people will have a real chance to achieve sound mental health. The concept of sin is the direct and indirect cause of virtually all neurotic disturbance. The sooner psychotherapists forthrightly begin to attack it the better their patients will be.

REFERENCES

Ellis, A. Outcome of employing three techniques of psychotherapy. J. clin. Psychol., 1957, 13:334–350.

Ellis, A., & Harper, R.A. A guide to rational living. Englewood Cliffs, N.J.: Prentice-Hall, 1961a.

Ellis, A., & Harper, R.A. Creative marriage. New York: Lyle Stuart, 1961b.

English, H.B., & English, Ava C. A comprehensive dictionary of psychological and psychoanalytical terms. New York: Longmans, Green, 1958.

Hartman, R.S. The measurement of value. Crotonville, N.Y.: General Electric Co., 1959.

Lewis, C. L. The nature of ethical disagreement. In H. Feigl & W. Sellars (Eds.) Readings in philosophical analysis. New York: Appleton-Century-Crofts, 1949.

Mead, G.H. Mind, self and society. Chicago: Univer. of Chicago Press, 1936.

Mowrer, O.H. Some constructive features of the concept of sin. J. counsel. Psychol., 1960a, 7:185–188.

Mowrer, O.H. "Sin," the lesser of two evils. Amer. Psychologist, 1960b, 15:301–304.

XVIII

PSYCHOLOGICAL DATA AND HUMAN VALUES

Abraham H. Maslow

Humanists for thousands of years have attempted to construct a naturalistic, psychological value system that could be derived from man's own nature, without the necessity of recourse to authority outside the human being himself. Many such theories have been offered throughout history. They have all failed for mass practical purposes exactly as all other theories have failed. We have about as many scoundrels in the world today as we have ever had, and many more neurotics, probably, than we have ever had.

These inadequate theories, most of them, rested on psychological assumptions of one sort or another. Today practically all of these can be shown, in the light of recently acquired knowledge, to be false, inadequate, incomplete or in some other way, lacking. But it is my belief that certain developments in the science and art of psychology, in the last few decades, make it possible for us for the first time to feel confident that this age-old hope may be fulfilled if only we work hard enough. We know how to criticize the old theories; we know, even though dimly, the shape of the theories to come, and most of all, we know where to look and what to do in order to fill in the gaps in knowledge, that will permit us to answer the age-old questions, "What is the good life? What is the good man? How can people be taught to desire and prefer the good life? How ought children to be brought up to be sound adults? etc." That is,

Reprinted by permission of the author and publisher from Abraham H. Maslow. *Toward a Psychology of Being* Princeton, N.J.: Van Nostrand, 1962.

we think that a scientific ethic may be possible, and we think we know how to go about constructing it.

The following section will discuss briefly a few of the promising lines of evidence and of research, their relevance to past and future value theories, along with a discussion of the theoretical and factual advances we must make in the near future. It is safer to judge them all as more or less probable rather than as certain.

FREE CHOICE EXPERIMENTS: HOMEOSTASIS

Hundreds of experiments have been made that demonstrate a universal inborn ability in all sorts of animals to select a beneficial diet if enough alternatives are presented from among which they are permitted free choice. This wisdom of the body is often retained under less usual conditions, e. g., adrenalectomized animals can keep themselves alive by readjusting their self-chosen diet. Pregnant animals will nicely adjust their diets to the needs of the growing embryo.

We now know this is by no means a perfect wisdom. These appetites are less efficient, for instance, in reflecting body need for vitamins. Lower animals protect themselves against poisons more efficiently than higher animals and humans. Previously formed habits of preference may quite overshadow present metabolic needs (Young, 1961). And most of all, in the human being, and especially in the neurotic human being, all sorts of forces can contaminate this wisdom of the body, although it never seems to be lost altogether.

The general principle is true not only for selection of food but also for all sorts of other body needs as the famous homeostasis experiments have shown (Cannon, 1932).

It seems quite clear that all organisms are more self-governing, self-regulating and autonomous than we thought 25 years ago. The organism deserves a good deal of trust, and we are learning steadily to rely on this internal wisdom of our babies with reference to choice of diet, time of weaning, amount of sleep, time of toilet training, need for activity, and a lot else.

But more recently we have been learning, especially from physically and mentally sick people, that there are good choosers and bad choosers. We have learned, especially from the psychoanalysts, much about the hidden causes of such behavior and have learned to respect these causes.

In this connection we have available a startling experiment (Dove, 1935), which is pregnant with implications for value theory. Chickens allowed to choose their own diet vary widely in their abil-

ity to choose what is good for them. The good choosers become
stronger, larger, more dominant than the poor choosers, which
means that they get the best of everything. If then the diet chosen
by the good choosers is forced upon the poor choosers, it is found
that they now get stronger, bigger, healthier and more dominant,
although never reaching the level of the good choosers. That is,
good choosers can choose better than bad choosers what is better
for the bad choosers themselves. If similar experimental findings
are made in human beings, as I think they will be (supporting clinical data are available aplenty), we are in for a good deal of reconstruction of all sorts of theories. So far as human value theory is
concerned, no theory will be adequate that rests simply on the statistical description of the choices of unselected human beings. To
average the choices of good and bad choosers, of healthy and sick
people is useless. Only the choices and tastes and judgments of
healthy human beings will tell us much about what is good for the
human species in the long run. The choices of neurotic people can
tell us mostly what is good for keeping a neurosis stabilized, just
as the choices of a brain injured man are good for preventing a catastrophic breakdown, or as the choices of an adrenalectomized animal may keep him from dying but would kill a healthy animal.

I think that this is the main reef on which most hedonistic value
theories and ethical theories have foundered. Pathologically motivated pleasures cannot be averaged with healthily motivated
pleasures.

Furthermore any ethical code will have to deal with the fact
of constitutional differences not only in chickens and rats but also
in men, as Sheldon (1942) and Morris (May et al., 1958) have
shown. Some values are common to all (healthy) mankind, but
also some other values will not be common to all mankind, but only
to some types of people, or to specific individuals. What I have
called the basic needs are probably common to all mankind and
are, therefore, shared values. But idiosyncratic needs generate
idiosyncratic values.

Constitutional differences in individuals generate preferences
among ways of relating to self, and to culture and to the world, i.e.,
generate values. These researches support and are supported by
the universal experience of clinicians with individual differences.
This is also true of the ethnological data that make sense of cultural diversity by postulating that each culture selects for exploitation, suppression, approval or disapproval, a small segment of
the range of human constitutional possibilities. This is all in line
with the biological data and theories and self-actualization theories

which show that an organ system presses to express itself, in a word, to function. The muscular person likes to use his muscles, indeed, <u>has</u> to use them in order to self-actualize, and to achieve the subjective feeling of harmonious, uninhibited, satisfying functioning which is so important an aspect of psychological health. People with intelligence must use their intelligence, people with eyes must use their eyes, people with the capacity to love have the <u>impulse</u> to love and the <u>need</u> to love in order to feel healthy. Capacities clamor to be used, and cease their clamor only when they <u>are</u> used sufficiently. That is to say, capacities are needs, and therefore are intrinsic values as well. To the extent that capacities differ, so will values also differ.

BASIC NEEDS AND THEIR HIERARCHICAL ARRANGEMENT

It has by now been sufficiently demonstrated that the human being has, as part of his intrinsic construction, not only physiological needs, but also truly psychological ones. They may be considered as deficiencies which must be optimally fulfilled by the environment in order to avoid sickness and subjective ill-being. They can be called basic, or biological, and likened to the need for salt, or calcium or vitamin D because—

a) The deprived person yearns for their gratification persistently.
b) Their deprivation makes the person sicken and wither.
c) Gratifying them is therapeutic, curing the deficiency-illness.
d) Steady supplies forestall these illnesses.
e) Healthy (gratified) people do not demonstrate these deficiencies.

But these needs or values are related to each other in a hierarchical and developmental way, in an order of strength and of priority. Safety is a more prepotent, or stronger, more pressing, more vital need than love, for instance, and the need for food is usually stronger than either. Furthermore, all these basic needs may be considered to be simply steps along the path to general self-actualization, under which all basic needs can be subsumed.

By taking these data into account, we can solve many value problems that philosophers have struggled with ineffectually for centuries. For one thing, it looks as if there were a single ultimate value for mankind, a far goal toward which all men strive. This is called variously by different authors self-actualization, self-realization, integration, psychological health, individuation, autonomy, creativity, productivity, but they all agree that this amounts to realizing the potentialities of the person, that is to say, becoming fully human, everything that the person can become.

But it is also true that the person himself does not know this. We, the psychologists observing and studying, have constructed this concept in order to integrate and explain lots of diverse data. So far as the person himself is concerned, all he knows is that he is desperate for love, and thinks he will be forever happy and content if he gets it. He does not know in advance that he will strive on after this gratification has come, and that gratification of one basic need opens consciousness to domination by another, "higher" need. So far as he is concerned, the absolute, ultimate value, synonymous with life itself, is whichever need in the hierarchy he is dominated by during a particular period. These basic needs or basic values therefore may be treated both as ends and as steps toward a single end-goal. It is true that there is a single, ultimate value or end of life and also it is just as true that we have a hierarchical and developmental system of values, complexly interrelated.

This also helps to solve the apparent paradox of contrast between Being and Becoming. It is true that human beings strive perpetually toward ultimate humanness, which itself may be anyway a different kind of Becoming and growing. It's as if we were doomed forever to try to arrive at a state to which we could never attain. Fortunately we now know this not to be true, or at least it is not the only truth. There is another truth which integrates with it. We are again and again rewarded for good Becoming by transient states of absolute Being, by peak-experiences. Achieving basic-need gratifications gives us many peak-experiences, each of which are absolute delights, perfect in themselves, and needing no more than themselves to validate life. This is like rejecting the notion that a Heaven lies someplace beyond the end of the path of life. Heaven, so to speak, lies waiting for us through life, ready to step into for a time and to enjoy before we have to come back to our ordinary life of striving. And once we have been in it, we can remember it forever, and feed ourselves on this memory and be sustained in times of stress.

Not only this, but the process of moment-to-moment growth is itself intrinsically rewarding and delightful in an absolute sense. If they are not mountain peak-experiences, at least they are foothill-experiences, little glimpses of absolute, self-validative delight, little moments of Being. Being and Becoming are not contradictory or mutually exclusive. Approaching and arriving are both in themselves rewarding.

I should make it clear here that I want to differentiate the Heaven ahead (of growth and transcendence) from the "Heaven" behind (of regression). The "high Nirvana" is quite different from the "low Nirvana" even though most clinicians confuse them (see also Weisskopf, 1958).

SELF-ACTUALIZATION: GROWTH

I have published in another place a survey of all the evidence that forces us in the direction of a concept of healthy growth or of self-actualizing tendencies (Maslow, 1954). This is partly deductive evidence in the sense of pointing out that unless we postulate such a concept, much of human behavior makes no sense. This is on the same scientific principle that led to the discovery of a hitherto unseen planet that <u>had</u> to be there in order to make sense of a lot of other observed data.

There is also some direct evidence, or rather the beginnings of direct evidence, which needs much more research to get to the point of certainty. The only direct study of self-actualizing people I know is the one I made, and it is a very shaky business to rest on just one study made by just one person when we take into account the known pitfalls of sampling error, of projection, etc. However, the conclusions of this study have been so strongly paralleled in the clinical and philosophical conclusions of Rogers, Fromm, Goldstein, Angyal, Murray, Moustakas, C. Buhler, Horney, Jung, Nuttin and many others that I shall proceed under the assumption that more careful research will not contradict my findings radically. We can certainly now assert that at least a reasonable, theoretical, and empirical case has been made for the presence within the human being of a tendency toward, or need for growing in a direction that can be summarized in general as self-actualization, or psychological health, and specifically as growth toward each and all of the sub-aspects of self-actualization, i.e., he has within him a pressure toward unity of personality, toward spontaneous expressiveness, toward full individuality and identity, toward seeing the truth rather than being blind, toward being creative, toward being good, and a lot else. That is, the human being is so constructed that he presses toward fuller and fuller being and this means pressing toward what most people would call good values, toward serenity, kindness, courage, honesty, love, unselfishness, and goodness.

Few in number though they be, we can learn a great deal about values from the direct study of these highly evolved, most mature, psychologically healthiest individuals, and from the study of the peak moments of average individuals, moments in which they become transiently self-actualized. This is because they are in very real empirical and theoretical ways, most fully human. For instance, they are people who have retained and developed their human capacities, especially those capacities which define the human being and differentiate him from, let us say, the monkey. (This accords with Hartman's (1959) axiological approach to the same problem of defining the good human being as the one who has more of the characteristics which define the concept "human being.") From a developmental point of view, they are more fully evolved because not fixated at immature or incomplete levels of growth. This is no more mysterious, or a priori, or question begging than the selection of a type specimen of butterfly by a taxonomist or the most physically healthy young man by the physician. They both look for the "perfect or mature or magnificent specimen" for the exemplar, and so have I. One procedure is as repeatable in principle as the other.

Full humanness can be defined not only in terms of the degree to which the definition of the concept "human" is fulfilled, i.e., the species norm. It also has a descriptive, cataloguing, measurable, psychological definition. We now have from a few research beginnings and from countless clinical experiences some notion of the characteristics both of the fully evolved human being and of the well-growing human being. These characteristics are not only neutrally describable; they are also subjectively rewarding, pleasurable and reinforcing.

Among the objectively describable and measurable characteristics of the healthy human specimen are—

1. Clearer, more efficient perception of reality.
2. More openness to experience.
3. Increased integration, wholeness, and unity of the person.
4. Increased spontaneity, expressiveness; full functioning; aliveness.
5. A real self; a firm identity; autonomy, uniqueness.
6. Increased objectivity, detachment, transcendence of self.
7. Recovery of creativeness.
8. Ability to fuse concreteness and abstractness.
9. Democratic character structure.
10. Ability to love, etc.

These all need research confirmation and exploration but it is clear that such researches are feasible.

In addition, there are subjective confirmations or reinforcements of self-actualization or of good growth toward it. These are the feelings of zest in living, of happiness or euphoria, of serenity, of joy, of calmness, of responsibility, of confidence in one's ability to handle stresses, anxieties, and problems. The subjective signs of self-betrayal, of fixation, of regression, and of living by fear rather than by growth are such feelings as anxiety, despair, boredom, inability to enjoy, intrinsic guilt, intrinsic shame, aimlessness, feelings of emptiness, of lack of identity, etc.

These subjective reactions are also susceptible of research exploration. We have clinical techniques available for studying them.

It is the free choices of such self-actualizing people (in those situations where real choice is possible from among a variety of possibilities) that I claim can be descriptively studied as a naturalistic value system with which the hopes of the observer absolutely have nothing to do, i.e., it is "scientific." I do not say, "He ought to choose this or that," but only, "Healthy people, permitted to choose freely, are observed to choose this or that." This is like asking, "What are the values of the best human beings," rather than, "What should be their values?" or, "What ought they be?" (Compare this with Aristotle's belief that "it is the things which are valuable and pleasant to a good man that are really valuable and pleasant.")

Furthermore, I think these findings can be generalized to most of the human species because it looks to me (and to others) as if most people (perhaps all) tend toward self-actualization (this is seen most clearly in the experiences in psychotherapy, especially of the uncovering sort), and as if, in principle at least, most people are capable of self-actualization.

If the various extant religions may be taken as expressions of human aspiration, i.e., what people would like to become if only they could, then we can see here too a validation of the affirmation that all people yearn toward self-actualization or tend toward it. This is so because our description of the actual characteristics of self-actualizing people parallels at many points the ideals urged by the religions, e.g., the transcendence of self, the fusion of the true, the good and the beautiful, contribution to others, wisdom, honesty and naturalness, the transcendence of selfish and personal motivations, the giving up of "lower" desires in favor of "higher" ones, the easy differentiation between ends (tranquility, serenity, peace) and means (money, power, status), the decrease of hostility, cruelty and destructiveness and the increase of friendliness, kindness, etc.

1. One conclusion from all these free-choice experiments, from developments in dynamic motivation theory and from examination of psychotherapy, is a very revolutionary one that no other large culture had even arrived at, namely, that our deepest needs are not, in themselves, dangerous or evil or bad. This opens up the prospect of resolving the splits within the person between Apollonian and Dionysian, classical and romantic, scientific and poetic, between reason and impulse, work and play, verbal and preverbal, maturity and childlikeness, masculine and feminine, growth and regression.

2. The main social parallel to this change in our philosophy of human nature is the rapidly growing tendency to perceive the culture as an instrument of need-gratification as well as of frustration and control. We can now reject, as a localism, the almost universal mistake that the interests of the individual and of society are of necessity mutually exclusive and antagonistic, or that civilization is primarily a mechanism for controlling and policing human instinctoid impulses (Marcuse, 1955). All these age-old axioms are swept away by the new possibility of defining the main function of a healthy culture as the fostering of universal self-actualization.

3. In healthy people only is there a good correlation between subjective delight in the experience, impulse to the experience, or wish for it, and "basic need" for the experience (it's good for him in the long run). Only such people uniformly yearn for what is good for them and for others, and then are able wholeheartedly to enjoy it, and approve of it. For such people virtue is its own reward in the sense of being enjoyed in itself. They spontaneously tend to do right because that is what they want to do, what they need to do, what they enjoy, what they approve of doing, and what they will continue to enjoy.

It is this unity, this network of positive intercorrelation, that falls apart into separateness and conflict as the person gets psychologically sick. Then what he wants to do may be bad for him; even if he does it he may not enjoy it, even if he enjoys it, he may simultaneously disapprove of it, so that the enjoyment is itself poisoned or may disappear quickly. What he enjoys at first he may not enjoy later. His impulses, desires, and enjoyments then become a poor guide to living. He must accordingly mistrust and fear the impulses and the enjoyments which lead him astray, and so he is caught in conflict, dissociation, indecision; in a word, he is caught in civil war.

So far as philosophical theory is concerned, many historical dilemmas and contradictions are resolved by this finding. Hedonistic theory does work for healthy people; it does not work for sick people. The true, the good and the beautiful do correlate some, but only in healthy people do they correlate strongly.

4. Self-actualization is a relatively achieved "state of affairs" in a few people. In most people, however, it is rather a hope, a yearning, a drive, a "something" wished for but not yet achieved, showing itself clinically as drive toward health, integration, growth, etc. The projective tests are also able to detect these trends as potentialities rather than as overt behavior, just as an X-ray can detect incipient pathology before it has appeared on the surface.

This means for us that that which the person is and that which the person could be exist simultaneously for the psychologist, thereby resolving the dichotomy between Being and Becoming. Potentialities not only will be or could be; they also are. Self-actualization values as goals exist and are real even though not yet actualized. The human being is simultaneously that which he is and that which he yearns to be.

GROWTH AND ENVIRONMENT

Man demonstrates in his own nature a pressure toward fuller and fuller Being, more and more perfect actualization of his humanness in exactly the same naturalistic, scientific sense that an acorn may be said to be "pressing toward" being an oak tree, or that a tiger can be observed to "push toward" being tigerish, or a horse toward being equine. Man is ultimately not molded or shaped into humanness, or taught to be human. The role of the environment is ultimately to permit him or help him to actualize his own potentialities, not its potentialities. The environment does not give him potentialities and capacities; he has them in inchoate or embryonic form, just exactly as he has embryonic arms and legs. And creativeness, spontaneity, selfhood, authenticity, caring for others, being able to love, yearning for truth are embryonic potentialities belonging to his species-membership just as much as are his arms and legs and brain and eyes.

This is not in contradiction to the data already amassed which show clearly that living in a family and in a culture are absolutely necessary to actualize these psychological potentials that define humanness. Let us avoid this confusion. A teacher or a culture doesn't create a human being. It doesn't implant within him the ability to love, or to be curious, or to philosophize, or to symbolize, or to be creative. Rather it permits, or fosters, or encourages or helps what exists in embryo to become real and actual. The same mother or the same culture, treating a kitten or a puppy in exactly the same way, cannot make it into a human being. The culture is sun and food and water: it is not the seed.

"INSTINCT" THEORY

The group of thinkers who have been working with self-actualization, with self, with authentic humanness, etc., have pretty firmly established their case that man has a tendency to realize himself. By implication he is exhorted to be true to his own nature, to trust himself, to be authentic, spontaneous, honestly expressive, to look for the sources of his action in his own deep inner nature.

But, of course, this is an ideal counsel. They do not sufficiently warn that most adults don't know how to be authentic and that, if the "express" themselves, they may bring catastrophe not only upon themselves but upon others as well. What answer must be given to the rapist or the sadist who asks "Why should I too not trust and express myself?"

These thinkers as a group have been remiss in several respects. They have implied without making explicit that if you can behave authentically, you will behave well, that if you emit action from within, it will be good and right behavior. What is very clearly implied is that this inner core, this real self, is good, trustworthy, ethical. This is an affirmation that is clearly separable from the affirmation that man actualizes himself, and needs to be separately proven (as I think it will be). Furthermore, these writers have as a group very definitely ducked the crucial statement about this inner core, i.e., that it must in some degree be inherited or else everything else they say is so much hash.

In other words, we must grapple with "instinct" theory or, as I prefer to call it, basic need theory, that is to say, with the study of the original, intrinsic, in part heredity-determined needs, urges, wishes and, I may say, values of mankind. We can't play both the biology game and the sociology game simultaneously. We can't affirm both that culture does everything and anything, and that man has an inherent nature. The one is incompatible with the other.

And of all the problems in this area of instinct, the one of which we know least and should know most is that of aggression, hostility, hatred, and destructiveness. The Freudians claim this to be instinctive; most other dynamic psychologists claim it to be not directly instinctive, but rather an ever-present reaction to frustration of instinctoid or basic needs. The truth is that we don't really know. Clinical experience hasn't settled the problem because equally good clinicians come to these divergent conclusions. What we need is hard, firm research.

THE PROBLEMS OF CONTROL AND LIMITS

Another problem confronting the morals-from-within theorists is to account for the easy self-discipline which is customarily found in self-actualizing, authentic, genuine people and which is not found in average people.

In these healthy people we find duty and pleasure to be the same thing, as is also work and play, self-interest and altruism, individualism and selflessness. We know they are that way, but not how they get that way. I have the strong intuition that such authentic, fully human persons are the actualization of what many human beings could be. And yet we are confronted with the sad fact that so few people achieve this goal, perhaps only one in a hundred, or two hundred. We can be hopeful for mankind because in principle anybody could become a good and healthy man. But we must also feel sad because so few actually do become good men. If we wish to find out why some do and some don't, then the research problem presents itself of studying the life history of self-actualizing men to find out how they get that way.

We know already that the main prerequisite of healthy growth is gratification of the basic needs. (Neurosis is very often a deficiency disease, like avitaminosis.) But we have also learned that unbridled indulgence and gratification has its own dangerous consequences, e.g., psychopathic personality, "orality," irresponsibility, inability to bear stress, spoiling, immaturity, certain character disorders. Research findings are rare but there is now available a large store of clinical and educational experience which allows us to make a reasonable guess that the young child needs not only gratification; he needs also to learn the limitations that the physical world puts upon his gratifications, and he has to learn that other human beings seek for gratifications, too, even his mother and father, i.e., they are not only means to his ends. This means control, delay, limits, renunciation, frustration-tolerance and discipline. Only to the self-disciplined and responsible person can we say, "Do as you will, and it will probably be all right."

REGRESSIVE FORCES: PSYCHOPATHOLOGY

We must also face squarely the problem of what stands in the way of growth; that is to say, the problems of cessation of growth and evasion of growth, of fixation, regression, and defensiveness, in a word the attractiveness of psychopathology, or as other people would prefer to say, the problem of evil.

Why do so many people have no real identity, so little power to make their own decisions and choices?

1. These impulses and directional tendencies towards self-fulfillment, though instinctive, are very weak, so that, in contrast with all other animals who have strong instincts, these impulses are very easily drowned out by habit, by wrong cultural attitudes toward them, by traumatic episodes, by erroneous education. Therefore, the problem of choice and of responsibility is far, far more acute in humans than in any other species.

2. There has been a special tendency in Western culture, historically determined, to assume that these instinctoid needs of the human being, his so-called animal nature, are bad or evil. As a consequence, many cultural institutions are set up for the express purpose of controlling, inhibiting, suppressing and repressing this original nature of man.

3. There are two sets of forces pulling at the individual, not just one. In addition to the pressures forward toward health, there are also fearful-regressive pressures backward, toward sickness and weakness. We can either move forward toward a "high Nirvana" or backward to a "low Nirvana."

I think the main factual defect in the value theories and ethical theories of the past and the present has been insufficient knowledge of psychopathology and psychotherapy. Throughout history, learned men have set out before mankind the rewards of virtue, the beauties of goodness, the intrinsic desirability of psychological health and self-fulfillment, and yet most people perversely refuse to step into the happiness and self-respect that is offered them. Nothing is left to the teachers but irritation, impatience, disillusionment, alternations between scolding, exhortation and hopelessness. A good many have thrown up their hands altogether and talked about original sin or intrinsic evil and concluded that man could be saved only by extra-human forces.

Meanwhile there lies available the huge, rich, and illuminating literature of dynamic psychology and psychopathology, a great store of information on man's weaknesses, and fears. We know much about why men do wrong things, why they bring about their own unhappiness and their self-destruction, <u>why</u> they are perverted and sick. And out of this has come the insight that human evil is largely (though not altogether) human weakness or ignorance, forgiveable, understandable and also curable.

I find it sometimes amusing, sometimes saddening that so many scholars and scientists, so many philosophers and theologians, who talk about human values, of good and evil, proceed in complete disregard of the plain fact that professional psychotherapists every day, as a matter of course, change and improve human nature, help people to become more strong, virtuous, creative, kind, loving, altruistic, serene. These are only some of the consequences of improved self-knowledge and self-acceptance. There are many others as well that can come in greater or lesser degree (Maslow, 1954; Rogers, 1960).

The subject is far too complex even to touch here. All I can do is draw a few conclusions for value theory.

1. Self-knowledge seems to be the major path of self-improvement, though not the only one.

2. Self-knowledge and self-improvement is very difficult for most people. It usually needs great courage and long struggle.

3. Though the help of a skilled professional therapist makes this process much easier, it is by no means the only way. Much that has been learned from therapy can be applied to education, to family life, and to the guidance of one's own life.

4. Only by such study of psychopathology and therapy can one learn a proper respect for and appreciation of the forces of fear, of regression, of defense, of safety. Respecting and understanding these forces makes it much more possible to help oneself and others to grow toward health. False optimism sooner or later means disillusionment, anger and hopelessness.

5. To sum up, we can never really understand human weakness without also understanding its healthy trends. Otherwise we make the mistake of pathologizing everything. But also we can never fully understand or help human strength without also understanding its weaknesses. Otherwise we fall into the errors of overoptimistic reliance on rationality alone.

If we wish to help humans to become more fully human, we must realize not only that they try to realize themselves but that they are also reluctant or afraid or unable to do so. Only by fully appreciating this dialectic between sickness and health can we help to tip the balance in favor of health.

REFERENCES

Cannon, W. B. Wisdom of the body. New York: Norton, 1932.

Dove, W. F. A study of individuality in the nutritive instincts. Amer. Naturalist, 1935, 69:469-544.

Hartman, R. The science of value. In A. H. Maslow (Ed.) New knowledge in human values. New York: Harper, 1959.

Marcuse, H. Eros and civilization. Boston: Beacon, 1955.

Maslow, A. H. Motivation and personality. New York: Harper, 1954.

May, R., et al. (Eds.) Existence. New York: Basic Books, 1958.

Rogers, C. R. A therapist's view of personal goals. Wallingford, Pa.: Pendle Hill Pamphlets, 1960.

Sheldon, W. H. The varieties of temperament. New York: Harper, 1942.

Weisskopf, W. Existence and values. In A. H. Maslow (Ed.) New knowledge in human values. New York: Harper, 1959.

Young, P. T. Motivation and emotion. New York: Wiley, 1961.

XIX

PSYCHOTHERAPY AND THE OBJECTIVIST ETHICS

Nathaniel Branden

The belief that moral values are the province of faith and that no rational, scientific code of ethics is possible, has had disastrous effects in virtually every sphere of human activity. But there is one profession for which the consequences of this belief have been particularly acute: the science of psychology.

As a theoretical discipline, psychology is concerned with studying and defining the nature of consciousness or mind; the volitional and automatic functions of mind, the source and nature of emotions, the principles of character-formation, the principles of motivation. As a therapeutic discipline, it is concerned with the diagnosis and treatment of the malfunctions of consciousness, of mental and emotional disturbances, of character and motivational disorders.

Central to the science of psychology is the issue or problem of <u>motivation</u>. The base of the science is the need to answer two fundamental questions: Why does a man act as he does? What would be required for a man to act differently? These questions are directed, not only at man's physical actions, but at the actions of his consciousness—at the whole of his mental life.

The key to motivation lies in the realm of <u>values</u>.

Within the context of his inherent needs and capacities as a specific kind of living organism, it is man's premises—specifically his <u>value</u>-premises—that determine his actions and emotions. Whether his value-premises are rational or contradictory and self-defeating, whether they are held consciously or subconscious-

This paper was originally delivered before the Michigan Society of Consulting Psychologists, November 24, 1965. It is based on material which appeared in the *Objectivist Newsletter* and *Who Is Ayn Rand?* (New York: Random House, 1962).

ly, whether they are explicit or implicit, whether they were chosen independently and by deliberation or were uncritically absorbed from other men by a process of cultural osmosis—it is a man's notion of what is for him or against him, what is conducive or inimical to his welfare, that determines the goals he will pursue and the emotions he will experience.

An emotion is the psychosomatic form in which man experiences his estimate of the relationship of things to himself. An emotion is a value-response. It is the automatic psychological result of a man's value-judgments.

Man's value-judgments are not innate. Having no innate knowledge of what is true or false, man can have no innate knowledge of what is good or evil. His values, and his emotions, are the product of the conclusions he has drawn or accepted, that is: of his basic premises.

If man chooses values that are consonant with the facts of reality and the needs of his own nature, these values will work in the service of his life. If he chooses values that are in contradiction to the facts of reality and to his nature, they will work for his destruction. No man whose values were consistently irrational could continue to exist. The majority of men hold values that are part-rational, part-irrational—part-consonant with and part-inimical to man's nature and needs—and they spend their lives in anxiously precarious fluctuation between life and destruction, neither dying immediately nor achieving their full human potential; they pay the price of their unresolved contradictions in frustration, in misery and in neurosis.

The existence of neurosis, of mental and emotional disturbances, is one of the most eloquent proofs that man needs an integrated, objective code of moral values—that a haphazard collection of subjective or collective whims will not do—that a rational ethical system is as indispensable to man's psychological survival as it is to his existential survival.

The paradox—and the tragedy—of psychology today is that values is the one issue specifically banned from its domain.

The majority of psychologists—both as theoreticians and as psychotherapists—have accepted the premise that the realm of science and the realm of ethics are mutually inimical, that morality is a matter of faith, not of reason, that moral values are inviolately subjective, and that a therapist must cure his patients without appraising or challenging their fundamental moral beliefs.

Ladies and gentlemen, it is this premise that I ask you to challenge.

Guilt, anxiety and self-doubt—the neurotic's chronic complaints—entail _moral_ judgments. The psychotherapist must deal with such judgments constantly. The conflicts that torture patients are _moral_ conflicts: Is sex evil, or is it a proper human pleasure?—Is the profit motive evil, or do men have the right to pursue their own interests?—Must one love and forgive everybody, or is it ever justifiable to feel violent indignation?—Must man blindly submit to the teachings of his religious authorities, or dare he subject their pronouncements to the judgment of his own intellect?—Is it one's duty to remain with the husband or wife one despises, or is divorce a valid solution?—Should a woman regard motherhood as her noblest function and duty, or may she pursue an independent career?—Is man "his brother's keeper," or does he have the right to live for his own happiness?

It is true that patients frequently repress such conflicts and that the repression constitutes the major obstacle to the conflict's resolution. But it is not true that merely bringing such conflicts into conscious awareness guarantees that the patients will resolve them. The answers to moral problems are not self-evident; they require a process of complex philosophical thought and analysis.

Nor does the solution lie in instructing the patient to "follow his deepest feelings." That frequently is the policy that brought him to disaster in the first place. Nor does the solution lie in "loving" the patient, and, in effect, giving him a moral blank-check (which is one of the approaches most commonly advocated today). Love is not a substitute for reason, and the suspending of all moral estimates will not provide the patient with the code of values that his mental health requires. The patient feels confused, he feels uncertain of his judgment, he feels he does not know what is right or wrong; if the therapist, to whom the patient has come for guidance, is professionally _committed_ to not knowing, the impasse is total.

To the extent that the therapist acts on the principle that he must be silent in moral issues, he passively confirms and sanctions the monopoly on morality held by mysticism—more specifically, by religion. Yet no conscientious therapist can escape the knowledge that religious teachings frequently are instrumental in _causing_ the patient's neurosis.

In fact, there is _no way_ for a psychotherapist to keep his own moral convictions out of his professional work. By countless subtle indications he reveals and makes the patient aware of his moral estimate—through his pauses, his questions, the things he chooses to say or not to say, etc. But because—for both parties—this process of communication is subconscious, the patient is being guided emotionally rather than intellectually; he does not form an independent, self-conscious appraisal of the therapist's value-premises; he can only accept them, if he accepts them at all, on faith, by feeling, without reasons or proof, since the issues are never named explicitly. This makes of the therapist, in effect, a religious authority—a subliminal religious authority, as it were.

A therapist who approaches moral problems in this manner will, most commonly, encourage conformity to and the acceptance of the prevailing moral beliefs of the culture, without regard for the question of whether or not those beliefs are compatible with psychological health. But even if the values the therapist communicates are rational, the method of "persuasion" is not—and thus fails to bring the patient any closer to authentic, independent rationality.

A code of ethics or morality is a code of values to guide one's choices and actions.

Effective psychotherapy requires a conscious, rational, scientific code of ethics—a system of values based on the facts of reality and geared to the needs of man's life on earth.

It is this that Ayn Rand has provided in her philosophy of Objectivism. For a detailed presentation of the Objectivist ethics, I refer you to Miss Rand's celebrated Atlas Shrugged (1957), to my own Who is Ayn Rand? (Branden, 1962), and to her most recent work, The Virtue of Selfishness (Rand, 1964).

My purpose here is not a detailed exposition of the Objectivist ethics, but rather a presentation of the base or foundation of this system of ethics: the method of deriving and justifying the Objectivist standard of value.

Ayn Rand does not begin by taking the phonomenon of "values" as a given; that is, she does not begin merely by observing that men pursue various values and by assuming that the first question of ethics is: What values ought man to pursue? She begins on a far deeper level, with the question: What are values and why does man need them? What are the facts of reality—the facts of existence and of man's nature—that necessitate and give rise to values?

A value is that which one acts to gain and/or keep. A value is the object of an action. "'Value' presupposes an answer to the question: of value to whom and for what? 'Value' presupposes a standard, a purpose and the necessity of action in the face of an alternative. Where there are no alternatives, no values are possible." (p. 1012)[1] An entity who—by its nature—had no purposes to achieve, no goals to reach, could have no values and no need of values. There would be no "for what." An entity incapable of initiating action, or for whom the consequences would always be the same, regardless of its actions —an entity not confronted with alternatives—could have no purposes, no goals, and hence no values. Only the existence of alternatives can make purpose—and therefore values—possible and necessary.

"There is only one fundamental alternative in the universe; existence or non-existence—and it pertains to a single class of entities: to living organisms. The existence of inanimate matter is unconditional, the existence of life is not: it depends on a specific course of action. Matter is indestructible, it changes its forms, but it cannot cease to exist. It is only a living organism that faces a constant alternative: the issue of life or death. Life is a process of self-sustaining and self-generated action. If an organism fails in that action, it dies; its chemical elements remain, but its life goes out of existence. It is only the concept of 'Life' that makes the concept of 'Value' possible. It is only to a living entity that things can be good or evil" (pp. 1012-13).

It is only a living entity that can have needs, goals, values— and it is only a living entity that can generate the actions necessary to achieve them.

A plant does not possess consciousness; it can neither experience pleasure and pain nor have the concepts of life and death; nevertheless, plants can die; a plant's life depends on a specific course of action. "A plant must feed itself in order to live; the sunlight, the water, the chemicals it needs are the values its nature has set it to pursue; its life is the standard of value directing its actions. But a plant has no choice of action; there are alternatives in the conditions it encounters, but there is no alternative in its function; it acts automatically to further its life, it cannot act for its own destruction" (p. 1013).

Animals possess a primitive form of consciousness; they cannot know the issue of life and death, but they can know pleasure and pain; an animal's life depends on actions automatically guided by its sensory mechanism. "An animal is equipped for sustaining its life; its senses provide it with an automatic code of action, an automatic knowledge of what is good for it or evil. It has no power to extend its knowledge or to evade it. In conditions where its knowledge proves inadequate, it dies. But so long as it lives, it

[1]This and all subsequent quotations are from Rand (1957).

acts on its knowledge, with automatic safety and no power of choice, it is unable to ignore its own good, unable to decide to choose the evil and act as its own destroyer" (p. 1013).

Given the appropriate conditions, the appropriate physical environment, all living organisms—with one exception—are set by their nature to originate automatically the actions required to sustain their survival. The exception is <u>man</u>.

Man, like a plant or an animal, must act in order to live; man, like a plant or an animal, must gain the values his life requires. But man does not act and function by automatic chemical reactions or by automatic sensory reactions; there is no physical environment on earth in which man could survive by the guidance of nothing but his involuntary sensations. And man is born without innate ideas; having no innate knowledge of what is true or false, he can have no innate knowledge of what is good for him or evil. <u>Man has no automatic means of survival</u>.

Man's basic means of survival is his mind, his capacity to reason. Reason is the faculty that identifies and integrates the material provided by the senses.

For man, survival is a question—a problem to be <u>solved</u>. The perceptual level of his consciousness—the level of passive sensory awareness, which he shares with animals—is inadequate to solve it. To remain alive, man must <u>think</u>—which means: he must exercise the faculty which he alone, of all living species, possesses: the faculty of abstraction, of <u>conceptualizing</u>. The conceptual level of consciousness is the human level, the level required for man's survival. It is upon his ability to think that man's life depends.

"But to think is an act of choice. The key to . . . human nature is the fact that <u>man is a being of volitional consciousness.</u> Reason does not work automatically; thinking is not a mechanical process; the connections of logic are not made by instinct. The function of your stomach, lungs or heart is automatic; the function of your mind is not. In any hour and issue of your life, you are free to think or to evade that effort. But you are not free to escape from your nature, from the fact that <u>reason</u> is your means of survival— so that for <u>you</u>, who are a human being, the question 'to be or not to be' is the question 'to think or not to think'" (p. 1012).

A being of volitional consciousness, a being without innate ideas, must discover, by a process of thought, the goals, the actions, the values on which his life depends. He must discover what will further his life and what will destroy it. If he acts against the facts of reality, he will perish. If he is to sustain his existence, he must discover the <u>principles of action</u> required to guide him in dealing with nature and with other men. His need of these principles is his need of a code of values.

Other species are not free to choose their values. Man is. "A code of values accepted by choice is a code of morality" (p. 1013).

The reason of man's need for morality determines the purpose of morality as well as the standard by which moral values are to be selected. Man needs a moral code in order to live; that is the purpose of morality—for every man as an individual. But in order to know what are the values and virtues that will permit him to achieve that purpose, man requires a standard. Different species achieve their survival in different ways. The course of action proper to the survival of a fish or an animal, would not be proper to the survival of man. Man must choose <u>his</u> values by the standard of that which is required for the life of a <u>human being</u>—which means: he must hold <u>man's life</u> (man's survival <u>qua</u> man) as his standard of value. Since reason is man's basic tool of survival, this means: the life appropriate to a rational being—or: that which is required for the survival of man <u>qua</u> rational being.

"All that which is proper to the life of a rational being is the good; all that which destroys it is the evil" (p. 1014).

To live, man must think, he must act, he must <u>produce</u> the values his life requires. This, metaphysically, is the human mode of existence.

"Man's life, as required by his nature, is not the life of a mindless brute, of a looting thug or a mooching mystic, but the life of a thinking being—not life by means of force or fraud, but life by means of achievement—not survival at any price, since there's only one price that pays for man's survival: reason" (p. 1014).

Thinking is man's basic virtue, the source of all his other virtues. Thinking is the activity of perceiving and identifying that which exists—of integrating perceptions into concepts, and concepts into still wider concepts, of constantly expanding the range of one's knowledge to encompass more and more of reality.

Evasion, the refusal to think, the willful rejection of reason, the willful suspension of consciousness, the willful defiance of reality, is man's basic vice—the source of all his evils.

Man, like every other living species, has a specific manner of survival which is determined by his nature. Man is free to act against the requirements of his nature, to reject his means of survival, his mind; but he is not free to escape the consequence: misery, anxiety, destruction. When men attempt to survive, not by thought and productive work, but by parasitism and force, by theft and brutality, it is still the faculty of reason that they are secretly counting on: the rationality that some moral man had to exercise in order to create the goods which the parasites propose to loot or expropriate. Man's life depends on thinking, not on acting blindly; on achievement, not on destruction; nothing can change that fact. Mindlessness, passivity, parasitism, brutality are not and cannot be principles of survival; they are merely the policy of those who do not wish to face the issue of survival.

"Man's life" means: life lived in accordance with the principle that make man's survival qua man possible.

Just as man is alive, physically, to the extent that the organs within his body function in the constant service of his life, so man is alive, as a total entity, to the extent that his mind functions in the constant service of his life. The mind, too, is a vital organ— the one vital organ whose function is volitional. A man encased in an iron lung, whose own lungs are paralyzed, is not dead; but he is not living the life proper to man. Neither is a man whose mind is volitionally paralyzed.

If man is to live, he must recognize that facts are facts, that A is A, that existence exists— that reality is an absolute, not to be evaded or escaped—and that the task of his mind is to perceive it, that this is his primary responsibility. He must recognize that his life requires the pursuit and achievement of rational values, values consonant with his nature and with reality—that life is a process of self-sustaining and self-generated action. He must recognize that self-value is the value without which no others are possible, but it is a value that has to be earned—and the virtue that earns it, is thinking. "To live, man must hold three things as the supreme and ruling values of his life: Reason—Purpose—Self-esteem. Reason, as his only tool of knowledge—Purpose, as his choice of the happiness which that tool must proceed to achieve—Self-esteem, as his inviolate certainty that his mind is competent to think and his person is worthy of happiness, which means: is worthy of living" (p. 1018).

The cardinal principle at the base of Ayn Rand's ethical system is the statement that "it is only the concept of 'Life' that makes the concept of 'Value' possible. It is only to a living entity that things can be good or evil." This is the identification that cuts through the Gordian knot of past ethical theorizing, that dissolves the mystical fog in the field of morality, and refutes the contention that a rational morality is impossible and that values cannot be derived from facts.

It is the nature of living entities—the fact that they must sustain their life by self-generated action—that makes the existence of values possible and necessary. For each living species, the course of action required is specific; what an entity is determines what it ought to do.

By identifying the context in which values arise existentially, Ayn Rand refutes the claim—especially prevalent today—that the ultimate standard of any moral judgment is "arbitrary," that normative propositions cannot be derived from factual propositions. By identifying the genetic roots of "value" epistemologically, she demonstrates that not to hold man's life as one's standard of moral judgment is to be guilty of a logical contradiction. It is only to a living entity that things can be good or evil; life is the basic value that makes all other values possible; the value of life is not to be justified by a value beyond itself; to demand such justification—to ask: Why should man choose to live?—is to have dropped the meaning, context and source of one's concepts. "Should" is a concept that can have no intelligible meaning, if divorced from the concept and value of life.

If life—existence—is not accepted as one's standard, then only one alternative standard remains: non-existence. But non-existence—death—is not a standard of value: it is the negation of values. The man who does not wish to hold life as his goal and standard is free not to hold it; but he cannot claim the sanction of reason; he cannot claim that his choice is as valid as any other. It is not "arbitrary," it is not "optional," whether or not man accepts his nature as a living being—just as it is not "arbitrary" or "optional" whether or not he accepts reality.

What are the major virtues man's survival requires, according to the Objectivist ethics? Rationality—Independence—Honesty—Integrity—Justice—Productiveness—Pride.

Rationality is the unreserved commitment to the perception of reality, to the acceptance of reason as an absolute, as one's only guide of knowledge, values and action. Independence is reliance upon one's own mind and judgment, the acceptance of intellectual responsibility for one's own existence. Honesty is the refusal to seek values by faking reality, by evading the distinction between the real and the unreal. Integrity is loyalty in action to the judgment of one's consciousness. Justice is the practice of identifying men for what they are, and treating them accordingly—of rewarding the actions and traits of character in men which are pro-life and condemning those which are anti-life. Productiveness is the act of supporting one's existence by translating one's thought into reality, of setting one's goals and working for their achievement, of bringing knowledge or goods into existence. Pride is moral ambitiousness, the dedication to achieving one's highest potential, in one's character and in one's life—and the refusal to be sacrificial fodder for the goals of others.

If life on earth is the standard, then it is not the man who sacrifices values who is moral, but the man who achieves them; not the man who renounces, but the man who creates; not the man who forsakes life, but the man who makes life possible.

The Objectivist ethics teaches that man—every man—is an end in himself, not a means to the ends of others. He is not a sacrificial animal. As a living being, he must exist for his own sake, neither sacrificing himself to others nor sacrificing others to himself. The achievement of his own happiness is man's highest moral purpose.

To live for his own happiness imposes a solemn responsibility on man: he must learn what his happiness objectively requires. It is a responsibility that the majority of men have not chosen to assume. No belief is more prevalent—or more disastrous—than that men can achieve their happiness by the pursuit of any random desires they experience. The existence of such a profession as psychotherapy is an eloquent refutation of that belief. Happiness is the consequence of living the life proper to man qua rational being, the consequence of pursuing and achieving consistent, life-serving values.

Thus, Objectivism advocates an ethics of rational self-interest.

Only reason can judge what is or is not objectively to man's self-interest; the question cannot be decided by feeling or whim. To act by the guidance of feelings and whims is to pursue a course of self-destruction; and self-destruction is not to man's self-interest.

To think is to man's self-interest; to suspend his consciousness, is not. To choose his goals in the full context of his knowledge, his values and his life, is to man's self-interest; to act on the impulse of the moment, without regard for his long-range context, is not. To exist as a productive being, is to man's self-interest; to attempt to exist as a parasite, is not. To seek the life proper to his nature, is to man's self-interest; to seek to live as an animal, is not.

In the light of the foregoing, let us turn now to a consideration of the issue of mental health.

It is a bromide of modern psychology that mental health cannot be defined. That which we call "healthy" or "normal," psychologists commonly declare, is determined by the culture or society in which one happens to live; what is healthy in one society is not healthy in another; it is all "relative"—there can be no universal and objective standard of mental health, they declare, just as there can be no universal and objective standard of moral values.

Psychological relativism is a corollary of moral relativism—and contains the same fallacies.

Just as the nature of mental health is not determined by individual preference, so it is not determined by social, cultural or historical preference; it is determined by the nature of man. That some hallucinating savage lives on an island where hallucinations are fashionable, does not alter the fact that hallucinations are the proof and the product of an aberrated mind. A leper cannot make himself healthy by joining a leper colony where his disease is shared by everyone; neither can a schizophrenic. Health is not adherence to a statistical norm. A healthy body is one whose organs function efficiently in maintaining the life of the organism; a diseased body is one whose organs do not. The standard by which health and disease are to be measured is life, for it is only the alternative of life or death that makes the concept of health or disease meaningful or possible. Just as medical science evaluates man's body by the standard of whether or not his body is functioning as man's life requires, so psychological science must uphold the standard of life in appraising the health or disease of a man's consciousness. The health of man's consciousness must be judged, like the health of any other organ, by how well it performs its proper function; and the function of consciousness is perception, cognition, and the initiation and direction of action.

An unobstructed consciousness, an integrated consciousness, a thinking consciousness, is a healthy consciousness. A blocked consciousness, an evading consciousness, a self-blinding consciousness, a consciousness disintegrated by fear or immobilized by depression, a consciousness dissociated from reality, is an unhealthy consciousness.

A psychologist cannot—and should not attempt to—force his views on a patient who is unwilling to accept them. Nothing can compel a mind to work, to think, to accept reason; that is a matter of a man's own choice. But this does not mean that health or disease—good or evil—are subjective and "personal." If a physician sees a patient who suffers from pneumonia wandering with inadequate clothing in the rain, he does not say: "It seems to me that is bad for the patient—but who am I to pass value-judgments?" But as psychotherapy is currently practiced, psychologists utter the equivalent of such statements every day, as when they declare that one must not "tamper" with a patient's religious beliefs. Or again: if an individual came to a physician and requested to be cured of a disease that had already infected two-thirds of the population, the physician would not reply: "Adjust to your environment. Do you want to be a non-conformist?" But what might a modern psychologist reply to his patient?

Neurotic and psychotic manifestations are the symptoms of a mind's malfunctioning. In order to learn whether a particular action or belief is an expression of such malfunctioning, it may be necessary to evaluate and interpret that action or belief in a social, cultural or historical context. This is an issue of diagnosis—not of the nature of mental health. It is not an indication of neurosis, for instance, for a man to believe, in the sixth century, that the earth is flat; but to believe it in the twentieth century, is. The diagnostician has to take into consideration the knowledge available to the patient (or person being studied). Ignorance or honest errors of knowledge are not intrinsic signs of disease; only errors due to evasion, to the rejection of available evidence, are. The concept of mental health pertains to the manner in which a consciousness functions; this determines the degree of its health.

I have said that man is a being of volitional consciousness. This means that man is free to exercise his rational faculty—or to suspend it; to act in accordance with his best, clearest and most conscientious judgment—or to act against it, moved by blind feelings; to preserve his intellectual independence and integrity—or to surrender in parasitical fear to the authority of others. This principle has the most profound implications for psychology in general, and psychotherapy in particular.

Man is the one living species who must, by volitional effort, make himself into an entity that is able to live and worthy of living. Self-esteem is the conviction that one has succeeded at this task. Self-esteem is the conviction that one is able to live and worthy of living—which means: that one's mind is competent to think and one's person is worthy of happiness.

Self-esteem is the hallmark of mental health. It is the consequence, expression and reward of a mind fully committed to reason. Commitment to reason is commitment to the maintenance of a full intellectual focus, to the constant expansion of one's understanding and knowledge, to the principle that one's actions must be consistent with one's convictions, that one must never attempt to fake reality, or place any consideration above reality, that one must never permit oneself contradictions—that one must never attempt to subvert or sabotage the proper function of consciousness.

In order to deal with reality successfully—to pursue and achieve the values which his life requires—man needs self-esteem: he needs to be confident of his efficacy and worth. Anxiety and guilt, the antipodes of self-esteem and the insignia of mental illness, are the disintegrators of thought, the distorters of values and the paralyzers of action. When a man of self-esteem chooses his values and sets his goals, when he projects the long-range purposes that will unify and guide his actions, it is like a bridge thrown to the future, across which his life will pass, a bridge supported by the conviction that his mind is competent to think, to judge, to value, and that he is worthy of enjoying values.

This sense of control over reality, of control over one's own existence, is not the result of special skills, ability or knowledge. It is not dependent on particular successes or failures. It reflects one's fundamental relationship to reality, one's conviction of fundamental efficacy and worthiness. It reflects the certainty that, in essence and in principle, one is right for reality.

It is this psychological state that traditional morality makes impossible, to the extent that a man accepts its tenets. And this is one of the foremost reasons why a psychotherapist cannot be indifferent to the question of moral values in his work.

Neither mysticism nor the creed of self-sacrifice is compatible with mental health or self-esteem. These doctrines are destructive existentially and psychologically.

(1) The maintenance of his life and the achievement of self-esteem require of man the fullest exercise of his reason—but morality, men are taught, rests on and requires faith.

Faith is the commitment of one's consciousness to beliefs for which one has no sensory evidence or rational proof.

When a man rejects reason as his standard of judgment, only one alternative standard remains to him: his feelings. A mystic is a man who treats his feelings as tools of cognition. Faith is the equation of feeling with knowledge.

To practice the "virtue" of faith, one must be willing to suspend one's sight and one's judgment; one must be willing to live with the unintelligible, with that which cannot be conceptualized or integrated into the rest of one's knowledge, and to induce a trancelike illusion of understanding. One must be willing to repress one's critical faculty and hold it as one's guilt; one must be willing to drown any questions that rise in protest—to strangle any thrust of reason convulsively seeking to assert its proper function as the protector of one's life and cognitive integrity.

Remember that all of man's knowledge and all his concepts have a hierarchical structure. The foundation and starting point of man's thinking are his sensory perceptions; on this base, man forms his first concepts, then goes on building the edifice of his knowledge by identifying and integrating new concepts on a wider and wider scale. If man's thinking is to be valid, this process must be guided by <u>logic</u>, "the art of non-contradictory identification"—(p. 1016)—and any new concept man forms must be integrated without contradiction into the hierarchical structure of his knowledge. To introduce into one's consciousness any idea that cannot be so integrated, an idea not derived from reality, not validated by a process of reason, not subject to rational examination or judgment—and worse: an idea that clashes with the rest of one's concepts and understanding of reality—is to sabotage the integrative function of consciousness, to undercut the rest of one's convictions and kill one's capacity to be certain of anything. This is the meaning of John Galt's statement in <u>Atlas</u> <u>Shrugged</u> that "the alleged shortcut to knowledge, which is faith, is only a short circuit destroying the mind" (p. 1018).

There is no greater self-delusion than to imagine that one can render unto reason that which is reason's and unto faith that which is faith's. Faith cannot be circumscribed or delimited; to surrender one's consciousness by an inch, is to surrender one's consciousness in total. Either reason is an absolute to a mind or it is not—and if it is not, there is no place to draw the line, no principle by which to draw it, no barrier faith cannot cross, no part of one's life faith cannot invade: then one remains rational only until and unless one's <u>feelings</u> decree otherwise.

Faith is a malignancy that no system can tolerate with impunity; and the man who succumbs to it, will call on it in precisely those issues where he needs his reason most. When one turns from reason to faith, when one rejects the absolutism of reality, one undercuts the absolutism of one's consciousness—and one's mind becomes an organ one cannot trust any longer. It becomes what the mystics claim it to be: a tool of distortion.

(2) Man's need of self-esteem entails the need for a sense of control over reality—but no control is possible in a universe which, by one's own concession, contains the supernatural, the miraculous and the causeless, a universe in which one is at the mercy of ghosts and demons, in which one must deal, not with the <u>unknown</u>, but with the <u>unknowable</u>; no control is possible if man proposes, but a ghost disposes; no control is possible if the universe is a haunted house.

(3) His life and self-esteem require that the object and concern of man's consciousness be reality and this earth—but morality, men are taught, consists of scorning this earth and the world available to sensory perception, and of contemplating, instead, a "different" and "higher" reality, a realm inaccessible to reason and incommunicable in language, but attainable by revelation, by special dialectical processes, by that superior state of intellectual lucidity known to Zen-Buddhists as "No-Mind," or by death.

There is only one reality—the reality knowable to reason. And if man does not choose to perceive it, there is nothing else for him to perceive; if it is not of this world that he is conscious, then he is not conscious at all.

The sole result of the mystic projection of "another" reality, is that it incapacitates man psychologically for this one. It was not by contemplating the transcendental, the ineffable, the undefinable—it was not by contemplating the nonexistent—that man lifted himself from the cave and transformed the material world to make a human existence possible on earth.

If it is a virtue to renounce one's mind, but a sin to use it; if it is a virtue to approximate the mental state of a schizophrenic, but a sin to be in intellectual focus; if it is a virtue to denounce this earth, but a sin to make it livable; if it is a virtue to mortify the flesh, but a sin to work and act; if it is a virtue to despise life, but a sin to sustain and enjoy it—then no self-esteem or control or efficacy are possible to man, nothing is possible to him but the guilt and terror of a wretch caught in a nightmare universe, a universe created by some metaphysical sadist who has cast man into a maze where the door marked "virtue" leads to self-destruction and the door marked "efficacy" leads to self-damnation.

(4) His life and self-esteem require that man take pride in his power to think, pride in his power to live—but morality, men are taught, holds pride, and specifically intellectual pride, as the gravest of sins. Virtue begins, men are taught, with humility; with the recognition of the helplessness, the smallness, the impotence of one's mind.

Is man omniscient?—demand the mystics. Is he infallible? Then how dare he challenge the word of God, or of God's representatives, and set himself up as the judge of—anything?

Intellectual pride is not—as the mystics preposterously imply it to be—a pretense at omniscience or infallibility. On the contrary, precisely because man must struggle for knowledge, precisely because the pursuit of knowledge requires an effort, the men who assume this responsibility properly feel pride.

Sometimes, colloquially, pride is taken to mean a pretense at accomplishments one has not in fact achieved. But the braggart, the boaster, the man who affects virtues he does not possess, is not proud; he has merely chosen the most humiliating way to reveal his humility.

Pride (as an emotional state) is one's response to one's power to achieve values, the pleasure one takes in one's own efficacy. And it is this that mystics regard as evil.

But if doubt, not confidence, is man's proper moral state; if self-distrust, not self-reliance, is the proof of his virtue; if fear, not self-esteem, is the mark of perfection; if guilt, not pride, is his goal—then mental illness is a moral ideal, the neurotics and psychotics are the highest exponents of morality, and the thinkers, the achievers, are the sinners, those who are too corrupt and too arrogant to seek virtue and psychological well-being through the belief that they are unfit to exist.

Humility is, of necessity, the basic virtue of a mystical morality; it is the only virtue possible to men who have renounced the mind.

Pride has to be earned; it is the reward of effort and achievement; but to gain the virtue of humility, one has only to abstain from thinking—nothing else is demanded—and one will feel humble quickly enough.

(5) His life and self-esteem require of man loyalty to his values, loyalty to his mind and its judgments, loyalty to his life —but the essence of morality, men are taught, consists of self-sacrifice: the sacrifice of one's mind to some higher authority, and the sacrifice of one's values to whomever may claim to require it.

It is not necessary, in this context, to analyze the almost countless evils entailed by the precept of self-sacrifice. Its irrationality and destructiveness have been thoroughly exposed in Atlas Shrugged. But there are two aspects of the issue that are especially pertinent to the subject of mental health.

The first is the fact that self-sacrifice means—and can only mean—mind-sacrifice.

A sacrifice means the surrender of a higher value in favor of a lower value or of a nonvalue. If one gives up that which one does not value in order to obtain that which one does value—or if one gives up a lesser value in order to obtain a greater one—this is not a sacrifice, but a gain.

All of man's values exist in a hierarchy; he values some things more than others; and, to the extent that he is rational, the hierarchical order of his values is rational: that is, he values things in proportion to their importance in serving his life and well-being. That which is inimical to his life and well-being, that which is inimical to his nature and needs as a living being, he disvalues.

Conversely, one of the characteristics of mental illness is a distorted value structure; the neurotic does not value things according to their objective merit, in relation to his nature and needs; he frequently values the very things that will lead him to self-destruction. Judged by objective standards, he is engaged in a chronic process of self-sacrifice.

But if sacrifice is a virtue, it is not the neurotic but the rational man who must be "cured." He must learn to do violence to his own rational judgment—to reverse the order of his value hierarchy—to surrender that which his mind has chosen as the good—to turn against and invalidate his own consciousness.

Do mystics declare that all they demand of man is that he sacrifice his happiness? To sacrifice one's happiness is to sacrifice one's desires; to sacrifice one's desires is to sacrifice one's values; to sacrifice one's values is to sacrifice one's judgment; to sacrifice one's judgment is to sacrifice one's mind—and it is nothing less than this that the creed of self-sacrifice aims at and demands.

If his judgment is to be an object of sacrifice—what sort of efficacy, control, freedom from conflict, or serenity of spirit will be possible to man?

The second aspect that is pertinent here, involves not only the creed of self-sacrifice but all the foregoing tenets of traditional morality.

An irrational morality, a morality set in opposition to man's nature, to the facts of reality and to the requirements of man's survival, necessarily forces men to accept the belief that there is an inevitable clash between the moral and the practical—that they must choose either to be virtuous or to be happy, to be idealistic or to be successful, but they cannot be both. This view establishes a disastrous conflict on the deepest level of man's being, a lethal dichotomy that tears man apart; it forces him to choose between making himself able to live and making himself worthy of living. Yet self-esteem and mental health require that he achieve both.

If man holds life on earth as the good, if he judges his values by the standard of that which is proper to the existence of a rational being, then there is no clash between the requirements of survival and of morality—no clash between making himself able to live and making himself worthy of living; he achieves the second by achieving the first. But there is a clash, if man holds the renunciation of this earth as the good, the renunciation of life, of mind, of happiness, of self. Under an anti-life morality, man makes himself worthy of living to the extent that he makes himself unable to to live—and to the extent that he makes himself able to live, he makes himself unworthy of living.

The answer given by many defenders of traditional morality is: "Oh, but people don't have to go to extremes!"—meaning: "We don't expect people to be <u>fully</u> moral. We expect them to smuggle <u>some</u> self-interest into their lives. We recognize that people have to live, after all."

The defense, then, of this code of morality is that few people will be suicidal enough to attempt to practice it consistently. <u>Hypocrisy</u> is to be man's protector against his professed moral convictions. What does <u>that</u> do to his self-esteem?

And what of the victims who are insufficiently hypocritical?

What of the child who withdraws in terror into an autistic universe because he cannot cope with the ravings of parents who tell him that he is guilty by nature, that his body is evil, that thinking is sinful, that question-asking is blasphemous, that doubting is depravity, and that he must obey the orders of a supernatural ghost because, if he doesn't, he will burn forever in hell?

Or the daughter who collapses in guilt over the sin of not wanting to devote her life to caring for the ailing father who has given her cause to feel only hatred?

Or the adolescent who flees into homosexuality because he has been taught that sex is evil and that women are to be worshiped, but not desired?

Or the businessman who suffers an anxiety attack because, after years of being urged to be thrifty and industrious, he has finally committed the sin of succeeding, and is now told that it shall be easier for the camel to pass through the eye of a needle than for a rich man to enter the kingdom of heaven?

Or the neurotic who, in hopeless despair, gives up the attempt to solve his problems because he has always heard it preached that this earth is a realm of misery, futility and doom, where no happiness or fulfillment is possible to man?

If the advocates of these doctrines bear a grave moral responsibility, there is a group who perhaps, bears a graver responsibility still: the psychologists and psychiatrists who see the human wreckage of these doctrines, but who remain silent and do not protest—who declare that philosophical and moral issues do not concern them, that science cannot pronounce value judgments—who shrug off their professional obligations with the assertion that a

<u>rational</u> code of morality is impossible, and, by their silence, lend their sanction to spiritual murder.

Mental health requires of man that he place no value above perception, which means: no value above consciousness, which means: no value above reality.

Every neurosis entails a break with reality. A neurotic is a man who, when his desires clash with reality, considers reality expendable. This is the attitude that the psychotherapist must seek to correct. But he cannot do so except by challenging (a) the patient's manner of using his consciousness, the abuses to which he subjects it, the evasions, the emotion-worshipping, the policy of mental inertia, and (b) the values that create the patient's emotions and set his purposes and goals.

If the patient is to be cured of his neurosis, he must learn to distinguish between a <u>thought</u> and a <u>feeling,</u> between a <u>fact</u> and a <u>wish,</u> and to recognize that nothing but destruction can result from sacrificing one's sight of reality to any other consideration. He must learn to seek his sense of self-esteem in the productive use of his mind, in the achievement of rational values, on whatever his level of ability. He must learn that the approval of others cannot be a substitute for self-esteem, and that only anxiety is possible to those who attempt such a substitution. He must learn not to seek the fraud of unearned love, and not to grant it. He must learn not to be afraid to question and challenge the prevalent beliefs of his culture. He must learn to reject the claims of those who demand his agreement <u>on faith</u>. He must learn to fight for his own happiness and to deserve it. He must learn that the irrational <u>will not work</u>—and that so long as any part of him desires it, that desire is the cause of his suffering.

He must learn to live as a rational being—and for guidance at this task, he needs a code of rational moral principles.

This is the reason I consider the Objectivist ethics indispensable to the practice of psychotherapy.

REFERENCES

Branden, N. <u>Who is Ayn Rand?</u> New York: Random House, 1962.
Rand, Ayn. <u>Atlas shrugged</u>. New York: Random House, 1957.
Rand, Ayn. <u>The virtue of selfishness</u>. New York: New American Library, 1964.

XX

THE CASE AGAINST RELIGION: A PSYCHOTHERAPIST'S VIEW

Albert Ellis

Before we can talk sensibly about religion—or almost anything else!—we should give some kind of a definition of what we are talking about. Let me, therefore, start with what I think are some legitimate definitions of the term religion. Other concepts of this term, of course, exist; but what I am talking about when I use it is as follows.

According to Webster's New World Dictionary, religion is: "1. belief in a divine or superhuman power or powers to be obeyed and worshipped as the creator(s) and ruler(s) of the universe. 2. expression of this belief in conduct and ritual."

English and English (1958), in their Comprehensive Dictionary of Psychological and Psychoanalytical Terms, define religion as "a system of attitudes, practices, rites, ceremonies, and beliefs by means of which individuals or a community put themselves in relation to God or to a supernatural world and often to each other, and from which the religious person derives a set of values by which to judge events in the natural world."

The Columbia Encyclopedia notes that "when a man becomes conscious of a power above and beyond the human, and recognizes a dependence of himself upon that power, religion has become a factor in his being."

These, then, are the definitions of religion which I accept and which I shall have in mind as I discuss the religious viewpoint in this paper. Religion, to me, must include some concept of a supernatural deity and some dependence on this deity. When the term is used merely to denote a system of beliefs, practices, or ethical values which are not connected with any assumed higher power, then I believe it is used loosely and confusingly: since such a non-

Reprinted by permission of the author and *The Independent*, October 1962, pp. 1–7.

supernatural system of beliefs can more accurately be described as a philosophy of life or a code of ethics, and it is misleading to confuse a believer in this general kind of philosophy or ethical code with a true religionist.

Every atheist, in other words, has some kind of philosophy and some code of ethics; and many atheists, in fact, have much more rigorous life philosophies and ethical systems than have most deists.

SOMEONE IS RELIGIOUS . . .

It therefore seems silly to say that someone is religious because he happens to be philosophic or ethical; and unless we rigorously use the term religion to mean some kind of faith unfounded on fact, or dependency on some assumed superhuman entities, we broaden the definition of the word so greatly as to make it practically meaningless.

If religion is defined as man's dependence on a power above and beyond the human, then, as a psychotherapist, I find it to be exceptionally pernicious. For the psychotherapist is normally dedicated to helping human beings in general and his patients in particular to achieve certain goals of mental health, and virtually all these goals are antithetical to a truly religious viewpoint.

Let us look at the main psychotherapeutic goals. On the basis of twenty years of clinical experience, and in basic agreement with most of my professional colleagues (such as Braaten, 1961; Dreikurs, 1955; Fromm, 1955; Goldstein, 1954; Maslow, 1954; Rogers, 1957; and Thorne, 1961), I would say that the psychotherapist tries to help his patients be minimally anxious and hostile; and to this end, he tries to help them to acquire the following kinds of personality traits:

1. Self-interest. The emotionally healthy individual should primarily be true to himself and not masochistically sacrifice himself for others. His kindness and consideration for others should be derived from the idea that he himself wants to enjoy freedom from unnecessary pain and restriction, and that he is only likely to do so by helping create a world in which the rights of others, as well as himself, are not needlessly curtailed.

2. Self-direction. He should assume responsibility for his own life, be able independently to work out most of his problems, and while at times wanting or preferring the cooperation and help of others, not need their support for his effectiveness or well-being.

3. Tolerance. He should fully give other human beings the right to be wrong; and, while disliking or abhorring some of their

behavior, still not blame them, as persons, for performing this dis-
likeable behavior. He should accept the fact that all humans are re-
markably fallible, never unrealistically expect them to be perfect,
and refrain from despising or punishing them when they make inevitable mistakes and errors.

4. Acceptance of uncertainty. The emotionally mature individual should completely accept the fact that we all live in a world
of probability and chance, where there are not nor probably ever
will be any absolute certainties, and should realize that it is not at
all horrible—indeed, in many ways it is fascinating and exciting—
to live in such a probabilistic, uncertain world.

5. Flexibility. He should remain intellectually flexible, be open
to change at all times, and unbigotedly view the infinitely varied
people, ideas, and things in the world around him.

6. Scientific thinking. He should be objective, rational, and
scientific; and be able to apply the laws of logic and of scientific
method not only to external people and events, but to himself and his
interpersonal relationships.

7. Commitment. He should be vitally absorbed in something
outside of himself, whether it be in people, things, or ideas; and
should preferably have at least one major creative interest, as well
as some outstanding human involvement, which is highly important
to him, and around which he structures a good part of his life.

8. Risk-taking. The emotionally sound person should be able
to take risks: to ask himself what he would really like to do in life,
and then to try to do this, even though he has to risk defeat or failure. He should be adventurous (though not necessarily fool-hardy);
be willing to try almost anything once, just to see how he likes it;
and look forward to some breaks in his usual life routine.

9. Self-acceptance. He should normally be glad to be alive, and
to like himself just because he is alive, because he exists, and because he (as a living being) invariably has some power to enjoy himself, to create happiness and joy. He should not equate his worth or
value to himself on his extrinsic achievements, or on what others
think of him, but on his personal existence: on his ability to think,
feel, and act, and thereby to make some kind of an interesting, absorbed life for himself.

These, then, are the kind of personality traits which a psychotherapist is interested in helping his patients achieve and which he
is also, prophylactically, interested in fostering in the lives of millions who will never be his patients.

How, now, does religion—by which, again, I mean faith unfounded on fact, or dependence on some supernatural deity—help

human beings to achieve these healthy traits and thereby to avoid becoming anxious, depressed, and hostile?

The answer, of course, is that it doesn't help at all; and in most respects it seriously sabotages mental health. For religion, first of all, is not self-interest: it is god-interest.

The religious person must, by virtual definition, be so concerned with whether or not his hypothesized god loves him, and whether he is doing the right thing to continue to keep in this god's good graces, that he must, at the very best, put himself second, and must sacrifice some of his most cherished interests to appease this god. If, moreover, he is a member of any organized religion, then he must choose his god's precepts first, those of his church and its clergy second, and his own views and preferences third.

NO VIEWS OF HIS OWN

In a sense, the religious person must have no real views of his own; and it is presumptuous of him, in fact, to have any. In regard to sex-love affairs, to marriage and family relations, to business, to politics, and to virtually everything else that is important in his life, he must try to discover what his god and his clergy would like him to do; and he must primarily do their bidding.

Masochistic self-sacrifice is an integral part of almost all organized religions: as shown, for example, in the various forms of ritualistic self-deprivation that Jews, Christians, Mohammedans, and other religionists must continually undergo if they are to keep in good with their assumed gods.

Masochism, indeed, stems from an individual's deliberately inflicting pain on himself in order that he may guiltlessly permit himself to experience some kind of sexual or other pleasure; and the very essence of most organized religions is the performance of masochistic, guilt-soothing rituals, by which the religious individual gives himself permission to enjoy life.

Religiosity, to a large degree, essentially is masochism; and both are forms of mental sickness.

In regard to self-direction, it can easily be seen from what has just been said that the religious person is by necessity dependent and other-directed rather than independent and self-directed. If he is true to his religious beliefs, he must first bow down to his god; second, to the clergy who run this god's church; and third, to all the other members of his religious sect, who are eagle-eyedly watching him to see whether he deflects an iota from the conduct his god and his church define as proper.

If religion, therefore, is largely masochism, it is even more dependency. For a man to be a true believer and to be strong and independent is impossible; religion and self-sufficiency are contradictory terms.

Tolerance, again, is a trait that the firm religionist cannot possibly possess. "I am the Lord thy God and thou shalt have no other Gods before me," sayeth Jehovah. Which means, in plain English, that whatever any given god and his clergy believe must be absolutely, positively true; and whatever any other person or group believes must be absolutely, positively false.

Democracy, permissiveness, and the acceptance of human fallibility are quite alien to the real religionist—since he can only believe that the creeds and commands of his particular deity should, ought, and must be obeyed, and that anyone who disobeys them is patently a knave.

Religion, with its definitional absolutes, can never rest with the concept of an individual's doing wrong or making mistakes, but must inevitably add to this the notion of his sinning and of his deserving to be punished for his sins. For, if it is merely desirable for you to refrain from harming others or committing other misdeeds, as any non-religious code of ethics will inform you that it is then if you make a mistake and do commit some misdeeds, you are merely a wrongdoer, or one who is doing an undesirable deed and who should try to correct himself and do less wrong in the future. But if it is god-given, absolutistic law that you shall not, must not, do a wrong act, and you actually do it, you are then a miserable sinner, a worthless being, and must severely punish yourself (perhaps eternally, in Hell) for being a wrongdoer, being a fallible human.

Religion, then, by setting up absolute, god-given standards, must make you self-depreciating and dehumanized when you err; and must lead you to despise and dehumanize others when they act badly. This kind of absolutistic, perfectionistic thinking is the prime creator of the two most corroding of human emotions: anxiety and hostility.

If one of the requisites for emotional health is acceptance of uncertainty, then religion is obviously the unhealthiest state imaginable: since its prime reason for being is to enable the religionist to believe in a mythical certainty.

Just because life is so uncertain, and because millions of people think that they cannot take its vicissitudes, they invent absolutistic gods, and thereby pretend that there is some final, invariant answer to things. Patently, these people are fooling themselves—

and instead of healthfully admitting that they do not <u>need</u> certainty, but can live comfortably in this often disorderly world, they stubbornly protect their neurotic beliefs by insisting that there <u>must</u> be the kind of certainty that they foolishly believe that they need.

This is like a child's believing that he <u>must</u> have a kindly father in order to survive; and then, when his father is unkindly, or perhaps has died and is nonexistent, he dreams up a father (who may be a neighbor, a movie star, or a pure figment of his imagination) and insists that this dream-father actually exists.

The trait of flexibility, which is so essential to proper emotional functioning, is also blocked and sabotaged by religious belief. For the person who dogmatically believes in god, and who sustains this belief with a faith unfounded in fact, which a true religionist of course must, clearly is <u>not</u> open to change and <u>is</u> necessarily bigoted.

If, for example, his scriptures or his church tell him that he shalt not even covet his neighbor's wife—let alone having actual adulterous relations with her!—he cannot ask himself "<u>Why</u> should I not lust after this woman, as long as I don't intend to do anything about my desire for her? What is <u>really</u> wrong about that?" For his god and his church have spoken; and there is no appeal from this arbitrary authority, once he has brought himself to accept it.

Anytime, in fact, anyone unempirically establishes a god or a set of religious postulates which have a superhuman origin, he can thereafter use no empirical evidence whatever to question the dictates of this god or these postulates, since they are (by definition) beyond scientific validation.

The best he can do, if he wants to change any of the rules that stem from his religion is to change the religion itself. Otherwise, he is stuck with the absolutistic axioms, and their logical corollaries, that he himself has initially accepted on faith. We may therefore note again that, just as religion <u>is</u> masochism, other-directedness, intolerance, and refusal to accept uncertainty, it also is mental and emotional inflexibility.

In regard to scientific thinking, it practically goes without saying that this kind of cerebration is quite antithetical to religiosity. The main canon of the scientific method—as Ayer (1947), Carnap (1953), Reichenbach (1953) and a host of other modern philosophers of science have pointed out—is that, at least in some final analysis, or in principle, all theories be confirmable by some form of human experience, some empirical referent. But all religions which are worthy of the name contend that their superhuman entities cannot be seen, heard, smelled, tasted, felt, or otherwise humanly experienced, and that their gods and their principles are therefore distinctly beyond science.

To believe in any of these religions, therefore, is to be unscientific at least to some extent; and it could well be contended that the more religious one is, the less scientific one tends to be. Although a religious person need not be entirely unscientific (as, for that matter, a raving maniac need not be either), it is difficult to see how he could be perfectly scientific.

While a person may be both scientific and religious (as he may also be at times sensible and at other times foolish), it is doubtful if an individual's attitude may simultaneously be truly pious and objective.

In regard to the trait of commitment, the religious individual may—for once!—have some advantages. For if he is truly religious, he is seriously committed to his god, his church, or his creed; and to some extent, at least, he thereby acquires a major interest in life.

Religious commitment also frequently has its serious disadvantages: since it tends to be obsessive-compulsive; and it may well interfere with other kinds of healthy commitments—such as deep involvements in sex-love relations, in scientific pursuits, and even in artistic endeavors. Moreover, it is a commitment that is often motivated by guilt or hostility, and may serve as a frenzied covering-up mechanism which masks, but does not really eliminate, these underlying disturbed feelings. It is also the kind of commitment that is based on falsehoods and illusions, and that therefore easily can be shattered, thus plunging the previously committed individual into the depths of disillusionment and despair.

Not all forms of commitment, in other words, are equally healthy. The Grand Inquisitors of the medieval Catholic church were utterly dedicated to their "holy" work; and Hitler and many of his associates were fanatically committed to their Nazi doctrines. But this hardly proves that they were emotionally stable human beings.

When religious individuals are happily committed to their faith, they often tend to be fanatically and dogmatically committed in an obsessive-compulsive way that itself is hardly desirable. Religious commitment may well be better for a human being than no commitment to anything. But religion, to a large degree, is fanaticism—which, in turn, is an obsessive-compulsive, rigid form of holding to a view point that invariably masks and provides a bulwark for the underlying insecurity of the obsessed individual.

In regard to risk-taking, it should be obvious that the religious person is highly determined not to be adventurous nor to take any of life's normal risks. He strongly believes in unvalidateable assumptions precisely <u>because</u> he does not want to risk following his <u>own</u> preferences and aims, but wants the guarantee that some higher power will back him.

Enormously fearing failure, and falsely defining his own worth as a person in terms of achievement, he sacrifices time, energy, and material goods and pleasures to the worship of his assumed god, so that he can at least be sure that this god loves and supports him. All religions worthy of the name are distinctly inhibiting: which means, in effect, that the religious person sells his soul, surrenders his own basic urges and pleasures, so that he may feel comfortable with the heavenly helper that he himself has invented. Religion, then, <u>is</u> needless inhibition.

Finally, in regard to self-acceptance, it should again be clear that the religious devotee cannot possibly accept himself just because he is alive, because he exists and has, by mere virtue of his aliveness, some power to enjoy himself. Rather, he must make his self-acceptance utterly contingent on the acceptance of his definitional god, the church and clergy who also serve this god, and all other true believers in his religion.

If all these extrinsic persons and things accept him, he is able —and even then only temporarily and with continued underlying anxiety—to accept himself. Which means, of course, that he defines himself only through the reflected appraisals of others and loses any real, existential self that he might otherwise keep creating. Religion, for such an individual, consequently <u>is</u> self-abasement and self-abnegation—as, of course, virtually all the saints and mystics have clearly stated that it is.

If we summarize what we have just been saying, the conclusion seems inescapable that religion is, on almost every conceivable count, directly opposed to the goals of mental health—since it basically consists of masochism, other-directedness, intolerance, refusal to accept uncertainty, unscientific thinking, needless inhibition, and self-abasement.

In the one area where religion has some advantage in terms of emotional hygiene—that of encouraging hearty commitment to a cause or project in which the person may be vitally absorbed— it even tends to sabotage this advantage in two important ways: (a) it drives most of its adherents to commit themselves to its tenets for the wrong reasons—that is, to cover up instead of to face and rid themselves of their basic insecurities; and (b) it encourages a fanatic, obsessive-compulsive kind of commitment that is, in its own right, a form of mental illness.

If we want to look at the problem of human disturbance a little differently, we may ask ourselves "What are the main irrational ideas which people believe and through which they drive themselves into severe states of emotional sickness?"

EXPLORING THE QUESTION

After exploring this question for many years, and developing a new form of psychotherapy which is specifically directed at quickly unearthing and challenging the main irrational ideas which make people neurotic and psychotic, I have found that these ideas may be categorized under a few major headings (Ellis, 1962; Ellis and Harper, 1961a, 1961b). Here, for example, are five irrational notions, all or some of which are strongly held by practically every seriously disturbed person; and here, along with these notions, are the connections between them and commonly held religious beliefs.

Irrational idea No. 1 is the idea that it is a dire necessity for an adult to be loved or approved by all the significant figures in his life. This idea is bolstered by the religious philosophy that if you cannot get certain people to love or approve you, you can always fall back on god's love. The thought, however, that it is quite possible for you to live comfortably in the world whether or not other people accept you is quite foreign to both emotionally disturbed people and religionists.

Irrational idea No. 2 is the idea that you must be thoroughly competent, adequate, and achieving in all possible respects, otherwise you are worthless. The religionist says that no, you need not be competent and achieving, and in fact can be thoroughly inadequate—as long as god loves you and you are a member in good standing of the church. But this means, of course, that you must be a competent and achieving religionist—else you are no damned good.

Irrational idea No. 3 is the notion that certain people are bad, wicked, and villainous and that they should be severely blamed and punished for their sins. This is the ethical basis, of course, of virtually all true religions. The concepts of guilt, blaming, and sin are, in fact, almost synonymous with that of revealed religion.

Irrational idea No. 4 is the belief that it is horrible, terrible, and catastrophic when things are not going the way you would like them to go. This idea, again, is the very core of religiosity: since the religious person invariably believes that just because he cannot stand being frustrated, and just because he must keep worrying about things turning out badly, he needs a supreme deity to supervise his thoughts and deeds and to protect him from anxiety and frustration.

Irrational idea No. 5 is the idea that human unhappiness is externally caused and that people have little or no ability to control their sorrows or rid themselves of their negative feelings. Once again, this notion is the essence of religion: since real religions invariably teach that only by your trusting in god and relying on and praying to him will you be able to control your sorrows or counteract your negative emotions.

Similarly, if we had the time to review all the other major irrational ideas that lead humans to become and to remain emotionally disturbed, we would quickly find that they are coexterminous with or are strongly encouraged by religious tenets.

If you think about the matter carefully, you will see that this close connection between mental illness and religion is inevitable and invariant: since neurosis or psychosis is something of a high-class name for childishness or dependency; and religion, when used correctly, is little more than a synonym for dependency.

In the final analysis, then, religion _is_ neurosis. This is why I remarked, at a symposium on sin and psychotherapy held by the American Psychological Association a few years ago, that from a mental health standpoint Voltaire's famous dictum should be reversed: for if there were a God, it would be necessary to uninvent Him.

If the thesis of this article is correct, religion goes hand in hand with the basic irrational beliefs of human beings. These keep them dependent, anxious, and hostile, and thereby create and maintain their neuroses and psychoses. What then is the role of psychotherapy in dealing with the religious views of disturbed patients? Obviously, the sane and effective psychotherapist should not—as many contemporary psychoanalytic Jungian, client-centered, and existentialist therapists have contended he should—go along with his patients' religious orientation and try to help these patients live successfully with their religions: for this is equivalent to trying to help them live successfully with their emotional illnesses.

EXCLUSIVE HOMOSEXUALITY

If a man is fearfully fixated on exclusive homosexuality, or obsessively engaged in hating his boss, or compulsively dependent on the love of his mother, no sensible psychotherapist would try to enable him to retain his crippling neurotic symptoms and still lead a happy life.

The effective therapist, instead, would of course try to help this man live successfully without his symptoms—and to this end would keep hammering away at the basic irrational philosophies of life which cause the patient to manufacture and to hang on to his manifestations of emotional illness.

So will the therapist, if he himself is not too sick or gutless, attack his patient's religiosity. Not only will he show this patient that he is religious—meaning, as we previously noted, that he is masochistic, other-directed, intolerant, unable to accept uncertainty, unscientific, needlessly inhibited, self-abasing, and fanatic —but he will also quite vigorously and forcefully question, challenge, and attack the patient's irrational beliefs that support these disturbed traits.

This is what is done in my own system of psychotherapy, which is called rational-emotive psychotherapy. Where other systems of therapy largely try to give the patient insight into the origins of his self-defeating beliefs (as, for example, the Freudians do) or try to help him accept himself with his self-sabotaging behavior (as the existential and client-centered therapists do), in rational therapy we give him insight and accept him in spite of his failings —but we also, and I think more importantly, clearly show him how he keeps maintaining his early-acquired irrationalities by indoctrinating himself over and over with nonsensical internalized sentences which sustain this nonsense; and show him how he can concretely challenge and contradict these internalized philosophies, by logically parsing and analyzing them, and by convincing himself that he must give them up if he is to regain emotional health.

Rational-emotive psychotherapy, in other words, goes distinctly beyond the usual insight-producing and patient-accepting methods of treatment in that it actively depropagandizes the patient, and teaches him how to keep depropagandizing himself for the rest of his life, so that the highly irrational, and essentially superstitious and religious, beliefs that he acquired from his parents and his culture can be thoroughly combatted until they are truly non-existent.

THE DISTURBED INDIVIDUAL

RT, as rational therapy is called for short, literally teaches the disturbed individual how he can apply the methods of scientific thinking to himself and his personal relationships with others; and it usually does so with many fewer sessions of psychotherapy than the more conventional psychoanalytic and other schools use. It is, however, an unusually depth-centered and thoroughgoing form of treatment, in that it is not interested in symptom removal or in release of feelings, but in an extensive and intensive reorganization of the patient's basic philosophy of life. While valuing the patient himself and his inalienable, existential right to happiness, it vigorously and most directly attacks his self-sabotaging values and his self-repeated irrational internal verbalizations which uphold these values. This is not the place to give the details of the theory and practice of rational-emotive psychotherapy, since they may be found in my recent book, Reason and Emotion in Psychotherapy (1962).

Not that RT is the only method of helping human beings to change their fundamental irrational and superstitious ideas about themselves, others, and the world. Various other depropagandizing techniques, including books, lectures, and works of literature, as well as other modes of psychotherapy, can also be most useful in this respect. The main point is, however, that the vast majority of people in contemporary society are basically irrational and religious in their thinking and feeling—and hence are more or less emotionally sick.

All true believers in any kind of orthodoxy—whether it be religious, political, social, or even artistic orthodoxy—are distinctly disturbed, since they are obviously rigid, fanatic, and dependent individuals (Hoffer, 1951). And many liberal religionists of various groups are distinctly less, but still quite definitely, emotionally childish. For that, again, is what all manner of religion essentially is: childish dependency. And that is what effective psychotherapy, along with all the other healing arts and informative sciences, must continue uncompromisingly to unmask and eradicate.

REFERENCES

Ayer, A. J. Language, truth and logic. New York: Dover Publications, 1947.

Braaten, L. J. The main theories of "existentialism" from the viewpoint of a psychotherapist. Ment. Hyg., 1961, 45: 10-17.

Carnap, R. Testability and meaning. In H. Feigl and M. Brodbeck (Eds.) Readings in the philosophy of science. New York: Appleton-Century-Crofts, 1953.

Dreikurs, R. The Adlerian approach on the changing scope of psychiatry. Chicago: Author, 1955.

Ellis, A. Reason and emotion in psychotherapy. New York: Lyle Stuart, 1962.

Ellis, A.,and Harper, R. A. Creative marriage. New York: Lyle Stuart, 1961.

Ellis, A., and Harper, R. A. A guide to rational living. Englewood Cliffs, N. J.: Prentice-Hall, 1961.

Fromm, E. The sane society. New York: Rinehart, 1955.

Hoffer, E. The true believer. New York: Harper, 1951.

Maslow, A. H. Motivation and personality. New York: Harper, 1954.

Reichenbach, H. The verifiability theory of meaning. In H. Feigl and M. Brodbeck (Eds.) Readings in the philosophy of science. New York: Appleton-Century-Crofts, 1953.

Rogers, C. R. The necessary and sufficient conditions of therapeutic personality change. J. consult. Psychol., 1957. 21: 459-461.

Thorne, F. C. Personality: a clinical eclectic view. Brandon, Vt.: Journal of Clinical Psychology, 1961.

Appendixes

ETHICAL STANDARDS

American Personnel and Guidance Association

Preamble

The American Personnel and Guidance Association is an educational, scientific, and professional organization dedicated to service to society. This service is committed to profound faith in the worth, dignity, and great potentiality of the individual human being.

The marks of a profession, and therefore of a professional organization, can be stated as follows:

1. Possession of a body of specialized knowledge, skills, and attitudes known and practiced by its members.

2. This body of specialized knowledge, skills, and attitudes is derived through scientific inquiry and scholarly learning.

3. This body of specialized knowledge, skills, and attitudes is acquired through professional preparation, preferably on the graduate level, in a college or university as well as through continuous in-service training and personal growth after completion of formal education.

4. This body of specialized knowledge, skills, and attitudes, is constantly tested and extended through research and scholarly inquiry.

5. A profession has a literature of its own, even though it may, and indeed must, draw portions of its content from other areas of knowledge.

6. A profession exalts service to the individual and society above personal gain. It possesses a philosophy and a code of ethics.

7. A profession through the voluntary association of its members constantly examines and improves the quality of its professional preparation and services to the individual and society.

8. Membership in the professional organization and the practice of the profession must be limited to persons meeting stated standards of preparation and competencies.

9. The profession affords a life career and permanent mem-

Reprinted by permission of the American Personnel and Guidance Association from "Ethical Standards," *Personnel and Guidance Journal,* October 1961, pages 206-209.

bership as long as services meet professional standards.

10. The public recognizes, has confidence in, and is willing to compensate the members of the profession for their services.

The Association recognizes that the vocational roles and settings of its members are identified with a wide variety of academic disciplines and levels of academic preparation. This diversity reflects the pervasiveness of the Association's interest and influence. It also poses challenging complexities in efforts to conceptualize:

    a. the characteristics of members;

    b. desired or requisite preparation or practice; and

    c. supporting social, legal and/or ethical controls.

The specification of ethical standards enables the Association to clarify to members, future members, and to those served by members the nature of ethical responsibilities held in common by its members.

The introduction of such standards will inevitably stimulate greater concern by members for practice and preparation for practice. It will also stimulate a general growth and identification with and appreciation for both the common and diverse characteristics of the definable roles within the world of work of Association members.

There are six major areas of professional activity which encompass the work of members of APGA. For each of these areas certain general principles are listed below to serve as guide lines for ethical practice. These are preceded by a general section which includes certain principles germane to the six areas and common to the entire work of the Association members.

Section A: General

1. The member exerts what influence he can to foster the development and improvement of the profession and continues his professional growth throughout his career.

2. The member has a responsibility to the institution within which he serves. His acceptance of employment by the institution implies that he is in substantial agreement with the general policies and principles of the institution. Therefore, his professional activities are also in accord with the objectives of the institution. Within the member's own work setting, if, despite his efforts, he cannot reach agreement as to acceptable ethical standards of conduct with his superiors, he should end his affiliation with them.

3. The member must expect ethical behavior among his professional associates in APGA at all times. He is obligated, in situations where he possesses information raising serious doubt as

to the ethical behavior of other members, to attempt to rectify such conditions.

4. The member is obligated to concern himself with the degree to which the personnel functions of non-members with whose work he is acquainted represent competent and ethical performance. Where his information raises serious doubt as to the ethical behavior of such persons, it is his responsibility to attempt to rectify such conditions.

5. The member must not seek self-enhancement through expressing evaluations or comparisons damaging to other ethical professional workers.

6. The member should not claim or imply professional qualifications exceeding those possessed and is responsible for correcting any misrepresentations of his qualifications by others.

7. The member providing services for personal remuneration shall, in establishing fees for such services, take careful account of the charges made for comparable services by other professional persons.

8. The member who provides information to the public or to his subordinates, peers, or superiors has a clear responsibility to see that both the content and the manner of presentation are accurate and appropriate to the situation.

9. The member has an obligation to ensure that evaluative information about such persons as clients, students, and applicants shall be shared only with those persons who will use such information for professional purposes.

10. The member shall offer professional services only, through the context of a professional relationship. Thus testing, counseling, and other services are not to be provided through the mail by means of newspaper or magazine articles, radio or television programs, or public performances.

Section B: Counseling

This section refers to practices involving a counseling relationship with a counselee or client and is not intended to be applicable to practices involving administrative relationships with the persons being helped. A counseling relationship denotes that the person seeking help retain full freedom of choice and decision and that the helping person has no authority or responsibility to approve or disapprove of the choices or decisions of the counselee or client. "Counselee" or "client" is used here to indicate the person (or persons) for whom the member has assumed a professional responsibility. Typically the counselee or client is the individual with whom the member has direct and primary contact. However, at times, "client" may include another person(s) when the other person(s) exercise significant control and direction over the individual being helped in connection with the decisions and plans being considered in counseling.

1. The member's <u>primary</u> obligation is to respect the integrity and promote the welfare of the counselee or client with whom he is working.

2. The counseling relationship and information resulting therefrom must be kept confidential consistent with the obligations of the member as a professional person.

3. Records of the counseling relationship including interview notes, test data, correspondence, tape recordings, and other documents are to be considered professional information for use in counseling, research, and teaching of counselors but always with full protection of the identity of the client and with precaution so that no harm will come to him.

4. The counselee or client should be informed of the conditions under which he may receive counseling assistance at or before the time he enters the counseling relationship. This is particularly true in the event that there exist conditions of which the counselee or client would not likely be aware.

5. The member reserves the right to consult with any other professionally competent person about his counselee client. In choosing his professional consultant the member must avoid placing the consultant in a conflict of interest situation, i.e., the consultant must be free of any other obligatory relation to the member's client that would preclude the consultant being a proper party to the member's efforts to help the counselee or client.

6. The member shall decline to initiate or shall terminate a counseling relationship when he cannot be of professional assistance to the counselee or client either because of lack of competence or personal limitation. In such instances the member shall refer his counselee or client to an appropriate specialist. In the event the counselee or client declines the suggested referral, the member is not obligated to continue the counseling relationship.

7. When the member learns from counseling relationships of conditions which are likely to harm others over whom his institution or agency has responsibility, he is expected to report <u>the condition</u> to the appropriate responsible authority, but in such a manner as not to reveal the identity of his counselee or clients.

8. In the event that the counselee or client's condition is such as to require others to assume responsibility for him, or when there is clear and imminent danger to the counselee or client or to

others, the member is expected to report this fact to an appropriate responsible authority, and/or take such other emergency measures as the situation demands.

9. Should the member be engaged in a work setting which calls for any variation from the above statements, the member is obligated to ascertain that such variations are justifiable under the conditions and that such variations are clearly specified and made known to all concerned with such counseling services.

Section C: Testing

1. The primary purpose of psychological testing is to provide objective and comparative measures for use in self-evaluation or evaluation by others of general or specific attributes.

2. Generally, test results constitute only one of a variety of pertinent data for personnel and guidance decisions. It is the member's responsibility to provide adequate orientation or information to the examinee(s) so that the results of testing may be placed in proper perspective with other relevant factors.

3. When making any statements to the public about tests and testing care must be taken to give accurate information and to avoid any false claims or misconceptions.

4. Different tests demand different levels of competence for administration, scoring, and interpretation. It is therefore the responsibility of the member to recognize the limits of his competence and to perform only those functions which fall within his preparation and competence.

5. In selecting tests for use in a given situation or with a particular client the member must consider not only general but also specific validity, reliability, and appropriateness of the test(s).

6. Tests should be administered under the same conditions which were established in their standardization. Except for research purposes explicitly stated, any departures from these conditions, as well as unusual behavior or irregularities during the testing session which may affect the interpretation of the test results, must be fully noted and reported. In this connection, unsupervised test-taking or the use of tests through the mails are of questionable value.

7. The value of psychological tests depends in part on the novelty to persons taking them. Any prior information, coaching, or reproduction of test materials tends to invalidate test results. Therefore, test security is one of the professional obligations of the member.

8. The member has the responsibility to inform the examinee(s) as to the purpose of testing. The criteria of examinee's welfare and/or explicit prior understanding with him should determine who the recipients of the test results may be.

9. The member should guard against the appropriation, reproduction, or modifications of published tests or parts thereof without express permission and adequate recognition of the original author or publisher.

Regarding the preparation, publication, and distribution of tests reference should be made to:

"Tests and Diagnostic Techniques"—Report of the Joint Committee of the American Psychological Association, American Educational Research Association, and National Council of Measurements used in Education. Supplement to Psychological Bulletin, 1954, 2, 1-38.

Section D: Research and Publication

1. In the performance of any research on human subjects, the member must avoid causing any injurious effects or after-effects of the experiment upon his subjects.

2. The member may withhold information or provide misinformation to subjects only when it is essential to the investigation and where he assumes responsibility for corrective action following the investigation.

3. In reporting research results, explicit mention must be made of all variables and conditions known to the investigator which might affect interpretation of the data.

4. The member is responsible for conducting and reporting his investigations so as to minimize the possibility that his findings will be misleading.

5. The member has an obligation to make available original research data to qualified others who may wish to replicate or verify the study.

6. In reporting research results or in making original data available, due care must be taken to disguise the identity of the subjects, in the absence of specific permission from such subjects to do otherwise.

7. In conducting and reporting research, the member should be familiar with, and give recognition to, previous work on the topic.

8. The member has the obligation to give due credit to those who have contributed significantly to his research, in accordance with their contributions.

9. The member has the obligation to honor commitments made to subjects of research in return for their cooperation.

10. The member is expected to communicate to other members the results of any research he judges to be of professional or scientific value.

Section E: Consulting and Private Practice

Consulting refers to a voluntary relationship between a professional helper and help-needing social unit (industry, business, school, college, etc.) in which the consultant is attempting to give help to the client in the solving of some current or potential problem.[1]

1. The member acting as a consultant must have a high degree of self-awareness of his own values and needs in entering a helping relationship which involves change in a social unit.

2. There should be understanding and agreement between consultant and client as to directions or goals of the attempted change.

3. The consultant must be reasonably certain that he or his organization have the necessary skills and resources for giving the kind of help which is needed now or that may develop later.

4. The consulting relationship must be one in which client adaptability and growth toward self-direction are encouraged and cultivated. The consultant must consistently maintain his role as a consultant and not become a decision maker for the client.

5. The consultant in announcing his availability for service as a consultant follows professional rather than commercial standards in describing his services with accuracy, dignity, and caution.

6. For private practice in testing, counseling, or consulting the ethical principles stated in all previous sections of this document are pertinent. In addition, any individual, agency, or institution offering educational and vocational counseling to the public should meet the standards of the American Board on Professional Standards in Vocational Counseling, Inc.

Section F: Personnel Administration

1. The member is responsible for establishing working agreements with supervisors and with subordinates especially regarding counseling or clinical relationships, confidentiality, distinction between public and private material, and a mutual respect for the

---

[1]This definition is adapted from "Dimensions of the Consultant's Job" by Ronald Lippitt, *The Journal of Social Issues*, Vol. XV, No. 2, 1959.

positions of parties involved in such issues.

2. Such working agreements may vary from one institutional setting to another. What should be the case in each instance, however, is that agreements have been specified, made known to those concerned, and whenever possible the agreements reflect institutional policy rather than personal judgment.

3. The member's responsibility to his superiors requires that he keep them aware of conditions affecting the institution, particularly those which may be potentially disrupting or damaging to the institution.

4. The member has a responsibility to select competent persons for assigned responsibilities and to see that his personnel are used maximally for the skills and experience they possess.

5. The member has responsibility for constantly stimulating his staff for their and his own continued growth and improvement. He must see that staff members are adequately supervised as to the quality of their functioning and for purposes of professional development.

6. The member is responsible for seeing that his staff is informed of policies, goals, and programs toward which the department's operations are oriented.

Section G: Preparation for Personnel Work

1. The member in charge of training sets up a strong program of academic study and supervised practice in order to prepare the trainees for their future responsibilities.

2. The training program should aim to develop in the trainee not only skills and knowledge, but also self-understanding.

3. The member should be aware of any manifestations of personal limitations in a student trainee which may influence the latter's provision of competent services and has an obligation to offer assistance to the trainee in securing professional remedial help.

4. The training program should include preparation in research and stimulation for the future personnel worker to do research and add to the knowledge in his field.

5. The training program should make the trainee aware of the ethical responsibilities and standards of the profession he is entering.

6. The program of preparation should aim at inculcating among the trainees, who will later become the practitioners of our profession, the ideal of service to individual and society above personal gain.

ETHICAL STANDARDS OF PSYCHOLOGISTS
American Psychological Association

The psychologist believes in the dignity and worth of the
individual human being. He is committed to increasing
man's understanding of himself and others. While pursuing this endeavor, he protects the welfare of any person who may seek his service or of any subject, human
or animal, that may be the object of his study. He does
not use his professional position or relationships, nor
does he knowingly permit his own services to be used by
others, for purposes inconsistent with these values.
While demanding for himself freedom of inquiry and communication, he accepts the responsibility this freedom
confers: for competence where he claims it, for objectivity in the report of his findings, and for consideration of the best interests of his colleagues and of society.

SPECIFIC PRINCIPLES

Principle 1. Responsibility. The psychologist,[1] committed to increasing man's understanding of man, places high value on objectivity and integrity, and maintains the highest standards in the
services he offers.

a. As a scientist, the psychologist believes that society will
be best served when he investigates where his judgment indicates investigation is needed; he plans his research in such a
way as to minimize the possibility that his findings will be
misleading; and he publishes full reports of his work, never
discarding without explanation data which may modify the interpretation of results.
b. As a teacher, the psychologist recognizes his primary obligation to help others acquire knowledge and skill, and to
maintain high standards of scholarship.
c. As a practitioner, the psychologist knows that he bears a
heavy social responsibility because his work may touch inti-
mately the lives of others.

Reprinted by permission of the American Psychological Association from
the *American Psychologist*, 18: 56-60, 1963.

[1] A student of psychology who assumes the role of psychologist shall be considered a psychologist for the purpose of this code of ethics.

Principle 2. Competence. The maintenance of high standards of professional competence is a responsibility shared by all psychologists, in the interest of the public and of the profession as a whole.

   a. Psychologists discourage the practice of psychology by unqualified persons and assist the public in identifying psychologists competent to give dependable professional service. When a psychologist or a person identifying himself as a pyschologist violates ethical standards, psychologists who know firsthand of such activities attempt to rectify the situation. When such a situation cannot be dealt with informally, it is called to the attention of the appropriate local, state, or national committee on professional ethics, standards, and practices.
   b. The psychologist recognizes the boundaries of his competence and the limitations of his techniques and does not offer services or use techniques that fail to meet professional standards established in particular fields. The psychologist who engages in practice assists his client in obtaining professional help for all important aspects of his problem that fall outside the boundaries of his own competence. This principle requires, for example, that provision be made for the diagnosis and treatment of relevant medical problems and for referral to or consultation with other specialists.
   c. The psychologist in clinical work recognizes that his effectiveness depends in good part upon his ability to maintain sound interpersonal relations, that temporary or more enduring aberrations in his own personality may interfere with this ability or distort his appraisals of others. There he refrains from undertaking any activity in which his personal problems are likely to result in inferior professional services or harm to a client; or, if he is already engaged in such an activity when he becomes aware of his personal problems, he seeks competent professional assistance to determine whether he should continue or terminate his services to his client.

Principle 3. Moral and Legal Standards. The psychologist in the practice of his profession shows sensible regard for the social codes and moral expectations of the community in which he works, recognizing that violations of accepted moral and legal standards on his part may involve his clients, students, or colleagues in damaging personal conflicts, and impugn his own name and the reputation of his profession.

Principle 4. <u>Misrepresentation</u>. The psychologist avoids misrepresentation of his own professional qualifications, affiliations, and purposes, and those of the institutions and organizations with which he is associated.

    a. A psychologist does not claim either directly or by implication professional qualifications that differ from his actual qualifications, nor does he misrepresent his affiliation with any institution, organization, or individual, nor lead others to assume he has affiliations that he does not have. The psychologist is responsible for correcting others who misrepresent his professional qualifications or affiliations.

    b. The psychologist does not misrepresent an institution or organization with which he is affiliated by ascribing to it characteristics that it does not have.

    c. A psychologist does not use his affiliation with the American Psychological Association or its Divisions for purposes that are not consonant with the stated purposes of the Association.

    d. A psychologist does not associate himself with or permit his name to be used in connection with any services or products in such a way as to misrepresent them, the degree of his responsibility for them, or the nature of his affiliation.

Principle 5. <u>Public Statements</u>. Modesty, scientific caution, and due regard for the limits of present knowledge characterize all statements of psychologists who supply information to the public, either directly or indirectly.

    a. Psychologists who interpret the science of psychology or the services of psychologists to clients or to the general public have an obligation to report fairly and accurately. Exaggeration, sensationalism, superficiality, and other kinds of misrepresentation are avoided.

    b. When information about psychological procedures and techniques is given, care is taken to indicate that they should be used only by persons adequately trained in their use.

    c. A psychologist who engages in radio or television activities does not participate in commercial announcements recommending purchase or use of a product.

Principle 6. <u>Confidentiality</u>. Safeguarding information about an individual that has been obtained by the psychologist in the course of his teaching, practice, or investigation is a primary obligation of the psychologist. Such information is not communicated to others unless certain important conditions are met.

a. Information received in confidence is revealed only after most careful deliberation and when there is clear and imminent danger to an individual or to society, and then only to appriate professional workers or public authorities.

b. Information obtained in clinical or consulting relationships, or evaluative data concerning children, students, employees, and others are discussed only for professional purposes and only with persons clearly concerned with the case. Written and oral reports should present only data germane to the purposes of the evaluation; every effort should be made to avoid undue invasion of privacy.

c. Clinical and other case materials are used in classroom teaching and writing only when the identity of the persons involved is adequately disguised.

d. The confidentiality of professional communications about individuals is maintained. Only when the originator and other persons involved give their express permission is a confidential professional communication shown to the individual concerned. The psychologist is responsible for informing the client of the limits of the confidentiality.

e. Only after explicit permission has been granted is the identity of research subjects published. When data have been published without permission for identification, the psychologist assumes responsibility for adequately disguising their sources.

f. The psychologist makes provision for the maintenance of confidentiality in the preservation and ultimate disposition of confidential records.

Principle 7. Client Welfare. The psychologist respects the integrity and protects the welfare of the person or group with whom he is working.

a. The psychologist in industry, education, and other situations in which conflicts of interest may arise among various parties, as between management and labor, or between the client and employer of the psychologist, defines for himself the nature and direction of his loyalties and responsibilities and keeps all parties concerned informed of these commitments.

b. When there is a conflict among professional workers, the psychologist is concerned primarily with the welfare of any client involved and only secondarily with the interest of his own professional group.

c. The psychologist attempts to terminate a clinical or consulting relationship when it is reasonably clear to the psychologist that the client is not benefiting from it.

d. The psychologist who asks that an individual reveal personal information in the course of interviewing, testing, or evaluation, or who allows such information to be divulged to him, does so only after making certain that the responsible person is fully aware of the purposes of the interview, testing, or evaluation and of the ways in which the information may be used.

e. In cases involving referral, the responsibility of the psychologist for the welfare of the client continues until this responsibility is assumed by the professional person to whom the client is referred or until the relationship with the psychologist making the referral has been terminated by mutual agreement. In situations where referral, consultation, or other changes in the conditions of the treatment are indicated and the client refuses referral, the psychologist carefully weighs the possible harm to the client, to himself, and to his profession that might ensue from continuing the relationship.

f. The psychologist who requires the taking of psychological tests for didactic, classification, or research purposes protects the examinees by insuring that the tests and test results are used in a professional manner.

g. When potentially disturbing subject matter is presented to students, it is discussed objectively, and efforts are made to handle constructively any difficulties that arise.

h. Care must be taken to insure an appropriate setting for clinical work to protect both client and psychologist from actual or imputed harm and the profession from censure.

<u>Principle 8. Client Relationship.</u> The psychologist informs his prospective client of the important aspects of the potential relationship that might affect the client's decision to enter the relationship.

a. Aspects of the relationship likely to affect the client's decision include the recording of an interview, the use of interview material for training purposes, and observation of an interview by other persons.

b. When the client is not competent to evaluate the situation (as in the case of a child), the person responsible for the client is informed of the circumstances which may influence the relationship.

c. The psychologist does not normally enter into a professional relationship with members of his own family, intimate friends, close associates, or others whose welfare might be jeopardized by such a dual relationship.

Principle 9. Impersonal Services. Psychological services for the purpose of diagnosis, treatment, or personalized advice are provided only in the context of a professional relationship, and are not given by means of public lectures or demonstrations, newspaper or magazine articles, radio or television programs, mail, or similar media.

a. The preparation of personnel reports and recommendations based on test data secured solely by mail is unethical unless such appraisals are an integral part of a continuing client relationship with a company, as a result of which the consulting psychologist has intimate knowledge of the client's personnel situation and can be assured thereby that his written appraisals will be adequate to the purpose and will be properly interpreted by the client. These reports must not be embellished with such detailed analyses of the subject's personality traits as would be appropriate only after intensive interviews with the subject. The reports must not make specific recommendations as to employment or placement of the subject which go beyond the psychologist's knowledge of the job requirements of the company. The reports must not purport to eliminate the company's need to carry on such other regular employment or personnel practices as appraisal of the work history, checking of references, past performance in the company.

Principle 10. Announcement of Services. A psychologist adheres to professional rather than commercial standards in making known his availability for professional services.

a. A psychologist does not directly solicit clients for individual diagnosis or therapy.

b. Individual listings in telephone directories are limited to name, highest relevant degree, certification status, address, and telephone number. They may also include identification in a few words of the psychologist's major areas of practice; for example, child therapy, personnel selection, industrial psychology. Agency listings are equally modest.

c. Announcements of individual private practice are limited to a simple statement of the name, highest relevant degree, certification or diplomate status, address, telephone number, office hours, and a brief explanation of the types of services rendered. Announcements of agencies may list names of staff members with their qualifications. They conform in other particulars with the same standards as individual announcements, making certain that the true nature of the organization is apparent.

d. A psychologist or agency announcing nonclinical professional services may use brochures that are descriptive of services rendered but not evaluative. They may be sent to professional persons, schools, business firms, government agencies, and other similar organizations.

e. The use in a brochure of "testimonials from satisfied users" is unacceptable. The offer of a free trial of services is unacceptable if it operates to misrepresent in any way the nature or the efficacy of the services rendered by the psychologist. Claims that a psychologist has unique skills or unique devices not available to others in the profession are made only if the special efficacy of these unique skills or devices has been demonstrated by scientifically acceptable evidence.

f. The psychologist must not encourage (nor, within his power, even allow) a client to have exaggerated ideas as to the efficacy of services rendered. Claims made to clients about the efficacy of his services must not go beyond those which the psychologist would be willing to subject to professional scrutiny through publishing his results and his claims in a professional journal.

Principle 11. Interprofessional Relations. A psychologist acts with integrity in regard to colleagues in psychology and in other professions.

a. A pyschologist does not normally offer professional services to a person receiving psychological assistance from another professional worker except by agreement with the other worker or after the termination of the client's relationship with the other professional worker.

b. The welfare of clients and colleagues requires that psychologists in joint practice or corporate activities make an orderly and explicit arrangement regarding the conditions of their association and its possible termination. Psychologists who serve as employers of other psychologists have an obligation to make similar appropriate arrangements.

Principle 12. Remuneration. Financial arrangements in professional practice are in accord with professional standards that safeguard the best interest of the client and the profession.

a. In establishing rates for professional services, the psychologist considers carefully both the ability of the client to meet the financial burden and the charges made by other professional persons engaged in comparable work. He is willing to contribute a portion of his services to work for which he receives little or no financial return.

b. No commission or rebate or any other form of remuneration is given or received for referral of clients for professional services.

c. The psychologist in clinical or counseling practice does not use his relationships with clients to promote, for personal gain or the profit of an agency, commercial enterprises of any kind.

d. A psychologist does not accept a private fee or any other form of remuneration for professional work with a person who is entitled to his services through an institution or agency. The policies of a particular agency may make explicit provision for private work with its clients by members of its staff, and in such instances the client must be fully apprised of all policies affecting him.

Principle 13. Test Security. Psychological tests and other assessment devices, the value of which depends in part on the naivete of the subject, are not reproduced or described in popular publications in ways that might invalidate the techniques. Access to such devices is limited to persons with professional interests who will safeguard their use.

a. Sample items made up to resemble those of tests being discussed may be reproduced in popular articles and elsewhere, but scorable tests and actual test items are not reproduced except in professional publications.

b. The psychologist is responsible for the control of psychological tests and other devices and procedures used for instruction when their value might be damaged by revealing to the general public their specific contents or underlying principles.

Principle 14. Test Interpretation. Test scores, like test materials, are released only to persons who are qualified to interpret and use them properly.

a. Materials for reporting test scores to parents, or which are designed for self-appraisal purposes in schools, social agencies, or industry are closely supervised by qualified psychologists or counselors with provisions for referring and counseling individuals when needed.

b. Test results or other assessment data used for evaluation or classification are communicated to employers, relatives, or other appropriate persons in such a manner as to guard against misinterpretation or misuse. In the usual case, an interpretation of the test result rather than the score is communicated.

c. When test results are communicated directly to parents and students, they are accompanied by adequate interpretive aids or advice.

Principle 15. Test Publication. Psychological tests are offered for commercial publication only to publishers who present their tests in a professional way and distribute them only to qualified users.

a. A test manual, technical handbook, or other suitable report on the test is provided which describes the method of constructing and standardizing the test, and summarizes the validation research.

b. The populations for which the test has been developed and the purposes for which it is recommended are stated in the manual. Limitations upon the test's dependability, and aspects of its validity on which research is lacking or incomplete, are clearly stated. In particular, the manual contains a warning regarding interpretations likely to be made which have not yet been substantiated by research.

c. The catalog and manual indicate the training or professional qualifications required for sound interpretation of the test.

d. The test manual and supporting documents take into account

the principles enunciated in the <u>Technical Recommendations</u>
<u>for Psychological Tests and Diagnostic Techniques</u>.

e. Test advertisements are factual and descriptive rather than
emotional and persuasive.

<u>Principle 16. Research Precautions</u>. The psychologist assumes
obligations for the welfare of his research subjects, both animal
and human.

a. Only when a problem is of scientific significance and it is
not practicable to investigate it in any other way is the psychologist justified in exposing research subjects, whether
children or adults, to physical or emotional stress as part of
an investigation.

b. When a reasonable possibility of injurious aftereffects
exists, research is conducted only when the subjects or their
responsible agents are fully informed of this possibility and
agree to participate nevertheless.

c. The psychologist seriously considers the possibility of
harmful aftereffects and avoids them, or removes them as
soon as permitted by the design of the experiment.

d. A psychologist using animals in research adheres to the
provisions of the Rules Regarding Animals, drawn up by the
Committee on Precautions and Standards in Animal Experi-
mentation and adopted by the American Psychological Association.

<u>Principle 17. Publication Credit</u>. Credit is assigned to those who
have contributed to a publication, in proportion to their contribution, and only to these.

a. Major contributions of a professional character, made by
several persons to a common project, are recognized by joint
authorship. The experimenter or author who has made the
principal contribution to a publication is identified as the first
listed.

b. Minor contributions of a professional character, extensive
clerical or similar nonprofessional assistance, and other
minor contributions are acknowledged in footnotes or in an introductory statement.

c. Acknowledgment through specific citations is made for unpublished as well as published material that has directly influenced the research or writing.

d. A psychologist who compiles and edits for publication the contributions of others publishes the symposium or report under the title of the committee or symposium, with his own name appearing as chairman or editor among those of the other contributors or committee members.

Principle 18. Responsibility toward Organization. A psychologist respects the rights and reputation of the institute or organization with which he is associated.

a. Materials prepared by a psychologist as a part of his regular work under specific direction of his organization are the property of that organization. Such materials are released for use or publication by a psychologist in accordance with policies of authorization, assignment of credit, and related matters which have been established by his organization.
b. Other material resulting incidentally from activity supported by any agency, and for which the psychologist rightly assumes individual responsibility, is published with disclaimer for any responsibility on the part of the supporting agency.

Principle 19. Promotional Activities. The psychologist associated with the development or promotion of psychological devices, books, or other products offered for commercial sale is responsible for ensuring that such devices, books, or products are presented in a professional and factual way.

a. Claims regarding performance, benefits, or results are supported by scientifically acceptable evidence.
b. The psychologist does not use professional journals for the commercial exploitation of psychological products, and the psychologist-editor guards against such misuse.
c. The psychologist with a financial interest in the sale or use of a psychological product is sensitive to possible conflict of interest in his promotion of such products and avoids compromise of his professional responsibilities and objectives.

304

A SELECTED BIBLIOGRAPHY OF BASIC TEXTS IN
COUNSELING AND PSYCHOTHERAPY

Adams, J. F. (Ed.) Counseling and guidance: a summary view.
(Paperback) New York: Macmillan, 1965.

Adams, J. F. Problems in counseling: a case study approach.
(Paperback) New York: Macmillan, 1962.

American Personnel and Guidance Association. Ethical standards.
Washington: A. P. G. A. , 1961.

American Psychological Association. Ethical standards of psychologists. Washington: A. P. A. , 1953.

Anderson, Camilla M. Beyond Freud. New York: Harper, 1957.

Arbuckle, D. S. Counseling: philosophy, theory and practice.
(2nd ed.) Boston: Allyn & Bacon, 1965.

Bakken, C. J. The legal basis for college student personnel work.
Washington: A. P. G. A. , 1961.

Balser, B. (Ed.) Psychotherapy of the adolescent. New York:
International Universities Press, 1957.

Barry, Ruth, & Wolf, Beverly. Modern issues in guidance-per-
sonnel work. New York: Teachers College (Columbia University),
1957.

Bingham, W. V. D. , & Moore, B. V. How to interview. (4th ed.)
New York: Harper, 1959.

Blaine, G. B. , Jr. , & McArthur, C. C. (Eds.) Emotional problems of the student. New York: Appleton-Century-Crofts, 1961.

Blum, M. L. , & Balinsky, B. Counseling and psychology. Englewood Cliffs, N.J.: Prentice-Hall, 1951.

Bordin, E. D. Psychological counseling. New York: Appleton-
Century-Crofts, 1955.

Bowers, Margaretta K. , et al. Counseling the dying. New York:
Thomas Nelson, 1964.

Boy, A. V. , & Pine, G. J. Client-centered counseling in the
secondary school. Boston: Houghton Mifflin, 1963.

Brammer, L. N. , & Shostrom, E. L. Therapeutic psychology:
fundamentals of counseling and psychotherapy. Englewood
Cliffs, N.J.: Prentice-Hall, 1960.

Brayfield, A. H. (Ed.) Readings in modern methods of counseling.
New York: Appleton-Century-Crofts, 1950.

Buhler, Charlotte. Values in psychotherapy. New York: Free
Press, 1962.

Burton, A. (Ed.) Case studies in counseling and psychotherapy. Englewood Cliffs, N.J.: Prentice-Hall, 1959.

Burton, A. (Ed.) Modern psychotherapeutic practice: innovations in technique. Palo Alto, Calif.: Science & Behavior Books, 1965.

Byrne, R. H. The school counselor. Boston: Houghton Mifflin, 1963.

Callis, R., et. al. A casebook of counseling. New York: Appleton-Century-Crofts, 1950.

Colby, K. A primer for psychotherapists. New York: Ronald, 1951.

Cottle, W. C., & Downie, N. M. Procedures and preparation for counseling. Englewood Cliffs, N.J.: Prentice-Hall, 1960.

Dugan, W. E. (Ed.) Counseling points of view. Minneapolis: Univer. of Minnesota Press, 1959.

Ellis, A. Reason and emotion in psychotherapy. New York: Lyle Stuart, 1962.

Ellis, A. (Ed.) The place of values in the practice of psychotherapy. Annals of Psychotherapy, Monogr. #2, 1959.

Ellis, A. (Ed.) What is psychotherapy? Annals of Psychotherapy, Monogr. #1, 1959.

Ellis, A., & Harper, R. A. A guide to rational living. Englewood Cliffs, N.J.: Prentice-Hall, 1961.

Erickson, C. E. The counseling interview. Englewood Cliffs, N.J.: Prentice-Hall, 1950.

Eysenck, H. J. (Ed.) Behavior therapy and the neuroses. New York: Pergamon, 1960.

Eysenck, H. J. Uses and abuses of psychology. London, Baltimore: Penguin (Pelican), 1953.

Evraiff, W. Helping counselors grow professionally. Englewood Cliffs, N.J.: Prentice-Hall, 1963.

Farwell, Gail P., & Peters, H. J. (Eds.) Guidance readings for counselors. Chicago: Rand McNally, 1960.

Ford, D. H., & Urban, H. B. Systems of psychotherapy. New York: Wiley, 1963.

Frank, J. D. Persuasion and healing. (Paperback) New York: Schocken, 1961.

Freeman, Ruth, & Freeman, H. A. Counseling: a bibliography with annotations. New York: Scarecrow Press, 1964.

Freud, S. An outline of psychoanalysis. (Paperback) New York: Norton, 1949.

Garrett, Annette. Interviewing: its principles and methods. New York: Family Service Association of America, 1942.

Glasser, W. Reality therapy. New York: Harper & Row, 1965.

Greenwald, H. (Ed.) The active psychotherapies. New York: Atherton, 1966.

Hadley, J. M. Clinical and counseling psychology. New York: Knopf, 1958.

Hahn, M. E., & MacLean, M. S. Counseling psychology. New York: McGraw-Hill, 1955.

Hamrin, Shirley A., & Paulson, Blanch B. Counseling adolescents. Chicago: Science Research Associates, 1950.

Hanfmann, Eugenia, et al. Psychological counseling in a small college. Cambridge, Mass.: Schenkman, 1963.

Harms, E., & Schreiber, P. (Eds.) Handbook of counseling techniques. New York: Pergamon, 1964.

Harper, R. A. Psychoanalysis and psychotherapy: 36 systems. (Paperback) Englewood Cliffs, N.J.: Prentice-Hall, 1959.

Holland, G. A. Fundamentals of psychotherapy. New York: Holt, Rinehart & Winston, 1965.

Horney, Karen. Neurosis and human growth. New York: Norton, 1950.

Jahoda, Marie. Current concepts of positive mental health. New York: Basic Books, 1958.

Johnson, W. People in quandaries: the semantics of personal adjustment. New York: Harper, 1946.

Lindner, R. Must you conform? (Paperback) New York: Grove, 1956.

Litwack, L., et al. Critical issues in student personnel work: a problem casebook. (Paperback) Chicago: Rand McNally, 1965.

London, P. The modes and morals of psychotherapy. New York: Holt, Rinehart & Winston, 1964.

Loughary, J. W. (Ed.) Counseling, a growing profession: report concerning the professionalization of counseling. Washington: A.P.G.A., 1965.

Marzolf, S. R. Psychological diagnosis and counseling in the schools. New York: Holt, 1956.

Maslow, A. H. Motivation and personality. New York: Harper, 1954.

Maslow, A. H. Toward a psychology of being. (Paperback) Princeton, N.J.: Van Nostrand, 1962.

May, R. (Ed.) Existential psychology. (Paperback) New York: Random House, 1961.

McCary, J. L. (Ed.) Six approaches to psychotherapy. (Paperback) New York: Grove, 1956.

McGowan, J. F., & Schmidt, L. D. (Eds.) Counseling: readings in theory and practice. New York: Holt, Rinehart & Winston, 1962.

McKinney, F. Counseling for personal adjustment in schools and colleges. Boston: Houghton Mifflin, 1958.

McKinney, F. Understanding personality: cases in counseling. Boston: Houghton Mifflin, 1961.

Moustakas, C. E. (Ed.) The self: explorations in personal growth. New York: Harper, 1956.

Mueller, Kate H. Student personnel work in higher education. Boston: Houghton Mifflin, 1961.

Mullahy, P. Oedipus myth and complex. New York: Hermitage, 1948.

Munroe, Ruth L. Schools of psychoanalytic thought. New York: Holt, Rinehart & Winston, 1955.

Nixon, R. E. The art of growing. (Paperback) New York: Random House, 1962.

Patterson, C. H. Counseling and psychotherapy: theory and practice. New York: Harper, 1959.

Pepinsky, H. B., & Pepinsky, Pauline N. Counseling: theory and practice. New York: Ronald, 1954.

Perez, J. F. Counseling: theory and practice. Reading, Mass.: Addison-Wesley, 1965.

Perls, F., et al. Gestalt therapy. (Paperback) New York: Dell, 1951.

Peters, H. J., et al. (Eds.) Counseling: selected readings. Columbus, Ohio: Merrill, 1962.

Porter, E. H. An introduction to therapeutic counseling. Boston: Houghton Mifflin, 1950.

Redl, F., & Wineman, D. The aggressive child. New York: Free Press, 1957.

Riessman, F., et al. (Eds.) Mental health of the poor: new treatment approaches for low-income people. New York: Free Press, 1964.

Robinson, F. P. Principles and procedures in student counseling. New York: Harper, 1950.

Rogers, C. R. Counseling and psychotherapy. Boston: Houghton Mifflin, 1942.

Rogers, C. R. Client-centered therapy. Boston: Houghton Mifflin, 1951.

Rogers, C. R. On becoming a person. Boston: Houghton Mifflin, 1961.

Rogers, C. R., & Dymond, Rosalind F. (Eds.) Psychotherapy and personality change. Chicago: Univer. of Chicago Press, 1954.

Rothmey, J., & Roens, B. Counseling the individual student.
New York: William Sloan, 1949.

Rutledge, A. Premarital counseling. Cambridge, Mass.:
Schenkman, 1965.

Sahakian, W. S. (Ed.) Psychology of personality: readings in
theory. Chicago: Rand McNally, 1965.

Satir, Virginia. Conjoint family therapy. Palo Alto, Calif.:
Science and Behavior Books, 1964.

Schofield, W. Psychotherapy: the purchase of friendship. (Paperback) Englewood Cliffs, N.J.: Prentice-Hall, 1964.

Singer, Erwin. Key concepts in psychotherapy. New York:
Random House, 1965.

Smith, G. E. Counseling in the secondary school. New York:
Macmillan, 1955.

Snyder, W. U. (Ed.) Casebook of non-directive counseling.
Boston: Houghton Mifflin, 1947.

Snyder, W. U. The psychotherapy relationship. New York: Macmillan, 1961.

Standal, S. W., & Corsini, R. J. (Eds.) Critical incidents in
psychotherapy. Englewood Cliffs, N.J.: Prentice-Hall, 1959.

Stefflre, B. (Ed.) Theories of counseling. New York: McGraw-
Hill, 1965.

Stein, M. T. (Ed.) Contemporary psychotherapies. New York:
Free Press, 1961.

Sullivan, H. S. The psychiatric interview. New York: Norton, 195-

Suttie, I. D. The origins of love and hate. London: Kegan Paul,
1935.

Thompson, Clara. Psychoanalysis: evolution and development.
New York: Hermitage, 1950.

Tolbert, E. L. Introduction to counseling. New York: McGraw-
Hill, 1959.

Tyler, Leona. The work of the counselor. (2nd ed.) New York:
Appleton-Century-Crofts, 1961.

Walker, N. A short history of psychotherapy in theory and practice. New York: Noonday, 1959.

Ware, Martha L. (Ed.) Law of guidance and counseling. Cincinnati: Anderson, 1964.

Warters, Jane. Techniques of counseling. (2nd ed.) New York:
McGraw-Hill, 1964.

White, R. W. Lives in progress. New York: Holt, Rinehart &
Winston, 1952.

Wolberg, L. R. (Ed.) Short-term psychotherapy. New York:
Grune & Stratton, 1965.

Wolberg, L. R. The technique of psychotherapy. New York:
Grune & Stratton, 1954.

Wolpe, J., et al. (Eds.) The conditioning therapies. New York:
Holt, Rinehart & Winston, 1964.

Zerfoss, K. P. (Ed.) Readings in counseling. New York: Association Press, 1952.

RELEVANT JOURNALS
For further articles on theories and issues in the field

Counselor Education and Supervision
    Published quarterly by the Association for Counselor Educa-
tion and Supervision, a division of the American Personnel
and Guidance Association, 1605 New Hampshire Avenue, N.W.,
Washington, D. C. 20009.

Educational and Psychological Measurement
    Published quarterly. Box 6907, College Station, Durham,
North Carolina.

Journal of Clinical Psychology
    Published quarterly by the Clinical Psychology Publishing Co.,
4 Conant Square, Brandon, Vermont 05733.

Journal of Consulting Psychology
    Published bimonthly by the American Psychological Associa-
tion, Inc., 1200 Seventeenth Street, N. W., Washington, D. C.
20036.

Journal of Counseling Psychology
    Published quarterly at 1945 N. High Street, Columbus, Ohio
43210.

Psychotherapy: Theory, Research and Practice
    Published quarterly by Psychologists Interested in the Advance-
ment of Psychotherapy, University of Chicago, 5730 Ellis
Avenue, Chicago 37, Illinois.

Rehabilitation Counseling Bulletin
    Published quarterly by the American Rehabilitation Counseling
Association, a division of the American Personnel and Guidance Association, 1605 New Hampshire Avenue, N. W., Washington, D. C. 20009.

310

The <u>Personnel</u> and <u>Guidance</u> Journal
   Published September through June by the American Personnel
   and Guidance Association, 1605 New Hampshire Avenue, N.W.,
   Washington, D. C. 20009.
The <u>School</u> <u>Counselor</u>
   Published in October, December, March and May by the Amer-
   ican School Counselor Association, a Division of the American
   Personnel and Guidance Association, 1605 New Hampshire
   Avenue, N.W., Washington, D.C. 20009.
<u>Vocational</u> <u>Guidance</u> <u>Quarterly</u>
   Published in September, December, March and June by the
   National Vocational Guidance Association, a division of the
   American Personnel and Guidance Association, 1605 New
   Hampshire Avenue, N.W., Washington, D.C. 20009.

A <u>Directory</u> of <u>Approved</u> <u>Counseling</u> <u>Agencies,</u> which includes all
   approved public, private, college and university centers, is
   published by the American Board on Counseling Services,
   1605 New Hampshire Avenue, N. W., Washington, D. C.
   20009.

Indexes

NAME INDEX

SUBJECT INDEX

ABOUT THE EDITOR

Dr. Ben N. Ard, Jr., received his B.A. from the University of California at Los Angeles with a major in psychology; his M.A. from Oregon State University, where he majored in counseling and guidance; his Ph. D. from the University of Michigan, an interdepartmental degree in education and psychology. He has taught at Michigan State University, the University of Michigan, and Central Michigan University, and was a fellow in marriage counseling and family life education at the Merrill-Palmer Institute in Detroit.

At present Dr. Ard is in private practice in San Francisco as a certified psychologist and a licensed marriage, family, and child counselor. He is also professor of counseling at San Francisco State College.

Dr. Ard is a member of the American Psychological Association, the American Personnel and Guidance Association, Psychologists Interested in the Advancement of Psychotherapy, Western Association of Counselor Educators and Supervisors, National Council on Family Relations, the Society for the Scientific Study of Sex, American Association of Marriage Counselors, and the San Francisco Psychological Association.